THE
NEW TESTAMENT
TODAY

THE
NEW TESTAMENT
TODAY

Mark Allan Powell

editor

Westminster John Knox Press
Louisville, Kentucky

© 1999 Westminster John Knox Press

Scripture quotations, unless otherwise noted, are from the New Revised Standard Version of the Bible, copyright © 1989 by the Division of Christian Education of the National Council of the Churches of Christ in the U.S.A., and are used by permission.

Book design by Sharon Adams
Cover design by Kevin Darst

First edition
Published by Westminster John Knox Press
Louisville, Kentucky

This book is printed on acid-free paper that meets the American National Standards Institute Z39.48 standard. ∞

PRINTED IN THE UNITED STATES OF AMERICA

99 00 01 02 03 04 05 06 07 08 — 10 9 8 7 6 5 4 3 2 1

Library of Congress Cataloging-in-Publication Data

The New Testament today / Mark Allan Powell, editor. — 1st ed.
    p. cm.
    Includes bibliographical references.
    ISBN 0-664-25824-7 (alk. paper)
    1. Bible. N.T—Criticism, interpretation, etc. I. Powell, Mark Allan, 1953– .
BS2393.N495   1999
225'.6—dc21   98-42329
                                                 CIP

Contents

Contributors

Mark Allan Powell is Robert and Phyllis Leatherman Professor of New Testament at Trinity Lutheran Seminary in Columbus, Ohio.

Fernando F. Segovia is Professor of New Testament and Early Christianity at the Divinity School of Vanderbilt University in Nashville, Tennessee.

John S. Kloppenborg Verbin is Professor of New Testament in the Faculty of Theology, University of St. Michael's College, and Professor of Religious Studies at the University of Toronto.

Donald A. Hagner is George Eldon Ladd Professor of New Testament at Fuller Theological Seminary in Pasadena, California.

Mary Ann Tolbert is George H. Atkinson Professor of Biblical Studies at Pacific School of Religion in Berkeley, California.

John T. Carroll is Professor of New Testament and Dean of Theology Faculty at Union Theological Seminary and Presbyterian School of Christian Education in Richmond, Virginia.

Gail R. O'Day is Almer H. Shatford Professor of Homiletics at Candler School of Theology at Emory University in Atlanta, Georgia.

Marion L. Soards is Professor of New Testament Studies at Louisville Presbyterian Seminary in Louisville, Kentucky.

James D. G. Dunn is Lightfoot Professor of Divinity at the University of Durham, England.

Richard P. Carlson is Associate Professor of Biblical Studies at Lutheran Theological Seminary, Gettysburg, in Gettysburg, Pennsylvania.

Pheme Perkins is Professor of Theology at Boston College in Boston, Massachusetts.

M. Eugene Boring is I. Wylie and Elizabeth M. Briscoe Professor of New Testament at Brite Divinity School, Texas Christian University, in Fort Worth, Texas.

Introduction

Mark Allan Powell

How shall we read the New Testament in the twenty-first century? The field of New Testament studies has become so complex and diversified that it threatens to overwhelm its practitioners. Indeed, some wonder whether the discipline can be called a *field* at all. Has it not become a network of loosely related *fields*—anthropology, history, literary criticism, philosophy, sociology, theology—all of which seem to have little in common except that, for one reason or another, their adherents have taken an interest in the writings of first-century Christians?

It's a wonderful problem! Today, we face an embarrassment of riches. The field (or fields) of New Testament research blossomed in the latter decades of the twentieth century to offer promises and challenges that had not been imagined. This is an exciting time to be a New Testament student.

We have witnessed, first, an incredible increase in knowledge. At a basic level, the achievements of archaeology in the last hundred years have surpassed those of the previous centuries combined. Highly publicized discoveries such as the Dead Sea Scrolls and the Nag Hammadi library, along with the more mundane dating of pottery shards, have brought a more exact awareness of what happened, *where* and *when*. The development of such sciences as cultural anthropology has served also to explain what happened, *why*. We now have methodological tools for interpreting first-century events in light of the cultural values intrinsic to that age. We know far more about the first-century world today than we did a few decades ago.

Along with this increase in knowledge has come an equally significant enhancement: the new accessibility of the available data. In the early 1980s, I sat in the office of Dr. Paul Achtemeier, one of my professors at Union Theological Seminary in Virginia. He was excited about a new toy he'd hooked up to his computer—a software program that connected him to a library of ancient Greco-Roman literature. At the moment, Achtemeier was reviewing a doctoral dissertation for which he had been asked to serve as an external examiner. A linchpin argument for this thesis involved a claim that the Apostle Paul had coined a certain expression that was found "nowhere else in the extant literature of the first century." Achtemeier spun around in his chair, tapped his keyboard a few times, and shook his head. "Nope, he's wrong. I found it three times."

Today, that anecdote records nothing amazing. The particular software program would be out of date, replaced by others that were in turn replaced by the Internet. But, back then, I *was* amazed. I knew that, somewhere, some poor student like me had just devoted two or three years of his life to scouring Greek manuscripts, reading them in the dusty halls of some library, looking in vain for the phrase Achtemeier had found three times in thirty seconds. I was not only amazed, but frightened. Achtemeier was intimidating enough already—what chance did a student have *now?* What I was a bit slower than some to realize, of course, was that *students* could use computers too. And so they did! During the last decade of the twentieth century, every doctoral student seemed to come equipped with a PC and a laptop, and most were more adept at using them than their professors.

Finally, the guild of New Testament scholarship has recently experienced a tremendous increase in diversity. The sheer number of those working in the field, or to be more precise, working *together* in the field has soared. At the school where I teach, my senior colleagues remember a time when the Society of Biblical Literature held its annual meetings in a hotel ballroom. A couple hundred scholars would attend and just about everyone knew everyone else. Today, that society still meets annually (in conjunction with the American Academy of Religion), but there are only a few cities in the country equipped to handle the dimensions of the gathering: eight thousand or so persons subdivided into numerous study groups, seminars, sections, and workshops. How did it become so huge, so fast?

For one thing, the Vatican Council II in the early 1960s opened the door for Roman Catholic scholars to study the Bible critically with their Protestant colleagues. For another, vast numbers of what are sometimes called "conservative evangelical" scholars came to reject the anti-intellectualism and/or dogmatic confessionalism of fundamentalist Christianity in favor of academic dialogue with scholars whose faith positions they might not share. At the same time, a shift of emphasis within the guild from seminary training to the teaching of religion in state universities brought to the fore numerous scholars whose interest in the New Testament has little to do with homiletical or devotional concerns. And then, in the last quarter of the century, the shape of what had traditionally been an "old boys' club" changed forever, as significant numbers of women swelled the ranks of New Testament scholarship. Add to this the many voices now being heard from scholars who represent third-world countries or marginalized minority groups and the transformation of the guild is complete. Not only are more voices being heard, but different voices.

So we have an embarrassment of riches. The availability of such resources and the inherent potential of their exploitation should inspire us to overcome the initially daunting aspects of being confronted with tasks more complicated than they once appeared. How can we make responsible use of the knowledge, the technology, and the diversity of scholarship that now confronts us?

For beginning students, the initial problem can be the simple matter of *catching up*. Almost every book, article, or thesis assumes acquaintance with other books, articles, and theses. Apparently distinct problems turn out to be interrelated. Cross-disciplinary expectations accumulate, and every topic for discussion seems to come with a history. On the other hand, for professionals who are no longer full-time students, the problem is *keeping up*. Those whose jobs and other commitments do not allow them to spend a couple of afternoons a week in the library may struggle with the sense that their hard-won expertise is slowly slipping away.

Most people who have an interest in New Testament scholarship soon discover a wonderful journal called *New Testament Abstracts,* which lists recent studies in the field, organizing them topically and offering very brief descriptions of their contents. Pastors, priests, and others may subscribe to this journal in the hope that it will help them keep up to date, but many complain that it also serves as a constant reminder of the extent to which they are falling behind. In 1997, *New Testament Abstracts* described 2,781 new contributions. No one has the time to read all 2,781 works. How do you know which ones are truly important?

Even the experts can be stymied by this magnitude of erudition. I have a friend who once confided in me regarding his own somewhat secret scheme for keeping up. An internationally acclaimed theologian, he found that when working in one area—such as the Gospels—he inevitably fell behind in research on other topics—such as the epistles. "I don't have time to read anything about Paul," he fumed once, while immersed in writing a book on John. Instead, he said, he relies on the assistance of colleagues. "Once or twice a year," he explained, "I take a Pauline scholar to lunch. I buy him a nice meal. Then, I sit back and say, 'Tell me what's happening with Paul these days.'"

Something like that may be the inspiration behind this book. Imagine that you have the opportunity, on successive days, to lunch with eleven prominent New Testament scholars, to sit back and to ask each of them, "What's happening in your field? What do I need to know about the current state of research? And what do you think is going to happen in the future?" The chapters of this volume provide answers to those questions. You don't even have to pick up the tab.

Before turning to the individual writings of the New Testament itself, we invite two scholars to offer introductory reflections on matters of overarching importance.

Fernando Segovia starts us off with a discussion of the topic that most scholars would agree underscores all developments in recent New Testament studies. The question is one of *method* and *theory,* of procedure and rationale: How do New Testament scholars go about doing what they do, and why do they go about it the way they do? Segovia details a process through which the field has moved from recognition of a single umbrella approach (historical criticism) through adoption of several disparate umbrella approaches (historical criticism, literary criticism, cultural criticism) to the eventual embracing of a new model (cultural studies) that strives to include all these approaches through a somewhat paradoxical affirmation of diversity. Segovia's tale is explicitly autobiographical. In a manner illustrative of what he now regards to be necessary, he is forthright about the prejudices that will inevitably affect not only his evaluation but also his description of the guild's traditional and current conceptions of method and theory. We should note that the diversity that Segovia identifies and celebrates as the hallmark of modern studies is evident in this very volume. Not all of the contributors would agree with Segovia's assessment that cultural studies offers the grand umbrella model for modern research, nor would they appreciate the apparent justification such a model offers for abandoning the "ideal of exegesis" and reconstruing the role of readers "as constructors rather than decipherers of texts." I suspect, however, that they would all acknowledge that Segovia's brief tour points up what are indeed the principal matters of hermeneutical debate—the issues that all students of the New Testament must confront.

The second introductory essay is John Kloppenborg Verbin's survey of modern research on the historical Jesus. Kloppenborg is one of the world's most prominent Q scholars, having done seminal work on the collection of Jesus' sayings that most scholars would identify as our earliest witness to Jesus. He is eminently qualified, then, to comment on the methodological and interpretive issues that modern historians face when trying to reconstruct the life and sayings of Jesus. Among the former, Kloppenborg highlights problems associated with establishing a database (What value is given to apocryphal gospels?), fixing a starting point (To begin with sayings or deeds?), assessing tradition (Does Mark carry more weight than Q?), and prioritizing criteria (Should primary weight be granted to "dissimilarity" or to "multiple attestation"?). As a result of differences on some of these fundamental concerns, recent historical Jesus scholars have produced divergent portraits of Jesus. Especially controversial are questions involving Jesus' eschatological stance (Did he anticipate an imminent, apocalyptic event? Did he speak of the kingdom in political, revolutionary terms?) and concerns relating to the type of Jewish matrix that offers the best framework for understanding him. Despite these difficulties, Kloppenborg has a hopeful outlook on the future of historical Jesus studies. The methodological questions are approaching resolution and, though the "war of competing Jesuses" may continue, the different images that are being proposed are not, in Kloppenborg's mind, completely opposed to each other.

Turning now to the canon of New Testament writings, we hear first from four scholars regarding each of the Gospels. In every case, the contributor is one who has made his or her own contributions to the study of the Gospel under consideration and who is well acquainted with the history of research on that book.

Donald Hagner, who has himself written one of the most widely used commentaries on Matthew's Gospel (a two-volume set in the Word Biblical Commentary series), notes the return to prominence that this Gospel has enjoyed in recent scholarship. Historical questions, while not altogether resolved, seem to be settled to the extent that there is little ongoing argument—except with regard to the question of whether Matthew's community was *intra muros* or *extra muros,* that is, inside or outside the walls of Judaism. Much of the contemporary work on what is called the "social history of the Matthean community" involves proposals for how the first evangelist was responding to this early identity crisis. Otherwise, Hagner discerns the most ferment in contemporary Matthean studies as deriving from the application of new interpretative methods that, in turn, originated in the new multidisciplinary approach to the field. His discussion of recent Matthean research parallels Segovia's account of developments in method and theory; new literary and sociocultural paradigms for understanding the text have at least diversified the process of interpretation, and, in some cases, have called into question the very goals of traditional exegesis. Hagner, however, does not share

Segovia's enthusiasm for reader-oriented hermeneutics. He recommends learning what can be learned from the new methods while retaining a solid commitment to understanding the intention of the work's historical author, which "remains of determinative importance for the church" (Segovia would not want to limit the reading audience of Matthew or of the New Testament to "the church"). Hagner concludes his essay with a brief survey of theological subjects that remain significant in Matthean studies, distinctive areas in which the Gospel will continue to make contributions or present problems in the next millennium.

Mary A. Tolbert's reflections on the Gospel of Mark begin with the observation that until recently that Gospel's fortunes in the scholarly world have risen or fallen in accord with its perceived usefulness for reconstructing Christian origins. Only in the past thirty years or so has Mark come to be valued on other grounds. The introduction of literary-critical approaches brought new insights for understanding such peculiar features as the negative depiction of the disciples and the anticlimactic ending. What were "problems" for historically oriented interpretation came to be viewed as aspects of a rhetorically effective strategy for engaging readers. Indeed, Mark's Gospel became a favorite document for testing the strategies of reader-response criticism in general and reader-oriented feminist criticism in particular. However, Tolbert concludes that the interest in Mark's effect on modern "flesh-and-blood readers" has not eclipsed the interest of scholars in discerning its potential effects on "historical readers" who would have read (or heard) the Gospel within the context of the first-century Greco-Roman world. We see here, again, a merging of interest in historical, literary, and social matters. Studies of Mark that relate the Gospel's persuasive possibilities to ancient rhetorical practices are one good example of such an interdisciplinary convergence. One implication of these approaches has been a move away from Mark as exemplary of a unique genre of literature (Christian Gospels) toward viewing it in comparison with other popular ancient Greco-Roman writings, including both novels and biographies. After discussing these definitive trends in Markan research, Tolbert concludes her essay by offering her own assessment of Mark's purpose in writing such a book, linking this both to the book's literary themes and to hypotheses regarding the social-historical circumstances of its origin.

John Carroll notes that Luke-Acts was characterized as a "storm center" in New Testament studies a generation ago, though for different reasons than might be considered today. The primary historical question that remains unresolved concerns the *nature* of the unity of the two books. Granted that they have the same author, are they theologically consistent, and do they belong to the same literary genre? This is a different way of addressing an old issue. Other questions come to the fore in light of the new literary and social-scientific studies being conducted; debate over the social context of Luke's writings feeds into discussions of how he uses the Jewish scriptures and how he regards the Jewish people. As for theological concerns, Carroll shows us that the emphasis has shifted decidedly away from Conzelmann's paradigm, which tended to disparage Luke's theological contributions, toward a recognition that Luke's theology can be appreciated for what it is if it is allowed to stand on its own. For instance, rather than dwelling on how Luke downplays the saving significance of the cross (from a Pauline perspective), recent scholars have focused on themes that are uniquely developed in Luke's account of the passion. Further, the significance of the delayed parousia theme—once so prominent in Lukan studies—has been muted, and the focus on Lukan christology has shifted away from preoccupation with analysis of titles and identification of a single dominant concept. The basic insight that Luke's story is first and foremost about *God* is partly responsible for these shifts. Luke's works are also now read with a strong interest in what Carroll calls "questions of ideology and culture." No other Gospel has provided as rich (or controversial) a basis for discussing issues involving the marginalized, wealth and poverty, the role of women, and the Christian evaluation of Judaism.

Gail O'Day bring us up to date on recent scholarship in the Johannine literature, with primary focus on the Gospel of John itself. She organizes her essay according to categories analogous to those employed in Segovia's discussion of methods and theories: historical criticism, literary criticism, social world criticism, and ideological criticism. Such a scheme evinces her belief that with this book—perhaps more than with any other—the most important developments in scholarship have been driven by the diversity of approaches. As such, Johannine scholarship functions almost as a paradigm of New Testament studies as a whole. The chief historical questions under debate are ones that are by now traditional: Is the Fourth Gospel literarily independent of the Synoptics (as those labels imply)? Is John a reliable source for historical knowledge of Jesus? How does the blatantly interpretative character of the book affect our understandings of the interrelationship of history and theology? Although these matters continue to be debated, newer approaches have often taken the focus elsewhere. O'Day discusses the tremendous gains literary criticism has brought with regard to appreciating the book on its own terms, the insights that social-world criticism has to offer vis à vis the vexing questions of John's supposed anti-Jewish polemic and sectarian character, and the promise that ideological modes of discourse offer for feminist studies in particular.

We have devoted three chapters to discussion of those portions of the New Testament written in the name of Paul. One reason, of course, is that the great majority of scholars do not think that all of these were written during Paul's lifetime. Furthermore, the "undisputed letters" have occupied a position of such importance in recent studies that the issues cannot all be dealt with in a single essay. We chose a somewhat artificial but workable distinction between "historical and literary matters" on the one hand and "theological matters" on the other.

Marion Soards tackles the first set of issues in a comprehensive survey of the questions that must be addressed before any of Paul's letters can be interpreted as part of the larger theological corpus. He summarizes current views regarding the form and purpose of letters in antiquity and also describes Paul's adaptations of that form and the role that these letters appear to have played in his total strategy for ministry. To understand the letters, we must know as much as we can about the letter-writer himself. But that task, Soards explains, is beset with its own set of problems. Indeed the "quest for the historical Paul" can quickly become as complicated as the search for Jesus that Kloppenborg discusses in chapter 2. Nevertheless, Soards explicates the methods used by most who attempt such a quest and then boldly presents a rough outline for Paul's life (complete with dates!) that would be accepted by a majority of those working in the field today. Of course, he does note points in the chronology that are disputed. Finally, and perhaps most important, Soards describes the three areas of ancient thought that have been proposed as representing the dominant matrix for comprehending Paul's life and writings: Pharisaic Judaism, Hellenistic Judaism, and Apocalyptic Judaism. As Soards notes, recent studies have tried to incorporate the influence of all of these perspectives rather than extolling one at the expense of the others. Still, he maintains that the third area (Apocalyptic Judaism), previously the most neglected element in Pauline studies, has risen now to become the most prominent.

James D. G. Dunn discusses recent developments in the study of Paul's theology in a way that parallels but only occasionally overlaps Soards' treatment. He begins with a scholarly retrospective, explaining how Pauline theology developed as a distinctive discipline in the nineteenth century and continued to typify concerns of the so-called "History of Religions school" throughout much of the twentieth century. During this period, a common assumption was that Paul's thinking was quite different from that of Jesus and could be best understood within the context of other religious movements (such as Gnosticism). Looking back, Dunn sees this period as "a relative calm," broken in the 1970s by two major developments. First, a new round of studies sought either to define the social situation addressed by Paul in each of his letters or to explicate the rhetorical features of those letters in ways that revealed their pragmatic objectives. Together, these sociological and literary studies served to ground Pauline scholarship in "the grittiness of social relations as they must actually have been" and this, in turn, served to preclude any understanding of Pauline theology as "a merely dogmatic or idealistic system." The second seventies watershed was E. P. Sanders' refutation of common Christian theological arguments that assumed Paul's version of the Christian gospel to be antithetical to the traditional Jewish understanding of the law. The post-Holocaust environment in which this reevaluation occurred lent a sobering urgency to the discussion.

Dunn turns his attention to the future, contemplating what now needs to be done to bring Paul's theology into clearer focus. He contends that, in spite of a current "crisis in confidence" that various hermeneutical concerns have produced, scholars must go beyond the level of theology discernible in the letters themselves to recognize allusions and echoes of what Paul and his readers would simply have taken for granted. He concludes by noting yet another development that is producing reassessments of Paul's theology, the charismatic renewal movement, which has redirected scholarly attention toward Paul's view of the Spirit and toward the significance of those views for Paul's broader theology.

Richard Carlson discusses the state of research in what are somewhat euphemistically called "the disputed letters of Paul." Until recently, most of the scholarship on these letters attempted either to demonstrate that they were not Pauline in origin or to argue that they were. As scholarly opinion moved increasingly toward the former option, the value of the letters also seemed to diminish: they were regarded, at best, as products of a lesser light, or, at worst, as outright forgeries. Carlson thinks that, as we move into a new millennium, discussion and evaluation of these letters is also moving to another plane. If Paul did not write them, who did and for what purposes? What types of rhetoric do they employ and to what genre should they each be assigned? What social situations are presupposed and how do each of the disputed letters address these? Acceptance of non-Pauline authorship actually broadens the possibilities for interpretation, in that proposals for these letters no longer need to be restricted by comparisons with the undisputed letters. This is especially true with regard to theological issues. When these letters are allowed to stand on their own, they may be seen to offer more satisfying and enduring theological contributions than when their perspective is shoe-horned into a scheme defined by the undisputed Pauline letters. Carlson identifies as especially promising the literary-critical tendency to interpret the letters from the perspective of their "implied authors," which means to read them with reference to the symbolic universe presented within the text itself. Looking to the future, Carlson concludes with his own prognosis about how issues of canonicity, authority, and relevance may figure in the discussion of these writings.

Pheme Perkins of Boston University discusses Hebrews and the several short books known as "the catholic epistles" (except for the Johannine letters, which are treated briefly by O'Day in chapter 6).This may have been the most difficult essay to write because the letters it is expected to cover are all quite distinct. Hebrews is an anonymous work addressed to Christians who have had to deal with waning commitment within their ranks and pressure (perhaps nonviolent persecution) from outside social forces. Noted for its use of cultic sacrificial metaphors to describe Christ's salvific work, the book also employs epideictic rhetoric to "transform shame into honor," to assure the beleaguered and despised believers that they belong to a glorious company of heroes and saints. The "catholic epistles" tend to be grouped together only for convenience. Nevertheless, Perkins begins by noting some features they have in common and possible relationships they may bear to other canonical writings. However she insists—in terms that echo Carlson's comments on disputed Pauline epistles—that the epistles be read on their own terms and valued for their distinctive witnesses to the diversity of early Christianity.

Perkins then offers comments on some of the individual letters. Contemporary discussion of 1 Peter revolves around the debate over the social status of the letter's addressees ("resident aliens") and the nature of the persecution that they may have been experiencing. In particular, the letter's apparent advice to accept unmerited suffering as potentially beneficial has inspired controversy over whether the writer is espousing a necessary strategy for survival or simply accommodating religion to a dominant cultural ethos. As Perkins notes, the issue highlights a methodological problem regarding the evaluation of New Testament material that departs from the fundamentally countercultural ethic seen in much of the New Testament. Turning to James, Perkins finds parallels to both Jewish and Greco-Roman ethical instruction and she indicates that the letter also makes some use of the Jesus tradition even though it does not explicitly identify Jesus as the source of its maxims. The letter of 2 Peter is viewed as challenging philosophical assumptions of the day in a way that has abiding relevance for modern theology.

Our last chapter is devoted to the book of Revelation, a text that is bound to enjoy a surge in popularity at the turning of millennia, although for reasons unsanctioned by scholarly inquiry. Eugene Boring summarizes the current state of research on Revelation in a series of seven theses. Though arguments remain, introductory issues (such as authorship and date) can now be discussed with less tendentious disagreement than marked the field a generation ago. On the other hand, the view that Revelation was addressed to persons suffering a terrible and violent persecution has been shattered. Boring indicates that what was once a broad assumption is now a minority view. Other developments include advances in the understanding of Christian prophecy as it relates to both Jewish and Greco-Roman phenomena and the literary studies that have focused on such issues as the relationship between the genres of "letter" and "narrative" (both of which seem to apply to this book). Other scholars have highlighted the political implications of this work and, specifically, indicated the particular meaning it assumes for readers whose social location includes experience of marginalization. Revelation has come to be understood as employing symbolic language that appeals to the imagination rather than code language that needs to be deciphered. Finally, recent studies on Revelation have emphasized its theological contributions to biblical eschatology and, surprisingly, to a vision of ultimately universal salvation.

I thought it best in fashioning this volume to allow each writer as much latitude as possible in shaping his or her work. Thus there is an inconsistency of style and format that may be unsettling to those who tend to be compulsive about such matters. I admit to such obsessions myself and, as an editor, I had to summon a good deal of resolve not to make one contribution look like another. Thus some writers offer an abundance of endnotes, others use no notes but append a bibliography, and still others simply identify works by author and date parenthetically in the text itself. One thing that we have all learned in the past thirty years is the truth of Marshall McLuhan's maxim, "The medium is the message." So, I think the somewhat chaotic formatting of these chapters symbolizes something important about the diversity of perspectives that currently typifies this field. Indeed, whether any of the modes of discourse adopted in this volume will continue to be followed is open to question. Already, scholarly papers are distributed via e-mail and discussed in internet chat rooms. How this will ultimately affect our text-oriented guild is hard to determine. Some voices claim that books and journals will themselves become things of the past. But, then, when I was in the fourth grade, the *Weekly Reader* said we'd all soon get flying cars or strap-on jet packs and live in cities on the ocean floor.

Although I asked every author to take a stab at predicting the future, you will note that they all are cautious about doing so. Who could have predicted the sweeping transformations (what Kuhn calls "paradigm shifts"; what Shakespeare called "sea changes") brought about through the introduction of reader-oriented literary hermeneutics or culture-oriented social-scientific methodologies? Who really knows what lies around the bend? If there is a dominant expectation in the guild, it is simply that the future will be surprising. To ask *how* it will be surprising, to seek definition of the kinds of surprises it will bring, is clearly a fool's errand. If we knew, we wouldn't be surprised.

Chapter 1

Methods for Studying
the New Testament

Fernando F. Segovia

At the center of any academic discipline, subject, or field of study lies the twofold question of method and theory. At its root are the interrelated and interdependent questions of procedure and rationale: the question of strategy, of *how to* go about doing whatever it is that one does or wishes to do; and the question of framework, of *why* go about doing what one does or wishes to do in the way that one does. As a subject or discipline, the study of the New Testament is no different. To enter the world of biblical criticism, the world of the academic reading of biblical and related texts, is perforce to enter the world of method and theory. Such has been the case since the beginning of the discipline, at the dawn of the nineteenth century, and is even more true today at the cusp of the twenty-first century. Several factors contribute to this heightened state of affairs.

METHOD AND THEORY: PRELIMINARY OBSERVATIONS

To begin with, as in the case of both the human and social sciences, the academic study of religion has undergone major transformations in the last quarter of the twentieth century. Such changes have affected the study of Christianity as a whole, including the study of its earliest texts—the New Testament. These changes in large part involve questions of method and theory, and have ultimately brought about a drastically different approach to the understanding and exercise of the discipline. As a result, what is expected of any practitioner today differs radically from what was expected of all practitioners even up to the 1970s.

If one word could be used to characterize this change in expectations, that word is *diversity*. Up to the 1970s, New Testament Studies called for expertise in a single "umbrella model" of interpretation—historical criticism. This approach may have involved a variety of reading strategies and theoretical frameworks, but it also provided a distinctive and overarching mode of discourse across all models and methods. At present, the field demands expertise in several such umbrella models, each of which comprises a variety of methods and models as well as related modes of discourse.

Two cultural indicators serve to drive the point home. First, from a curricular point of view, courses with a focus on method and theory have come into being, by and large, only after the development of this diversity and plurality of umbrella models. Previously, such courses were unnecessary: method and theory could be absorbed through the various curricular offerings, all of which represented variations within the same umbrella model of interpretation. Today, and for the foreseeable future, such courses are indispensable. Second, from a personal point of view, my own life as a critic during the period in question proves highly instructive. My own graduate education (1972–78) involved training in one long-established critical formation. During the course of my first professional appointment (1972–84), two revisionary currents developed, demanding thorough revisioning on my part. In the course of my second professional appointment (1984–present), a further critical formation emerged, demanding yet further revisioning on my part. Such revisioning and multivisioning are only bound to increase.

A concomitant and important result of these changes involving method and theory in New Testament Studies has been a reconsideration of the tradition of academic reading or criticism as such. Up to the 1970s, consensus opinion among practitioners looked upon academic reading of the Bible as both inherently superior and hermeneutically privileged, as the one proper and correct reading of the texts. Such a view, while certainly elitist, was by no means gnostic: this was a reading that called for systematic and arduous training but that was also open to anyone able and willing to undergo such training. At present, this view finds itself under challenge from different, though related, directions. Academic reading is now approached as *a* tradition of reading, subject to critical analysis with regard to its origins, presuppositions, strategies, results, and agenda. It is but one among several traditions of reading, all similarly long-standing and comprehensive. Claims of hermeneutical privilege and inherent superiority are no longer a critical given but are themselves subject to analysis.

After all, as has often been pointed out, *academic* reading is a fairly recent tradition of reading the Bible. Today, scholars must study not only the history of academic reading as a discipline but also other traditions of reading the Bible. Such study has to include at least three such traditions: 1) the theological or churchly tradition, encompassing such different modes as dogmatic, fundamentalist, denominational, and liberationist; 2) the religious or devotional tradition, covering many beloved and enduring practices observed in daily life; and, 3) the cultural or popular tradition, encompassing the broad appropriation and use of biblical motifs, situations, and themes in cultural production at large.

Finally, a further and significant result of these changes in method and theory in New Testament Studies has been the emergence of introductions to method as a distinctive genre of scholarly writing. Up to the 1970s, introductions to method were uncommon, and introductions to the field as a whole focused only briefly, if at all, on questions of method. Moreover, discussion of method was seldom accompanied by discussion of the theory behind the method. Introductions to method have now become popular, and broader discussions of method in general introductions to the field have also become *de rigueur*. Such discussions, moreover, tend to focus as much on theory as on method, if not more.

The rapid proliferation of this genre of scholarly writing parallels a similar trend in other fields, both in the social and human sciences. In effect, methods and theories have become so numerous and so complex that introductions to method and theory have become indispensable tools for any field of study and research. For New Testament Studies, a field that by nature feeds on other fields of study and research, this development can only mean more extensive and disciplined attention to ongoing discussions in other disciplines. Today, one must become familiar with the origin, parameters, reception, and development of whatever reading strategy is adopted. As a result, New Testament Studies has become much more explicitly interdisciplinary in nature.

The advent of diversity, then, has brought about profound transformations in the definition and contours of the field. In matters of method and theory, practitioners are, first, called upon now to look intensively inward. At the same time, diversity has wrought profound transformations in the delineation and circumscription of the field, forcing a reconsideration of the discipline as one way of reading among several such ways of reading. Thus, practitioners are now forced to look outward as well as inward, toward other approaches to biblical texts and even toward the discourses and practices of other disciplines.

In the field of New Testament Studies, therefore, the twofold question of method and theory has not only become more prominent and absorbing but also more intricate and consuming over the last twenty-five years. Following major tectonic movements at work across the entire disciplinary terrain of the human and social sciences, the study of the New Testament has been compelled to reconsider and revision its approach to texts (its methods and models), its self-conception as a tradition of reading (its academic contextualization and perspective), and its location in the academy (its relationship to and engagement with other fields of study). A driving force behind such shifts has been the issue of diversity, which always exacts a heavy price. For the field as a whole, diversity has meant a heightened demand in matters methodological and theoretical, a need for ever greater sophistication, conceptual as well as practical, on the part of all practitioners. This state of affairs is bound not only to perdure but also to intensify.

IRRUPTION OF DIVERSITY: READING THE DISCIPLINE

Given such a state of affairs, such a legacy from the past and such a charter for the future, clearly little choice exists—short of a deliberate option for disciplinary blinders—but to come to terms with these major transformations in the discipline and the resultant need for ever broader sophistication in matters of method and theory. One way to do so is to approach or read the discipline like a story, constructing a narrative about its recent path, its present outlook, and its future prospects.

Needless to say, a variety of such stories is inevitable, but such variety is actually to be welcomed. First, it further brings to the fore the diversity that has permeated the discipline of late; the given multiplicity of methods and models is matched by a corresponding multiplicity of narratives striving to account for changes in the discipline. Second, it shows pointedly that there are different ways of tracing and accounting for the irruption of diversity. Third, it allows for comparative analysis among the various accounts advanced in terms of construction, strategy, and perspective.

Such is the approach I shall follow. By way of preface, I should explain that my tale of the discipline proceeds from an observing participant, a critic who has both witnessed and engaged in all of the tectonic shifts in question. The point of view from which this story is constructed looks upon it as a tale of progress and rejoices in the gradual unfolding of diversity. The plot of this story involves a threefold movement: 1) a period of stability, involving an initial umbrella model, sole and entrenched; 2) a period of crisis, involving the emergence of two other umbrella models, which effectively displace the hegemony of the existing model and begin to make of the discipline a competitive arena; and, 3) a period of resolution, of unstable stability as it were, involving the rise of another umbrella model, which turns the discipline even further into a competitive arena, while offering a full-fledged justification for the phenomenon of diversity as such. I characterize these three stages as follows: Diversity Bound; Diversity Unbinding; Diversity Unbound.

Diversity Bound: Historical Criticism. I have referred to historical criticism as the dominant umbrella model through the 1970s. In fact, a historical approach to the texts of the New Testament reigned supreme for about 150 years, from the formation of the discipline in the first half of the nineteenth century through the third quarter of the twentieth century—from that period of intellectual ferment after the French Revolution, when the study of Christian beginnings turns to the similarly nascent discipline of history for grounding, to that other period of intellectual ferment after the upheavals of the 1960s, when such study begins to look elsewhere for grounding. Remarkable internal stability characterized this period.

For reading the New Testament today, knowledge of this *historical* mode of discourse remains crucial for practitioners, not only because of its long duration but also because understanding the recent turn of events is impossible without a grasp of what preceded and motivated them. In its modernist attempt to break free of dogma and tradition, historical criticism sought to study the New Testament in the light of its context, broadly understood—historical, literary, social, religious. A variety of perspectives were available, depending on the specific focus of study: textual criticism; source criticism; comparative criticism involving matters religious, literary, or social; form criticism; redaction and composition criticism. Underlying all of these different approaches was a specific view of the relationship between practitioner and field—the ideal of "exegesis."

A wide historical as well as cultural gulf separated text and critic: the text was "out there"; the critic was "over here." The text represented historical evidence from and for the time of composition and called for contextualization. As such, it was to be read on its own terms, within its own context, and as evidence for the reconstruction of that context. Its meaning was univocal and objective, as was the path of history itself. To retrieve its meaning and to reconstruct history, however, required a decontextualization of the critic. Such retrieval and such reconstruction could be achieved only by means of a scientific method that guaranteed neutrality and impartiality on the part of the critic. For anyone to attain such a level of reading, a process of divestiture was in order: taking off presuppositions and taking on objectivity. With regard to critics, therefore, diversity remained bound: all practitioners were to become alike—universal and informed readers. While historical criticism pursued with relish the diversity of Christian beginnings as reflected in the New Testament, it frowned severely upon diversity at the level of interpretation.

Knowledge of this umbrella model remains essential today. From the point of view of historical criticism, reading the New Testament today requires a measure of sophistication in both the history of historiography, so that the model followed by historical criticism can be compared with other competing models, and contemporary historiography, a field that has witnessed enormous transformations as well.

Diversity Unbinding: Literary and Cultural Criticisms. I have also pointed to the emergence of two other umbrella models in the 1970s as the beginnings of a drastic change in the state of affairs of the discipline; I refer to literary criticism and cultural criticism. Voices of dissatisfaction with the traditional historical approach to the New Testament texts began to surface in the mid-1970s, swiftly developed into major critical formations through the 1980s, and continued to expand in diversity and sophistication in the 1990s. These voices of dissent came from different quarters, addressed different perceived shortcomings of historical criticism, and remained for the most part independent of one another. The result was a period of crisis that ultimately signaled the end of historical criticism as the dominant umbrella model and the rise of a plurality of such models.

Dissatisfaction was expressed with the way in which historical criticism approached *texts*. The fracturing (emphasis on textual rupture), excavative (emphasis on the preliterary stages of the text), and atomistic (emphasis on verse-by-verse analysis) tendencies of historical criticism began to be viewed as overlooking the text as such. The text, it was now argued, was worthy of analysis in and of itself, as text, with a focus on its formal features. Dissatisfaction was also expressed with the way in which historical criticism approached *context*. The pointilistic tendencies of historical criticism began to be seen as unstructured, impressionistic, even ethnocentric. The context, it was now argued, was worthy of analysis in and of itself, as context, with a focus on its social and cultural features. These voices of dissatisfaction produced an instability in New Testament Studies, such that practitioners began to look to other disciplines for grounding. Those concerned with texts looked often to the human sciences—literary, rhetorical, and psychological studies; those concerned with context looked to the social sciences—economics, sociology, and anthropology. In the process, the long-standing and exclusive association between New Testament Studies and historical studies drew rapidly to a close.

For reading the New Testament today, knowledge of the *literary* and the *cultural* modes of discourse proves essential for practitioners, not only because of their prominence and vigor but also because of their pivotal role in the recent turn of events. Gradually, a broad variety of approaches came into being, again depending on the particular focus of study in question. From the point of view of literary criticism, one finds structuralism, psychoanalytic criticism, narrative criticism, rhetorical criticism, reader-response criticism; and deconstruction. From the point of view of cultural criticism, one finds socioeconomic (neo-Marxist) criticism, sociological criticism, and anthropological criticism.

With regard to the prevailing view of the relationship between practitioner and field in all of these approaches, a distinction is in order. For the most part, the ideal of exegesis remained unquestioned. In fact, both literary criticism and cultural criticism determined to outdo historical criticism by seeking to advance a more secure foundation and strategy for dealing with the text as text and the context as context. The basic perception was, in effect, that the task of contextualization—of reading the text on its own terms, within its own context, and as evidence for the reconstruction of that context—had not been properly executed.

At the same time, certain developments within both formations pointed to the first cracks in this ideal of exegesis. From the perspective of literary criticism, the concepts of univocality and objectivity did yield some ground, given the increasing emphasis on the plurality of interpretations, due to the polysemy of texts and the agency of readers. From the perspective of cultural criticism, both concepts yielded further ground, given the increasing focus on the socioeconomic and sociocultural dimensions of readers. Thus, while the scientific goals of retrieval and reconstruction as well as neutrality and impartiality prevailed, a certain erosion of these goals was evident. Consequently, while both umbrella models continued to pursue unreservedly the diversity of Christian beginnings, the first hints of diversity at the level of interpretation began to surface.

With respect to critics, then, this was a case of diversity unbinding. First, expectations regarding practitioners witnessed a fundamental change from one umbrella model to various such models. Second, expectations regarding the ideal of exegesis began, ever so slightly, to be relaxed. Needless to say, knowledge of these two umbrella models proves necessary today. Reading the New Testament today demands a measure of expertise in the broad traditions of literary and social studies, if one is to be self-conscious in approaching a text and dealing with context. Such expertise calls for critical awareness regarding the recent history and currents of the disciplines in question as well as the history of their use in New Testament Studies.

Diversity Unbound: Cultural Studies. I have further referred to the appearance in more recent times of another umbrella model—cultural studies—as the entrenchment of the drastic change in the discipline. It was not long before other voices of dissatisfaction came to the fore, now with regard to the literary and cultural critiques and programs as well. Such voices came both from inside and outside these recent critical formations, gathering strength through the 1980s and coming into their own in the 1990s. From the inside, the initial cracks noted above with regard to the traditional ideals of exegesis began to widen and deepen. From the outside, a momentous change was taking place in the ranks of a discipline that up to this point had been male, clerical, and Western. These two developments coincided with and reinforced one another and, in so doing, not only created a distinctive umbrella model but also justified the plurality of competing models. This was a period of resolution, therefore, involving stability—not the stability of uniformity, to be sure, but the unstable stability of pluralism. The discipline finds itself in this period today.

Dissatisfaction from the inside was inevitable, as the focus on the plurality of interpretations and the agency of the reader in interpretation continued to intensify. A number of voices began to argue that behind all retrievals of meaning and reconstructions of history—behind all methods and models—stand the real flesh-and-blood readers, who are always and inescapably contextualized and perspectival. Dissatisfaction from the outside became inevitable as well, as more and more outsiders to the discipline joined its ranks: Western women, men and women from the non-Western world, and women and men from non-Western minority groups in the West. Such voices insisted on the agency as well as the contextualization and perspective of real readers. In both quarters, such rumblings were directly aided by similar discussions across the disciplinary spectrum of the human and social sciences, which came together to form the subject of cultural studies, with its focus on issues of representation, power, and ideology.

For reading the New Testament today, knowledge of this *ideological* mode of discourse is absolutely indispensable. First, as the end result of the recent turn of events, it cannot but serve as the foundation for all future development. Also, this mode of discourse is where the discussion continues to rage in the academy at large, seeking the freedom to contextualize the reader as much as the text in any number of ways: gender, ethnic or racial provenance, socioeconomic standing, sociopolitical status and affiliation, socioreligious tradition, socioeducational level, socioacademic tradition, and so forth.

With this emphasis on the agency of contextualized and perspectival readers, the prevailing view of the relationship between practitioner and field leaves behind altogether the sense of the wide gulf separating text and critic—the text as "out there" and the critic as "over here"—and with it the ideal of exegesis. The basic perception of this model is that the traditional task of reading the text on its own terms, within its own context, and as evidence for the reconstruction of that context is fundamentally defective. Behind this task lies not, as required, a neutral and impartial reader but rather a reader that is very much involved, in any number of ways, in the task of retrieval and reconstruction. Indeed, for cultural studies such a reader is ultimately engaged in the construction of texts and contexts, and, given the enormous variety of real readers engaged in such a task, such constructions can only be expected to show widespread and conflicting diversity. As a result, the phenomenon of diversity is both explained and justified at a foundational level. For cultural studies, in the end, the task of contextualization becomes far more complex, equally applicable as it is to texts and critics; in fact, exegesis and eisegesis now go hand in hand.

With regard to critics, therefore, this is a case of diversity unbound. First, another umbrella model becomes part of the disciplinary repertoire, adding to the methodological and theoretical diversity already unleashed. Second, within this umbrella model, practitioners are called upon to contextualize themselves as much as the text—to acknowledge and analyze their social location and agenda as sharply as those of the text and to examine the relationship between such a text and such a reader. Finally, this umbrella model justifies diversity on the basis of readers as constructors rather than decipherers of texts.

Without a doubt, knowledge of this umbrella model is crucial today. From the point of view of cultural studies, reading the New Testament today calls for a measure of expertise in the congeries of studies that form cultural studies, if one is to be self-conscious in the construction of texts and contexts. Such expertise requires critical sophistication in the ongoing discussions regarding questions of representation, power, and ideology both inside and outside the discipline.

METHOD AND THEORY: CONCLUDING COMMENTS

I referred at the beginning to a heightened state of affairs in matters methodological and theoretical within the discipline at the present time and accounted for it in terms of the diversity that has come to permeate the discipline in the last twenty-five years. In the preceding narrative of this turn of events, I proceeded to trace the irruption of diversity in terms of three stages involving a process of unbinding. The result of such unbinding, I have argued, has been a heightened demand on all practitioners with regard to method and theory: a need for ever greater sophistication in an ever wider array of reading strategies, theoretical frameworks, and umbrella models of interpretation—both inside and outside the discipline. Such, I have pointed out, is the heavy price always exacted by any process of diversity.

Yet diversity always proves enormously uplifting as well, and this is no less true with regard to New Testament Studies. Its benefits for the discipline can be readily outlined. Diversity has forced practitioners to become ever more self-conscious in their use of method and theory; ever more interdisciplinary in their understanding and exercise of the discipline—tying them closer to the human and social sciences and thus to the academy itself; and ever more self-conscious regarding their own contextualization and perspective in the world, where increasing globalization goes hand in hand with increasing differentiation.

Reading the New Testament today has become a far more challenging and exciting task. If the demands in method and theory have increased a hundredfold, so have their rewards. For now, such demands and such rewards are bound to continue and multiply, making the field even more challenging and exciting in the years to come.

BIBLIOGRAPHY

History

Collins, Raymond F. *Introduction to the New Testament.* Garden City, N.Y.: Doubleday & Co., 1983.
Morgan, Robert, with John Barton. *Biblical Interpretation.* The Oxford Bible Series. Oxford: Oxford University Press, 1988.

Method and Theory

McKenzie, S. L., and S. R. Haynes, eds. *To Each Its Own Meaning: An Introduction to Biblical Criticisms and Their Application.* Louisville, Ky.: Westminster/John Knox Press, 1993.
Green, J. B., ed. *Hearing the New Testament: Strategies for Interpretation.* Grand Rapids: Wm. B. Eerdmans Publishing Co., 1995.
Porter, S., and D. Tombs, eds. *Approaches to New Testament Study.* Journal for the Study of the New Testament Supplement Series 120. Sheffield: Sheffield Academic Press, 1995.
Watson, F., ed. *The Open Text: New Directions for Biblical Studies.* London: SCM Press, 1993.

Historical Criticism

Krentz, E. *The Historical-Critical Method.* Philadelphia: Fortress Press, 1975.
McKnight, E. V. *What is Form Criticism?* Philadelphia: Fortress Press, 1969.
Perrin, N. *What is Redaction Criticism?* Philadelphia: Fortress Press, 1969.

Literary Criticism

Beardslee, W. A. *Literary Criticism of the New Testament.* Philadelphia: Fortress Press, 1970.
Mack, B. *What is Rhetorical Criticism?* Minneapolis: Fortress Press, 1990.
McKnight, E. V., and E. Struthers Malbon, eds., *The New Literary Criticism and the New Testament.* Valley Forge, Penn.: Trinity Press International, 1994.
Moore, S. D. *Literary Criticism and the Gospels: The Theoretical Challenge.* New Haven, Conn.: Yale University Press, 1989.
Powell, M. A. *What Is Narrative Criticism?* Minneapolis: Fortress Press, 1990.

Cultural Criticism

Elliott, J. H. *What is Social-Scientific Criticism?* Minneapolis: Fortress Press, 1992.
Esler, P. *The First Christians in Their Social Worlds. Social-Scientific Approaches to New Testament Interpretation.* London: Routledge, 1994.
Esler, P. F., ed. *Modelling Early Christianity: Social-Scientific Studies of the New Testament in Its Context.* London: Routledge, 1995.

Cultural Studies

Adam, A. K. M. *What is Postmodern Biblical Criticism?* Minneapolis: Fortress Press, 1995.
The Bible and Culture Collective, *The Postmodern Bible.* New Haven, Conn.: Yale University Press, 1995.
Segovia, F. F., and Mary Ann Tolbert. *Reading from This Place. Volume 1: Biblical Interpretation and Social Location in the United States.* Minneapolis: Fortress Press, 1995.
Segovia, F. F., and Mary Ann Tolbert. *Reading from This Place. Volume 2: Biblical Interpretation and Social Location in the Global Scene.* Minneapolis: Fortress Press, 1995.

Chapter 2

The Life and Sayings of Jesus

John S. Kloppenborg Verbin

The last two decades have witnessed a virtual avalanche of books and articles on the life and teachings of Jesus, offering widely divergent conceptions of him. In recent scholarship, Jesus has been depicted as a liberal Pharisee, a Galilean holy man, a restorationist prophet, a visionary, an advocate of village renewal, a subversive sage, and a Jewish Cynic. The purpose of this essay is to provide a road map of this rather wild and varied country and to describe common points of departure and the places where paths diverge.

Since the beginning of the nineteenth century, there is broad agreement that Gospel portraits of Jesus bear the impress of the interests of those who first transmitted the Jesus tradition and the evangelists who composed the Gospels. This means it is imperative to be able to distinguish within the Jesus tradition those elements that reflect the teaching and practice of Jesus from those that represent the interests of the tradents of the material. Disagreements, however, exist at two levels, one methodological and the other interpretive. The first has to do with the starting point(s) of historical Jesus scholarship and its criteria: What sources define the corpus of the Jesus tradition and how does one best extract "authentic" materials from those sources? The second level is a broader issue. Once individual units of tradition have been identified, how does one assemble these units into a coherent portrait and what interpretive framework responds best to the data?

METHODOLOGICAL ISSUES

Defining the Jesus Tradition. The first methodological problem arises from the sheer bulk of the sayings ascribed to Jesus and stories told about him. John Dominic Crossan's inventory of the Jesus tradition (both sayings of Jesus and anecdotes about Jesus) comprises more than five hundred items and contains materials from both intracanonical and early noncanonical gospels.[1] Especially noteworthy are items from the *Gospel of Thomas,* the *Gospel of Peter,* the *Egerton Gospel* and *P. Oxyrhynchus* 1224.[2] No one would seriously propose a portrait of Jesus based on the whole of this inventory, especially since there are many conflicting sayings and stories within this collection. The critical issue is how to define the corpus of

Jesus traditions so as to ensure that significant data are not omitted from consideration, but also that the portrait of Jesus is not skewed by irrelevant or idiosyncratic materials.

The simplest expedient is to dismiss the noncanonical gospels. Joachim Gnilka, for example, acknowledges that a few scattered sayings of Jesus (called *agrapha*) have been preserved in intracanonical writings outside the Gospels, in text-critical variants to the Gospels and Acts, and in the Apostolic Fathers, but dismisses the more substantial collections of sayings such as the *Gospel of Thomas* as a product of fantasy and heretical (gnostic) developments.[3] A similar judgment is reflected in Rudolf Schnackenburg's treatment of the evangelists' representations of Jesus, a study that simply sidesteps other gospels by declaring that the traditions contained in these second-, third-, and fourth-century documents cannot be compared with those in the four intracanonical Gospels.[4] Others scholars do not even raise the possibility of noncanonical gospels as sources or proceed as if they were simply irrelevant.[5]

The dismissal of the noncanonical gospels is troubling for several reasons. First, it confuses a theological category (the canon) with a historiographic category (materials bearing on an historical figure). There are no *a priori* grounds for supposing that noncanonical gospels are less reliable historically simply because, for whatever reasons, they did not find their way into the Christian canon. Nor is it justified to suppose that intracanonical documents are more historically reliable simply because they were chosen in the late second, third, and fourth centuries as theologically authoritative. Second, the fact that the manuscripts of noncanonical gospels are second century or later is true but irrelevant. The manuscript of the *Egerton Gospel* is from the early second century—the same time as our first scrap of the Fourth Gospel. The earliest papyri of the *Gospel of Thomas* (*P. Oxy.* 1, 655) and the *Gospel of Peter* (*P. Oxy.* 2949, 4009) date from about 200 C.E., or about the same time as our earliest manuscripts of Matthew and Luke. *P. Oxy.* 1224 is dated not long after our first attestation of Mark. Needless to say, no one would dismiss the intracanonical Gospels merely because their first manuscript attestations come from the early third century. Third, even if noncanonical gospels were composed, say, in the early second century, the traditions they embody might well be considerably earlier, just as the traditions contained in Matthew and Luke, composed towards the end of the first century, nonetheless contain historically reliable data. Finally, to observe, as Gnilka and others do, that the *Gospel of Thomas* is "gnostic"—an assertion that is itself debatable—settles nothing at all, since *all* of our Gospels betray the theological influences of their editors. It is normal to take into account the theology of an evangelist and to adjust for it when isolating historical tradition; in this regard, the *Gospel of Thomas* is no different from any other Gospel.

In contrast to these hasty, perhaps *a priori,* dismissals of noncanonical gospels, North American scholarship has with some exceptions[6] adopted a more careful position. E. P. Sanders suggests that "only some of the sayings in the *Gospel of Thomas* are worth consideration."[7] John P. Meier devotes an entire chapter to *agrapha* and apocryphal gospels, but concludes that upon analysis these documents offer nothing new or authentic that is independent of the intracanonical Gospels.[8] Meier's conclusions regarding both the *Gospel of Peter* and the *Gospel of Thomas* are based on an argument that these documents betray knowledge of the redactional elements of the Synoptics and therefore must be posterior to them.[9] The approach is correct, but Meier's conclusion are in doubt, for certain passages in the *Gospel of Thomas*—for example, the Parable of the Tenants (Mark 12:1–12/*Gos. Thom.* 65–66)—reflect none of the evangelists' redaction. The more probable hypothesis is that Thomas is here independent of the Synoptics.

This conclusion of course cannot automatically be extrapolated to the *Gospel of Thomas* as a whole, much less to other noncanonical gospels. Since the *Gospel of Thomas* has a complex transmission history, involving early Greek and later Coptic recensions, one has to reckon with the possibility that versions of sayings from the intracanonical Gospels influenced the transmission and/or translation of Thomas, just as early manuscripts of the intracanonical Gospels already display the scribal tendency to harmonize one Gospel with another. The sayings in the *Gospel of Thomas* (and other noncanonical gospels) must be examined individually to determine the extent of interference from the Synoptic Gospels. They must also be subjected to the same tests of authenticity that are applied to the Synoptic sayings (see below). Such examination has indeed made a strong case that the *Gospel of Thomas* does contain *some* independent material,[10] including *some* authentic Jesus tradition. Such material provides another "window" on the early Jesus tradition.

The inclusion of noncanonical materials in the database implies the possibility that some sayings or stories completely unattested in the intracanonical Gospels might contribute to a portrait of Jesus. In practice, however, only a very small number of such sayings have survived scrutiny, and even these do not introduce a radically new perspective on Jesus.[11] The more significant effect of considering noncanonical gospels is to underscore through multiple attestation the foundational importance of certain sayings or aspects of Jesus' teachings. In doing so, they also provide an indication of the extent to which some sayings already known from the Synoptics have been subordinated to other interests in the intracanonical Gospels or even filtered out of later portraits of Jesus, perhaps because they did not fit the tendencies of the theologies of the second and subsequent centuries.

Crossan's use of the *Gospel of Thomas* nicely illustrates the point. Crossan begins his discussion of the reign of God in Jesus' preaching with two multiply attested sayings, the saying about children and the kingdom, which has four independent attestations (*Gos. Thom.* 22; Mark 10:13–16; Matt. 18:3; John 3:1–10), and the blessing of the poor, with three independent attestations (*Gos. Thom.* 54; James 2:5; Q 6:20b [Note: Q texts are normally cited by Lukan versification; thus Q6:20b refers to the Q text found in the parallel verses of Luke 6:20b and Matt. 5:3]). These two units exemplify for Crossan a fundamental aspect of Jesus' view of the kingdom as a "Kingdom of Nobodies"—a view of the kingdom in sharp contrast to the triumphalistic and nationalistic views espoused in some other sectors of Second Temple Judaism.[12] These sayings–units are foundational in Crossan's treatment, precisely because the multiple independent attestations indicate their wide impact.

When one turns to scholars who ignore or downplay noncanonical gospels—E. P. Sanders, B. F. Meyer, J. Gnilka, B. Witherington, and N. T. Wright[13]—the contrast with Crossan is striking. These authors cite Q 6:20b only in passing, and Mark 10:13–16 and its parallels are not used at all as part of an effort to characterize Jesus' view of the reign of God.

The effect of ignoring Mark 10:13–16 is noteworthy. By itself, Q 6:20b can be read as an expression of the expectation that God will intervene in the near future on behalf of the poor and oppressed.[14] But when Q 6:20b is interpreted alongside Mark 10:13–16, what becomes more visible is the contrast between statuses: the rich (who are usually thought to be blessed) *versus* the poor; and adults and other persons with status *versus* insignificant, non statusy persons. Thus, the kingdom as defined by Q 6:20b and Mark 10:13–16 is not just about God's eventual elevation of the poor and lowly, but is a *threat* in the present to the customary valuations of hierarchy, wealth, and power. Crossan's "Kingdom of Nobodies" includes a critical nuance that is lacking in the more usual constructions of the Kingdom based on Q 6:20b. Without using the noncanonical gospels to import *new* sayings, Crossan's procedure allows him to lift up authentic *intracanonical* sayings that, because of their radical character, are in danger of being ignored by those who base their portraits solely on the intracanonical Gospels.

Sayings or Deeds? A second methodological issue has to do with starting points, once the corpus is determined. Although most treatments of Jesus begin with the sayings, E. P. Sanders has observed that not only have the sayings been conformed to later ecclesial interests in ways that probably cannot be assessed with precision, but that the usual tests of authenticity (see below) are rendered problematic by the various lacunae in our knowledge of Second Temple Judaism. Sanders's alternative is to begin with events that, in his view, are indisputably secure: that Jesus was baptized by John, that he was a Galilean who preached and healed; that he called disciples and spoke of there being twelve; that he confined his activities to Israel; that he engaged in a controversy about the Temple; that he was crucified by a Roman prefect; that his followers continued after his death; and that the Jesus movement experienced at least some persecution at the hands of some fellow Jews.[15]

Sanders regards these as unassailable starting points and selects the action against the temple (Mark 11:15–19) and the traditions about the choosing of the Twelve as the bases for suggesting that Jesus is best understood as a prophet who expected the eschatological restoration of Israel and enacted the symbolic destruction and renewal of the Temple.[16] Having determined the Temple incident as a starting point, Sanders can then introduce sayings that relate to the Temple (Mark 13:1–2; 14:57–58), viewing them through the lens of restorationist eschatology.

Yet neither the historicity of the Temple act nor its significance has gone unquestioned. Even if the incident is regarded as historical, it is scarcely unambiguous: the action of overturning tables in the forecourt of the Temple is not obviously a "symbolic destruction" and that it was a sign of expected restoration is even less obvious. Jesus' baptism by John presents similar problems. John was an ascetic preacher with a message of a coming fiery judgment (Q 3:7–9, 16–17) associated with the arid Jordan valley, while Jesus was more regularly connected with the large towns of the Galilee, and was evidently not an ascetic. Hence, the erstwhile association of Jesus with John, while historically likely, does not in the final analysis provide an unambiguous characterization of Jesus.

The Synoptic Problem. A third problem in starting points has to do with the way the Jesus tradition is assessed. In an earlier era influenced by form criticism, Gospel material could be treated as if the order of composition of the Gospels did not matter much, because form criticism assumed that the evangelists contributed little to the Gospels apart from the juxtaposition of individual units of tradition. With the advent of redaction criticism, the editorial contribution of the evangelists became more important, and the issue of the literary relationship among the Gospels (called "the Synoptic Problem") took on new significance.

The most commonly accepted hypothesis, the Two Document hypothesis, holds that Matthew and Luke each independently used two written sources: the Gospel of Mark and a nonnarrative document, now called the Sayings Gospel Q. Dieter Lührmann has observed that despite the very widespread acceptance of the Two Document hypothesis, with its corollaries of the priority of Mark and Q, historical Jesus scholarship has turned again and again to *Matthew's* portrait of Jesus and privileged the Matthean issues of Jesus and the Torah.[17] This methodological inconsistency has to some extent been faced in some of the newer wave of historical Jesus studies. Integral to the very fabric of Crossan's method is careful attention to stratigraphy and source criticism. He disciplines himself by a rigorous adherence to the principle of multiple, early, and independent attestations of traditions about Jesus. This means that traditions attested in several *independent* documents (for example, Mark and Q and the *Gospel of Thomas*) are weighted more heavily than singly attested materials (for example, the Lukan Parable of the Good Samaritan). His attention to stratigraphy, which parcels out the tradition into several strata, is expressly connected to his acceptance of the Two-Document hypothesis and of the essential independence of the *Gospel of Thomas* from the Synoptics. Whether one agrees with these source-critical judgments or not is not the point here; rather, the point is that for Crossan, the Synoptic problem has affected his understanding of the Jesus tradition in a way that it did not in earlier generations of historical Jesus studies.[18]

The influence of source criticism can also be seen on E. P. Sanders's recent *The Historical Figure of Jesus.* Sanders does not adhere to the Two Document hypothesis but instead adopts a form of the Farrer-Goulder hypothesis, which asserts Markan priority but holds that Matthew used Mark and that Luke used both. (This obviates the need for the positing of Q.) This helps to account for the fact that Sanders's book follows essentially the outline of Mark (although he is far from uncritical in his use of Mark). Similarly, William Farmer's *The Gospel of Jesus* privileges Matthew in what he says about Jesus for the reason that Farmer advocates a Two-Gospel hypothesis, which places Matthew first, makes Luke directly dependent on Matthew, and Mark a conflation of Matthew and Luke.[19] The point here, again, is not whether either the Farrer-Goulder or the Two-Gospel hypotheses are adequate descriptions of synoptic relationships; I do not think that they account for the data as adequately as the Two-Document hypothesis. But both Sanders and Farmer have taken seriously their own source-critical convictions in a way that others have not.

Criteria of Authenticity. The issue of the criteria used to differentiate authentic Jesus tradition from other materials ascribed to Jesus is, on the surface, less controverted. Although there are some variations in designation and enumeration of the criteria, a large degree of common ground exists. Dennis Polkow's helpful survey divides these into preliminary, primary, and secondary criteria.[20]

1) Preliminary Criteria. In the first place, some sayings and stories or elements of these units coincide strongly with the editorial interests of the evangelists and with the interests of earlier Christian communities and should for that reason be discounted. As Sanders has put it, whatever is "too much with the grain" should be suspect. For example, redactional analysis shows that Mark maximizes pro-Gentile elements in this Gospel in spite of a general paucity of sayings having to do with Gentiles, suggesting that sayings such as Mark 13:10 (which predicts a Gentile mission) are so congenial with Mark's own interests that they cannot easily be ascribed to Jesus. By contrast, a saying such as Mark 7:27 (Jesus' saying about feeding the children before the dogs), which depicts Jesus as hesitant in dealings with Gentiles, goes against the grain of Mark's intention. For this reason it is unlikely to be Mark's creation, although that does not mean that it comes from Jesus. On the other hand, Sanders suggests that Matt. 10:23 (the prediction that the mission to Israel will not be completed before the Parousia) coincides with the interests of Jewish Christians who systematically opposed a Gentile mission. Thus neither the programmatically pro-Gentile Mark 13:10 nor the anti-Gentile Matt. 10:23 goes back to Jesus. Such endorsements are the work of later tradents.[21]

2) Primary Criteria. Once the editorializing of the evangelists and the tendencies of the earliest tradents are bracketed, three primary criteria are relevant.

A. The first is generally called the criterion of *dissimilarity* (also called "discontinuity" [Meier] or "uniqueness" [Sanders]).[22] This criterion isolates materials that are dissimilar, both to the *characteristic* emphases of contemporary Judaism and of primitive Christianity. Thus, for example, the injunction "let the dead bury the dead" in response to a request of a would-be follower first to bury his father (Luke 9:59–60) is shocking in the context of Second Temple Judaism (and, indeed, the Mediterranean world). It is hardly a piece of common lore taken over from the culture and placed on Jesus' lips, and it would hardly have been formulated by early Christians, who displayed no inclination to challenge contemporary burial practices.

Closely related to dissimilarity is Meier's criterion of "embarrassment," which looks for materials that proved embarrassing to early Christians—for example, the fact that Jesus was baptized by John—and which the evangelists tried to rationalize in various ways.[23] The embarrassment felt by the evangelists is usually taken as a good indication that such materials would not have been invented by early Christians but came from Jesus himself. The criterion of dissimilarity and embarrassment isolate a small set of highly distinctive materials—indispensable for any portrait, but insufficient in themselves for a comprehensive picture of Jesus.

There are, of course, disagreements among those who accept the criteria of dissimilarity over whether particular sayings qualify. For example, many critics treat Mark 7:15 (on what defiles) as authentic because it stands out so sharply in the context of the dietary customs of Second Temple Judaism.[24] But the decision turns both on the interpretation of the saying and how much dissimilarity the critic is prepared to allow Jesus. Both Funk and Witherington, for example, understand Mark 7:15 to be an explicit rejection of *kashruth* (that is, dietary regulations regarding what is "kosher"). Witherington thinks that Jesus declared portions of the Torah to be invalid.[25] Mark's Gentile community, which did not observe *kashruth* in the first place, would have no reason to invent the saying and the saying is hardly a common aphorism placed on Jesus' lips. Hence, for Witherington, the saying meets the criterion of dissimilarity. Sanders also takes the saying to be about *kashruth* (as Mark plainly does) but concludes that the saying is "too revolutionary" to have come from Jesus.[26]

B. The second primary criterion is *multiple attestation,* which isolates materials that appear in more than one independent *source* (Mark, Q, Paul), or motifs or phrases that appear in more than one *form* of discourse (parable, chreia, aphorism).[27] As noted above, a saying concerning children and the kingdom appears in multiples sources: in Mark (10:13–16), special Matthean material (18:3), the *Gospel of Thomas* (22) and in John (3:3, 5). The parable of the mustard seed appears in Q (13:18–19), Mark (4:30–32), and the *Gospel of Thomas* (20); and Jesus' saying on divorce is attested in Mark (10:11–12), Q (16:18), 1 Cor. 7:10–11. The "reign of God" appears not only in several independent sources, but in a variety of discursive forms: beatitudes (Q 6:20b; *Gos. Thom.* 54); admonitions (Q 10:9; 12:31); aphorisms (Q 7:28; Matt. 18:3), parables (Mark 4:30; Matt. 13:44, 47); a prayer (Q 11:2); prophetic sayings (Mark 9:1; Q 13:28–29); and chriae (Luke 17:20–21). Similarly, Jesus' association with toll collectors is found in call stories (Mark 2:14); controversy chriae (Mark 2:16–17); aphorisms (Q 7:34); parables (Luke 18:10–13); and anecdotes (Luke 19:1–11). Of course the mere fact that a particular motif is multiply attested does not mean every occurrence of that motif is authentic. Nor does the multiple attestation of a story or saying imply that there are not elements in those units that are redactional or secondary. But multiple attestation does indicate that the saying or motif in question is not simply the creation of the evangelist, and it shows that it was commonly enough associated with Jesus to have become part of several streams of tradition or types of sayings.

C. The third primary criterion, coherence, is really dependent upon the first two. It isolates sayings that are not obviously dissimilar or multiply attested, but which nevertheless cohere with the core Jesus tradition.[28]

The criterion of coherence is normally understood as pertaining to content: sayings or stories that are materially consistent with sayings otherwise judged to be authentic can also be included within the corpus of historical Jesus materials. Robert Funk has in effect proposed a criterion of stylistic or rhetorical coherence, identifying as authentic those sayings that are characterized by exaggeration, typification, caricature, or reversal, or that are antithetic couplets, parodies, or paradoxes.[29] Thus, for example, the Lukan story of the Pharisee and the toll collector

(18:10–14a) exhibits both caricature—Pharisees are not in fact especially hypo-critical and toll collectors are not that humble—and reversal. This criterion, of course, is rather subjective: presumably Jesus had no monopoly on caricature, antithetic parallelism, or exaggeration. As in the case of dissimilarity, critics will inevitably differ on whether a particular saying is coherent enough, either materially or rhetorically, with other Jesus tradition to be included.

3) Secondary criteria. In addition to these three primary criteria,[30] Polkow lists secondary criteria—coherence with Palestinian culture and the Aramaic language. There are obvious caveats with both: since Jesus' first followers were also Palestinian and (presumably) spoke Aramaic, the presence of Aramaisms in a saying or its coherence with Palestinian culture does not automatically imply authentic material. Moreover, it is often difficult to distinguish "semitisms" from Septuagintalisms and both from simple colloquial Greek; hence, linguistic criteria can at best be corroborative and never primary.

Polkow also lists as secondary stylistic criteria that are distinguishable from the rhetorical elements which I have treated under the heading of coherence. C. F. Burney and Joachim Jeremias looked to features such as the use of the "divine passive" and semitic style—parallelism, rhythm and rhyme—as indications of authenticity.[31] As with linguistic criteria, however, this criterion tacitly assumes that only Jesus used a semitizing style, which is hardly likely to have been the case.

Eugene Boring suggests two interrelated criteria, "plausible tradition history" and "hermeneutical potential."[32] Both begin with diversity—the diversity of forms of sayings, and the diversity of interpretations of Jesus generated by the tradition. Just as in text criticism, where the best reading accounts for all others, these two criteria in effect attempt to identify the earliest forms and versions of sayings by reconstructing a stemma that arranges all versions of a saying or motif in such a way as to derive less original forms from more original forms, and to suggest the basis on which hermeneutical diversity originated.[33]

Although there is an impressive degree of agreement on the relevant criteria, the application of the criteria differs from one critic to another. As noted above, Crossan privileges multiple independent attestation over other criteria. Using this standard, a saying such as Luke 9:60, which Sanders treats as indubitably authentic, is not mentioned by Crossan because it is attested in only one source (Q). Conversely, the sayings about children and the kingdom, ignored by Sanders and Meier, are given a prominent place in Crossan's book. The virtue of Crossan's procedure is its measure of objectivity[34] insofar as it requires the interpreter to face numerically well-attested traditions and discourages the founding of a portrait of Jesus on a singly attested saying or story.

On the other hand, one might argue that the materials that are multiply attested are not necessarily the most distinctive or characteristic aspects of Jesus, only what happened to be most widely disseminated. It also seems a defensible procedure, therefore, to begin with what is judged to be the most characteristic items of the inventory. For this reason, presumably, Funk begins with Jesus' parables, whether or not they are multiply attested, and then moves to other materials.[35] Other scholars, such as Sanders and Meier, begin with those items that they regard to be the most historically certain—the disruption of the Temple (Sanders) and Jesus' baptism by John (Meier)—and then by a synthetic process accumulate related materials into a fuller portrait.[36] Such procedures trade the discipline provided by multiple attestation for the security afforded by strong arguments from dissimilarity or embarrassment.

INTERPRETIVE ISSUES

Some of the variation in scholarly reconstructions of Jesus derives from differences over the methodological issues noted above—whether one includes noncanonical gospels or not, whether one begins with the sayings or the deeds of Jesus, whether one adopts the Two-Document hypothesis or not (and takes its implications seriously), and whether one privileges multiple attestation or dissimilarity. These disagreements account for many of the differences in current portraits of Jesus. Other variations derive from the fact that since our sources are fragmentary and since the available data have "blanks" that must be filled, the blanks can be filled in a variety of ways. Another dimension of the problem, however, has to do with the way scholars move from the isolation of authentic Jesus materials to the synthetic enterprise of producing a coherent portrait. Many decisions relating to this exercise are functions of theoretical or ideological (theological) commitments.[37]

In saying this I wish to make clear that I am *not* speaking about personal commitments or about individual psychology (though a few recent reviewers seem tempted to reduce disagreements to such factors). Most of those who have contributed major works to historical Jesus studies are well-trained scholars who employ critical methods precisely to obtain a measure of control on their own tendencies and preferences.[38] To reduce disagreements among scholars to personal "preferences" trivializes their work and needlessly impugns their integrity as scholars. What I have in mind are the larger interpretive frameworks within which portraits of Jesus are offered and the fundamental choices that define these frameworks—choices that do not derive directly from historical data. Let me illustrate.

A representative selection of current portraits of Jesus reveals differing emphases regarding several basic issues, of which I will mention three: (1) whether Jesus' "eschatology" should be treated as a defining issue and whether Jesus expected an imminent and dramatic intervention by God and a corresponding transformation of human affairs; (2) whether the principal locus of transformation represented by the reign of God (whatever it was and whenever it was expected) should be seen as individual and personal, or whether it pertained more broadly to "Israel" or some other large entity (related to this is the question of whether Jesus' "reign of God" was something to be awaited more or less passively, or whether it was to be expressed in a set of social, political, and economic transformations in the lives of its adherents); and (3) whether the data of the Jesus tradition should be read against the background of "Judaism" (and if so, which "Judaism"), Galilean regionalism, or the typicalities of Mediterranean peasant culture.

Put so starkly, these beg many questions of definition and represent false dichotomies. To take only the last issue: Jesus, of course, was an Israelite, a Galilean, and lived in an eastern Mediterranean culture. The Torah was a key part of Israelite identity, as were the typical Mediterranean dynamics of honor and shame, patronage, and the notion that all goods (material and nonmaterial) were in limited supply. The interpretive issue, however, is which of these frameworks the interpreter chooses to privilege as *primary*. Nothing in the data about Jesus tells us how to frame our reconstruction; there is no neutral or objective or self-evidently correct framework. The choice of frameworks is interpretive and a function of the theoretical issues that each interpreter sees as being at stake in historical Jesus studies.

Reconstruction involves acts of comparison with three dimensions. The scholar first decides which data are most reliable on the basis of the criteria indicated above. Then, s/he sets these data within a comparative framework (Second Temple apocalyptic Judaism; early scribalism; Mediterranean village culture; Greco-Roman Cynicism), noting similarities and certain differences. Thus, one can conclude that Jesus was "like" a classical Hebrew prophet or a Cynic or an apocalypticist in certain specifiable ways, notwithstanding clear differences. But such a comparison is done for specific (though often unstated) theoretical reasons.[39] This third member in the comparative act, the scholar's theoretical interests, helps to render intelligible *why* a certain comparison is ventured and what interpretive interest is being served. It is necessary to insist that it is not possible or even theoretically desirable to work without such interests. The presence of such interests does not render the comparative work "subjective" or otherwise flawed. Indeed, the scholar's theoretical interests are what make the comparison productive of meaning.

Jesus and Apocalyptic Eschatology. Much recent historical Jesus scholarship has given special prominence to a link between Jesus' preaching and imminent eschatological expectation. It is not that Jesus expected the "end of the world" in the sense of the dissolution of the cosmos; rather, the reign of God he expected involved a decisive intervention of God in human history and an empirically visible (and dramatic) transformation. Among those who underscore this feature of Jesus' expectations, disagreements exist as to whether Jesus can be described as an apocalypticist who (mistakenly) expected this transformation in the near future, or whether he had a less specific, but nonetheless definite, temporal expectation. Dale Allison and E. P. Sanders are willing to embrace a Jesus who made such a mistake.[40] Gnilka and Meier, on the other hand, avoid the embarrassment of Jesus being wrong about the coming of the kingdom by rejecting such obviously predictive sayings as Mark 9:1; 13:30 and Matt. 10:23 as nonauthentic. They insist, nonetheless, on a twofold character of Jesus' preaching: first, that Jesus expected the future coming of the reign of God and, second, that he also thought that reign of God was somehow being actualized of mediated in his own activities.

Other scholars, however, downplay significantly Jesus' eschatology. Marcus Borg observes that a majority of modern scholars reject the authenticity of the future Son of Man sayings (e.g., Mark 8:38; 13:27; 14:62; Matt. 10:23; Q 12:40; 17:24, 26–30), which formerly had been employed to illustrate Jesus' futuristic orientation. Without such sayings to provide an interpretive context, Jesus' sayings about the reign of God lose any strong connection with imminent end-expectation.[41] It is not that the kingdom sayings are not about a crisis, but for Borg that crisis is the "end of the world of conventional wisdom as a basis for existence, as well as the threatened end of the 'social world' of Judaism (including the threat of war and the destruction of Jerusalem and the temple)."[42] Rather than being an apocalypticist, Borg's Jesus is a teacher of "world-subverting wisdom."

What is at stake in this debate? Almost a century ago, Albert Schweitzer proposed an apocalyptic Jesus, basing this understanding on the apocalyptic documents of Second Temple Judaism.[43] His Jesus was thus consistent with the supposedly thoroughly apocalyptic climate of the first century. Schweitzer's Jesus, however, was a stranger to the world of the early 1900s, for at the time Schweitzer wrote apocalypticism was alien to European culture and was regarded with distaste and disdain.

Ironically, since Schweitzer's time a complete reversal has occurred. The terms "eschatological" and "apocalyptic"—usually stripped of their most blatantly predictive aspects—are regularly used in order to *distinguish* Jesus from his environment. Thus, for example, Martin Hengel's study of discipleship uses the category of "eschatological charismatic" in order to render Jesus incomparable and unique within Judaism and the Hellenistic world.[44] But at the same time, eschatology was elevated to a central theological category by such systematic theologians as Wolfhart Pannenberg and Jürgen Moltmann, so that Jesus' announcement of an imminent and decisive transformation of human reality happily coincides with what is seen to be at the heart of the Christian theological project. Hence, the emphasis on the eschatological orientation of Jesus serves to cement the historical Jesus to contemporary Christian theological interests rather than to distance him from modern sensibilities.

Seán Freyne is one of the rare exegetes to declare his theological interests in the historical Jesus. The insistence on the eschatological nature of Jesus' career, he says,

> arises from my concern regarding the claims of ultimacy that Christian faith makes in terms of Jesus. . . . In the absence of an eschatological dimension to Jesus' utterances it would be impossible to see how any *christological claims* could be grounded in his earthly life, which is precisely the issue that gave rise to the quest for the historical Jesus in the first place as both an ecclesial and academic exercise.[45]

This admission is both welcome and weighty for it makes clear the theoretical interest—christology and ultimacy—that Freyne sees as being served by highlighting Jesus' eschatology. "Eschatology" stands as a cipher for finality and ultimacy. Freyne expresses hesitations about this admission, fearing that it will destroy the credibility of his historical reconstruction. It should have no such effect. In Freyne's case there is little danger of him being accused of engaging in covert apologetics or of smuggling theology into his historical analysis. But his admission clarifies why eschatology—however it is construed—has achieved so central a place in some treatments of the historical Jesus.[46]

In making this observation, I want to be clear that I am not suggesting that those reconstructions that underscore the future aspects of the "reign of God" necessarily do so out of a theoretical concern for christology. E. P. Sanders, for example, stresses the future aspects of Jesus' proclamation and thinks that Jesus probably regarded himself as God's agent, but doubts that he thought the reign of God to be especially present in his own ministry or that he can be thought to be unique.[47] Sanders's theoretical concern is not christology, however; rather, it is to root Jesus and his activities firmly within Second Temple Judaism and to disallow a portrait of Jesus as "against" or "superseding" "Judaism." Géza Vermès likewise insists on Jesus' wholehearted endorsement of the Baptist's eschatological expectations, but not for christological reasons.[48] On the contrary, Vermès wants to rescue Jesus, whom he describes as a Galilean holy man, from Christianity.[49] While both Sanders and Vermès might approve of Hengel's category of "eschatological charismatic," that designation makes him comparable and commensurable, not incommensurable and unique.

Eschatology can be stressed in a portrait of Jesus for a number of reasons. Some might have to do with understanding the relation between Jesus' activities and traditional christological assertions; or, they may have to do with an effort to root Jesus firmly in the life and expectations of Second Temple Judaism and thus obviate the strong tendency of New Testament scholars (at least in the past) to define Jesus over against "Judaism."

On the other hand, those portraits that do not stress future eschatology are not necessarily devoid of christological interests. Future expectations play little role in Elizabeth Schüssler Fiorenza's treatment of Jesus. Instead, she focuses on Jesus' liberative practice in the present, his critique of patriarchy (also in the present) and his retrieval of wisdom theology and his role as a prophet of Sophia.[50] Marcus Borg, perhaps the most vocal advocate of a nonapocalyptic Jesus, offers an alternative portrait of Jesus as a "holy person," "person of the Spirit," and "charismatic wisdom prophet"—each with evident christological potential. For both Fiorenza and Borg, Jesus' concrete engagement with social and political realities of his day are essential to any portrait of the historical figure and to any christology that flows from that portrait. The standard portrait of an apocalyptic prophet too easily disconnects Jesus from that environment.[51]

To observe that theoretical interests are at work in the construction of various portraits of Jesus is *not* necessarily to imply that the various reconstructions are *reducible* to those interests; it does suggest, however, that a critical reading of those reconstructions must attend to the comparative project that is being ventured.

A Revolutionary Kingdom? A second obvious difference in historical Jesus studies concerns whether Jesus is understood as engaged in a project of corporate renewal of Israel (or some "large" entity) or whether his appeal was mainly to individual persons. Entangled with this question is another one: whether the kingdom Jesus proclaimed was to be awaited passively, or whether it symbolized a set of alternative, perhaps radical or revolutionary, postures.

Sanders argues that Jesus stood in a tradition of restorationist prophecy. In Sanders's view, the action against the Temple and the calling of the Twelve were symbolic actions that pointed to the imminent restoration and renewal of Israel.[52]

As noted above, Sanders rejects the idea that Jesus programmatically opposed the Torah. What set him off from other sectors of Second Temple Judaism was his view on repentance. Whereas repentance and observance of the commandments were normally assumed to be a precondition for entry into the Kingdom, Sanders's Jesus held that "God showed his mercy to those who heard and responded to him and his message even while they lived outside the framework of at least some of the Mosaic ordinances; that is, while they were still 'tax-gatherers and sinners.' "[53]

Despite the fact that Jesus' reign of God, according to Sanders, would involve a future renewed social order in which sinners were included and while it would include a reversal of important social values,[54] there is little evidence from Sanders's description that in the present the kingdom implied any social transformation. The reign of God involved so dramatic a change—including the "miraculous" recreation of Israel and reconstitution of the ten lost tribes—that it would be unimaginable that Jesus could have thought that this would be accomplished by social and political reforms.[55] Thus, the miraculous and otherworldly nature of the coming kingdom in effect pushes out any meaningful this-worldly anticipation of the kingdom that is less than miraculous.

The same is true of Meier's Jesus. Meier thinks that Jesus' ministry had the corporate aim of reconstituting the scattered people of God and that he expected a dramatic intervention by God in which the poor would be exalted and justice established. But for Meier, Jesus expected God *alone* to act; "humans can only wait for it"; the reign of God "is a revolution wrought by God alone as this present world comes to an end."[56] Thus Jesus was neither a revolutionary nor a social reformer.[57] This postponing of the reign of God into the future has the odd effect of giving Jesus a dramatic *message,* but leaves him strangely devoid of concrete impact, except at the level of ideas.

A very different portrait emerges in the works of Marcus Borg and especially Richard Horsley. It is perhaps significant that neither emphasizes the futuristic and otherworldly character of the reign of God; indeed, Borg argues against this. Borg's Jesus is a visionary with "world subverting wisdom" who was critical of "the politics of holiness"—a set of social and political arrangements predicated on distinctions of pure and impure. In its place, Jesus advocated "compassion as alternate paradigm for the transformation of Israel's life."[58] Jesus' critique challenged the dangerous nationalism driven by the politics of holiness, and in this sense Jesus' social vision constituted a real threat to the established order.[59]

Horsley provides an even more nuanced reading of the Jesus tradition through the lens of the politics of agrarian societies under foreign control. Understanding the basic fault lines of Jewish Palestine to run between the taxers and the taxed, the governors and the governed, Horsley views Jesus as invoking the covenantal and prophetic traditions of Israel in support of the plight of the poor. Horsley is critical of readings that suppose that Jesus expected a "miraculous change," arguing that these are designed to divert attention from the social and political dimensions of Jesus' message. Since "religion" in the ancient world was not a realm separate from political and social relations, such a diversion is also anachronistic. According to Horsley, apocalyptic texts are not fantasies about future transformations but have a historical orientation and must be given a sociopolitical reading. They express "in ordinary language eager hopes for an anti-imperial revolution."[60] Thus, for example, the prediction of the destruction of the Temple and other anti-Temple sayings amount to a judgment of the ruling institutions of Israel and an attack on the ruling families.[61] In place of a hierarchical, imperial and exploitative model of society, Jesus substituted a model of local (village) cooperation that encouraged solidarity (rather than the divisive social relations created by exploitation), debt cancellation, local autonomy, and a form of egalitarianism.[62]

It is unfair to Borg, Horsley, and Fiorenza to caricature their view of Jesus as that of a "social reformer." The term presupposes the structures of modern politics and the modern compartmentalizing of "religion," "politics," and "economics" into discrete and separate divisions of culture—something that was not part of the ancient Mediterranean world. Borg and Horsley affirm the concrete social and political *implications* in the message of Jesus and hence do not postpone his "revolution" to the apocalyptic future. Their Jesus embodied a real threat to established power precisely because the reign of God, active in the present, constituted a set of practices of resistance to domination and exploitation or to social arrangements predicated on purity distinction. This Jesus was dangerous at the level of praxis, not just ideas.

It is not difficult to see that just as theoretical concerns to relate Jesus to later christological assertions, or to the theological streams of "Judaism," are supported by reconstructions that underscore Jesus' eschatology, so the reconstructions of Borg, Horsley, and Fiorenza are designed to address the question of how and where Jesus fit (or failed to fit) into the society of Jewish Palestine. Part of the reason for differing configurations of the data is that the questions are different. Borg, Horsley, and Fiorenza begin with sociopolitical rather than theological or ideological questions. Such questions are a needed correction to the tendency of earlier generations of biblical scholars who often treated "theology" as the central aspect of texts, ignoring the intimate relationship between theological assertions and social location and treating discourse about the "reign of God," forgiveness, and justice as if they could be detached from the present experience of foreign domination, injustice, debt, and subsistence.

Which "Judaism"? A final theoretical issue that informs scholarly constructs of the historical Jesus concerns the issue of which "Judaism" provides the most suitable interpretive framework for understanding Jesus: early scribalism? apocalyptic movements? Qumran? Galilean village culture? As I have suggested above, nothing tells us which one is the most appropriate; in fact, different comparative frameworks are appropriate to different tasks.

It is a truism that Jesus was a Jew. Most interpreters accordingly pay attention to the history and culture of Jewish Palestine at least in general terms. Most recognize important differences between the culture(s) of Palestine and those of other parts of the empire, and some are aware of finer distinctions: for example, between Greek cities and Roman cities or colonies; between autonomous (for example, Tyre) and nonautonomous cities (for example, Jerusalem and Tiberias); and between the cities (*poleis*), their attached city-regions, and the hinterland. Sophisticated analyses now

understand that we can no longer divide the Mediterranean into two cultural
spheres—Jewish and Hellenistic—as earlier generations of scholars did; we must be
prepared to see multiple competing cultures and layers of culture, both outside Palestine and within Jewish Palestine. Judaism in rural Galilee was not identical with the
Judaism of urban elites of Jerusalem, or of rural Judaea, or of the inhabitants of Qumran, or of Caesarea Maritima, or of Sepphoris, and so forth. The selection of any one
of these cultures as the comparative framework for understanding Jesus has important consequences, both in what may become visible and in what is obscured.

To insist that Jesus be situated firmly within Second Temple Judaism reflects
in part a salutary resolve to guard against the earlier tendencies to see Jesus as tran-
scending and even rejecting fundamental aspects of "Judaism" and as somehow
not, or no longer, "Jewish." The Holocaust has made painfully clear the hideous
consequences of supersessionist readings of the Jesus tradition. The works of
Sanders and others who have underscored Jesus "within" Judaism are important
efforts to rid historical Jesus studies of the toxin of antisemitism. In this regard, it
must be observed that the perfectly legitimate *historiographical* goal of understanding how Jesus may have been *distinct* in his context can easily slip into in-
vidious caricatures of Jewish culture(s), especially when the inquiry is tied to
theological concerns to make Jesus *unique*. Christian scholarship on Jesus has often been criticized as potentially or actually antisemitic, and more recently some
have observed that feminist treatments of Jesus' liberative praxis are sometimes
constructed at the expense of "Judaism," which is caricatured as "patriarchal" and
"oppressive."[63]

To agree that Jesus belongs to Second Temple Judaism does not, however, set-
tle the issue of a more specific historical location. Vermès and Sanders have shown
by careful comparison of Jesus' sayings with the first-century antecedents of rabbinic Judaism that Jesus' views of the Torah would hardly have placed him outside
the orbit of first-century Judaism. Although some have even attempted to make of
Jesus a liberal Pharisee,[64] a more compelling portrait treats Jesus as non-Pharisaic
teacher whose view of the Torah, nonetheless, was either fully within the range of
Second Temple discussions of the Torah (Vermès) or largely so (Sanders).[65]

A seemingly divergent portrait of Jesus has been offered by Crossan and Mack,
who compare Jesus with Greco-Roman Cynics.[66] The comparison is not intended
to constitute a claim that Jesus was "influenced" by Cynics or was a "member" of
a Cynic "school." In fact, no unified Cynic "school" existed. Neither Crossan nor
Mack is oblivious to differences between largely urban Cynics and the Jesus of
Galilean town and village culture: Jesus and the Jesus movement had, unlike the
Cynics, something of a social vision and social program.[67] Nevertheless, the *comparison* with Cynicism serves to underscore the countercultural, even "deviant"
character of Jesus' activity. This portrayal represents in many ways only an ex-
trapolation of earlier representations of Jesus as embodying "novel," "striking,"
"countercultural," "marginal," or "world-subverting" sayings and practices—depictions that are nearly ubiquitous in historical Jesus studies.

The reaction engendered by the "Cynic hypothesis" is striking in its vigor;
clearly, a deep nerve has been probed. Extraordinary efforts have been taken to

"demonstrate" that no Cynics were present in Galilee (something that the "Cynic hypothesis" does not in fact require). Indeed, the proponents and opponents of the hypothesis often argue at cross purposes; thus, it is asserted that Jesus was a Jew, as if this somehow means that he could not have been Cynic-*like*. But, as William Arnal rightly observes, "the issue cannot be whether Jesus was either 'Jewish' or 'Cynic/Hellenistic,' in spite of it being framed this way far too frequently; it is instead *what kind of Jew* Jesus was."[68]

The assertion that "Jesus was a Jew" of course rightly locates Jesus in the history, culture, and institutions of Israel. But all too often it also embodies a tacit assumption that "Jew" means "religious Jew" and that "religion" is a discrete and bounded realm of cultural discourse, separate from social (family, village) and political structures. Thus, the assertion serves to isolate Jesus, not only from the context of the other cultural discourses of the Mediterranean, but from the social and political culture of Jewish Galilee. The Cynic comparison, like the social and political approaches of Horsley and Borg, assumes that religion was "embedded" in other cultural and social forms and hence, that the tensions between Jesus and his culture which the criterion of dissimilarity isolate should not be interpreted as narrowly defined "religious" opposition, isolated from other cultural possibilities. Without ceasing to be a Galilean Jew, Jesus may *also* have been simultaneously part of an intersecting discourse critical of certain institutions and patterns of his culture and *analogous to* (not influenced by) Cynic criticism of Greek urban culture.[69] The Cynic comparison implicitly resists compartmentalization, either of "religion" with ancient society, or of "Judaism" within the ancient world, but instead attempts to locate Jesus at the conjunction of multiple intersecting discourses.

CONCLUSION

The purpose of this survey of methodological and interpretive problems in historical Jesus studies has not been to encourage readers to "pick and choose" among the various divergent portraits of Jesus, but to understand, first, the somewhat differing methodological foundations on which such portraits are constructed and, second, the important theoretical questions that drive the quest of the historical Jesus. At the level of methodology, scholars are near a consensus in the description (though not the application) of the criteria of authenticity, but differ in important ways in defining the scope of Jesus tradition. Still, it is perhaps not too much to hope that continued debate will bring more agreement, even on such issues as the relevance of the *Gospel of Thomas* or the role of the Synoptic Problem in historical Jesus scholarship. The other set of issues represent a more difficult problem. For until scholars are prepared to acknowledge *why* particular comparisons are ventured and *how* they enlighten particular aspects of the Jesus tradition, historical Jesus studies may be forever locked in a war of competing Jesuses, each having special explanatory power with respect to a given theoretical problem (the foundations of christological doctrine, the history of Christian antisemitism, or significance of "religion" within culture), but each seemingly—though not in fact, I think—completely opposed to the others.

NOTES

1. John Dominic Crossan's *Sayings Parallels: A Workbook for the Jesus Tradition* (Philadelphia: Fortress Press, 1986) listed 502 discrete sayings, some of them multiply attested, while his later inventory of the "Jesus tradition" (which includes stories as well as sayings) contained 522 items. See Crossan, *The Historical Jesus: The Life of a Mediterranean Jewish Peasant* (San Francisco: Harper & Row, 1991), 434–50.

2. For convenient translations of these documents, see Ron Cameron, *The Other Gospels* (Philadelphia: Westminster Press, 1982) or J. K. Elliott, *The Apocryphal New Testament* (Oxford: Clarendon Press, 1993).

3. Joachim Gnilka, *Jesus of Nazareth: Message and History* (Peabody, Mass.: Hendrickson Publishers, 1997), 12–25, esp. 15.

4. Rudolf Schnackenburg, *Jesus in the Gospels: A Biblical Christology* (Louisville, Ky.: Westminster/John Knox Press, 1995), 323.

5. Pierre Grelot (*Jésus de Nazareth, Christ et Seigneur. Tome 1* [Paris: Editions du Cerf, 1997], 215, 264) cites the *Gospel of Thomas* twice, but only to note that it contains parallels to synoptic sayings. N. T. Wright (*Jesus and the Victory of God,* Christian Origins and the Question of God 2 [Minneapolis: Fortress Press, 1996], 47–48) refers to the *Gospel of Thomas* at many points (see 728 *s.v.* "Gospel of Thomas"), but his use of Thomas has no critical function in his argument. Wright's treatment of the *Gospel of Thomas* in *The New Testament and the People of God* (Christian origins and the question of God 1 [Minneapolis: Fortress Press, 1992], 435–39) likewise avoids the key issue of source criticism.

6. For example, Luke Timothy Johnson, *The Real Jesus: The Misguided Quest for the Historical Jesus and the Truth of the Traditional Gospels* (San Francisco: HarperSanFrancisco, 1996), 89, and Ben Witherington, *The Jesus Quest: The Third Search for the Jew of Nazareth* (Downers Grove, Ill: InterVarsity Press, 1995), 49.

7. E. P. Sanders, *The Historical Figure of Jesus* (Harmondsworth, Middlesex: Penguin Books, 1993), 64. Similarly, James H. Charlesworth and Craig A. Evans, "Jesus in the Agrapha and Apocryphal Gospels," *Studying the Historical Jesus: Evaluations of the State of Current Research,* ed. Bruce Chilton and Craig A. Evans; New Testament Tools and Studies 19; (Leiden: E. J. Brill, 1994), 496–503, citing the cautiously positive evaluation of some sayings in the *Gospel of Thomas* by Bruce Chilton, "The Gospel according to Thomas as a Source of Jesus' Teaching," *The Jesus Tradition Outside the Gospels,* ed. David Wenham; Gospel Perspectives 5 (Sheffield: JSOT Press, 1985), 155–75.

8. John P. Meier, *A Marginal Jew: Rethinking the Historical Jesus,* 2 vols. (New York: Doubleday, 1991, 1994), 1:112–66, esp. 139–40. Meier's position, however, is quite moderate: "I will always keep one eye on the sayings in this gospel [the *Gos. Thom.*] as a check on my own interpretation of the data in the canonical Gospels. Even if the *Gospel of Thomas* represents only a gnostic reworking of the Synoptic tradition, what Thomas does to that tradition may highlight certain aspects of it that otherwise might be overlooked."

9. Meier, *Marginal Jew,* 1:123–39; idem, "Dividing Lines in Jesus Research Today: Through Dialectical Negation to a Positive Sketch," *Interpretation* 50/4 (1996): 357, referring to the work of Christopher M. Tuckett, "Thomas and the Synoptics," *Novum Testamentum* 30/2 (1988): 132–57.

10. See Francis T. Fallon and Ron Cameron, "The Gospel of Thomas: A Forschungsbericht and Analysis," *Aufstieg und Niedergang der römischen Weld* II.25.6 (1988): 4195–251.

11. The most cited references that lack clear Synoptic parallels are *Gos. Thom.* 97 (parable of the jar of meal) and 98 (parable of the assassin). Robert W. Funk (*Honest to Jesus: Jesus for a New Millennium* [San Francisco: HarperSanFrancisco, 1996], 331)

adds to these only *Gos. Thom.* 42 ("Become passersby") on which the Jesus Seminar was evenly divided (and hence treated it as "gray").

12. Crossan, *Historical Jesus,* 265–76.

13. Ben F. Meyer, *The Aims of Jesus* (London: SCM Press, 1979).

14. Compare Meier (*Marginal Jew,* 2: 317–36), who, unlike Sanders, Meyer, Gnilka, Witherington, and Wright, gives Q 6:20b considerable attention and makes it a fundamental part of his characterization of the kingdom.

15. Sanders, *Jesus and Judaism* (Philadelphia: Fortress Press, 1985), 11.

16. Sanders, *Jesus and Judaism,* 61–119.

17. Dieter Lührmann, "Die Logienquelle und die Frage nach dem historischen Jesus" (unpublished paper presented at the Fall 1991 Meeting of the Westar Institute, Edmonton, Alberta, 1991).

18. Although Burton L. Mack's *A Myth of Innocence: Mark and Christian Origins* (Philadelphia: Fortress Press, 1988) was intended as a book on Mark (despite widespread misreadings that took it to be a book on Jesus), Mack's brief treatment of Jesus (53–77) took source criticism seriously in a way not seen since the time of Harnack. See further, Burton L. Mack, "Q and a Cynic-Like Jesus," *Whose Historical Jesus?* ed. William E. Arnal and Michel Desjardins (Waterloo, Ont.: Wilfrid Laurier University Press, 1997), 25–36.

19. William R. Farmer, *The Gospel of Jesus* (Louisville, Ky.: Westminster/John Knox, 1994).

20. Dennis Polkow, "Method and Criteria for Historical Jesus Research," *Society of Biblical Literature 1987 Seminar Papers,* ed. Kent H. Richards (Atlanta: Scholars Press, 1987), 336–56.

21. The need to bracket the evangelists' editorializings and materials generated during the period of oral transmission of the Jesus tradition is recognized explicitly or implicitly by virtually all scholars. See Polkow ("Method and Criteria," 343–45; E. P. Sanders and Margaret Davies, *Studying the Synoptic Gospels* (Philadelphia: Trinity Press International, 1989), 304–15; Funk, *Honest to Jesus,* 144, 146–47, 162–63.

22. Polkow, "Method and Criteria," 347–50; Meier, *A Marginal Jew,* 1: 171–74; Sanders and Davies, *Studying the Synoptic Gospels,* 316–23; Funk, *Honest to Jesus,* 145.

23. Similarly, Funk, *Honest to Jesus,* 138.

24. Marcus J. Borg, *Conflict, Holiness & Politics in the Teachings of Jesus,* Studies in the Bible and Early Christianity 5 (New York: Edwin Mellen Press, 1984), 96–99; Bruce Chilton, *Pure Kingdom: Jesus' Vision of God* (Grand Rapids: Wm. B. Eerdmans Publishing Co., 1996), 123; Crossan, *Historical Jesus,* 262, 436; Funk, *Honest to Jesus,* 204, 246–47, 330; Robert W. Funk, Roy W. Hoover, and the Jesus Seminar, *The Five Gospels: The Search for the Authentic Words of Jesus* (New York: Macmillan, 1993), 69. Gnilka, *Jesus,* 215–17; Meier, *Marginal Jew,* 1: 173; Ben Witherington III, *The Christology of Jesus* (Minneapolis: Fortress Press, 1993), 63–65. Wright, *Jesus,* 397.

25. Funk, *Honest to Jesus,* 204–06. Witherington, *Christology,* 63–64. Both suggest that this reading of Mark 7:15 is not contradicted by the controversy in Acts 15 and Galatians (see below), suggesting that some of Jesus' sayings were not immediately understood by his disciples. Wright (*Jesus,* 396) also sees the matter as directly touching food laws: Jesus insisted that "genuine purity is a matter of the heart, for which the normal laws of purity . . . are irrelevant."

26. E. P. Sanders, *Jewish Law from Jesus to the Mishnah: Five Studies* (Philadelphia: Trinity Press International, 1990), 28. In *Jesus and Judaism* (266), he argues that the later positions of the "false brethren" of Galatians would be unintelligible had Jesus actually have made a statement such as Mark 7:15, and in *Studying* (314) he adds that the saying is not multiply attested (but see *Gos. Thom.* 14!).

27. Polkow, "Method and Criteria," 350–51; Meier, *Marginal Jew,* 1: 174–75; Sanders and Davies, *Studying the Synoptic Gospels,* 323–30.

28. Charles E. Carlston, "A *Positive* Criterion of Authenticity," *Bible Review* 7 (1962):

33–44; Polkow, "Method and Criteria," 350; Meier, *Marginal Jew*, 1: 174–175; Funk, *Honest to Jesus*, 138. Sanders and Davies, *Studying the Synoptic Gospels*, do not treat this as a separate criterion.

29. Funk, *Honest to Jesus*, 149–58.
30. Meier (*Marginal Jew*, 1: 177) adds the criterion of "rejection and execution," which he does not apply to individual sayings or deeds, but to the resulting portrait of Jesus. A convincing portrait of Jesus, says Meier, must be able to account for the fact that Jesus did "threaten, disturb, and infuriate people." Sanders and Davies (*Studying the Synoptic Gospels*, 330–34) use details that were agreed upon by "friend and foe"—for example, that Jesus was a miracle worker and that he made claims about a kingdom. One might add here that he associated with tax collectors, since this theme is found in both accusatory sayings (Q 7:34) and in positive depictions of Jesus' activities (Mark 2:14, 16–17).
31. C. F. Burney, *The Poetry of Our Lord* (Cambridge: Cambridge University Press, 1925); Joachim Jeremias, *New Testament Theology: The Proclamation of Jesus* (London: SCM Press; New York: Charles Scribner's Son, 1971), 9–29.
32. Compare Crossan, "Materials and Methods in Historical Jesus Research," *Forum* 4/4 (1988):3–24, esp. 11, who describes a "criterion of adequacy": "that is original which best explains the multiplicity engendered in the tradition."
33. M. Eugene Boring, "The Historical-Critical Method's 'Criteria of Authenticity': The Beatitudes in Q and Thomas as a Test Case," *Semeia* 44 (1988): 23–24.
34. Compare Harvey K. McArthur, "The Burden of Proof in Historical Jesus Research," *Expository Times* 82 (1971): 116–19, esp. 118, who regards multiple attestation as the most objective criterion and as the proper starting point for arguments for authenticity.
35. Funk, *Honest to Jesus*, 165–96. Polkow ("Method and Criteria," 351) also treats multiple attestation as procedurally secondary to dissimilarity and coherence, serving mainly as corroboration of materials already identified by dissimarility and coherence, and to attest the authenticity of materials that do not meet the criteria of dissimarility and coherence.
36. The weakness of Sanders's procedure, as noted above, is that Sanders not only concludes that the Temple incident is historical but also assumes an *interpretation* of the significance of that event. It is the interpretation (as a prophetic sign of destruction and restoration), which is neither the only interpretation possible nor even the most likely, that governs the rest of his reconstruction. Meier (*Marginal Jew*, 2:100–77) makes a strong argument for the historicity of the original association of Jesus with John and concludes from this that Jesus "carried John's eschatology, concern for sinful Israel facing God's imminent judgment, call to repentance, and baptism with him throughout his own ministry, however much he recycled and reinterpreted this inheritance" (176). But Meier (along with Sanders, Crossan, and others) must argue that Jesus was measurably different from John (ibid., 401). Hence the relation between the elements characteristic of John and the historical Jesus becomes problematic.
37. I do not wish to suggest a unidirectional relationship between the technical phase of isolating historical Jesus tradition and the construction of synthetic portraits; in actual practice, one never comes to the technical phase *tabula rasa*, and the results of historical criticism conversely have the potential to influence one's ideological commitments.
38. See the remarks of Meier (*Marginal Jew*, 1: 6; 2: 5–6), who acknowledges that the application of the criteria of authenticity forced him to conclusions he had not foreseen. For similar remarks, see Sanders, *Jesus and Judaism*, 334–35, and Crossan, *Historical Jesus*, xxviii.
39. Jonathan Z. Smith (*Drudgery Divine: On the Comparison of Early Christianities and the Religions of Late Antiquity* [Chicago: University of Chicago Press, 1990], 115) puts it thus: "[C]omparison, in its strongest form, brings differences together solely

within the space of the scholar's mind. It is the individual scholar, for his or her own good theoretical reasons, who imagines their cohabitation, without even requiring that they be consenting adults. . . ."

40. For example, Dale C. Allison, "A Plea for Thoroughgoing Eschatology," *Journal of Biblical Literature* 113/4 (1994): 651–68, who is critical both of those who embrace an imminent eschatology but who reinterpret such sayings as Mark 9:1 and Mark 13:30 in order to avoid the "humiliating discovery" that Jesus proclaimed a divinely wrought end of the world (Wright and Witherington), and of those who deny or attenuate the futuristic component to Jesus' preaching (Crossan, Borg, and Mack).

41. The most obvious exceptions are Mark 1:15 and 9:1. Most scholars treat Mark 1:15 as a redactional summary, and many (including Meier) consider 9:1 as nonauthentic. Borg (*Jesus in Contemporary Scholarship* [Valley Forge, Penn.: Trinity Press International, 1994], 54) notes that even if it is authentic (which he doubts) it is slender evidence upon which to base an entire reading of the Kingdom sayings.

42. Borg, *Jesus in Contemporary Scholarship,* 59.

43. Albert Schweitzer, *The Kingdom of God and Primitive Christianity,* ed. Ulrich Neuenschwander (London: Adam & Charles Black, 1968), 90–96.

44. Martin Hengel, *The Charismatic Leader and his Followers* (New York: Crossroad, 1981), 69.

45. Seán Freyne, "Galilean Questions to Crossan's Mediterranean Jesus," *Whose Historical Jesus?*, 90 (emphasis added).

46. It does not seem to me self-evident that christological discourse is compromised by Borg's nonapocalyptic Jesus (and Borg himself certainly does not think so). Traditional christologies, which underscore the mediational nature of Jesus' activity, might be endangered by Crossan's Jesus (who proclaims a brokerless kingdom).

47. Sanders, *Jesus and Judaism,* 153, 240. Sanders (ibid., 154) suggests that part of the reason that scholars emphasize the presence of the kingdom in Jesus' teaching is that thereby Jesus' message is rendered more relevant and "problem of his mistake about the immediate future is muted."

48. Géza Vermès, *The Religion of Jesus the Jew* (Minneapolis: Fortress Press, 1993), 146–49.

49. Vermès, *Religion of Jesus,* 5–6. See Larry W. Hurtado, "A Taxonomy of Recent Historical-Jesus Work," *Whose Historical Jesus?,* 277–79.

50. Elisabeth Schüssler Fiorenza, *Jesus: Miriam's Child, Sophia's Prophet: Critical Issues in Feminist Christology* (New York: Continuum, 1994).

51. Borg (*Jesus in Contemporary Scholarship,* 194) suggests that the construal of Jesus as an "eschatological prophet"—and, one might add, the attempts to make Jesus incomparable—has led to theological appropriations which either rendered Jesus silent or which, by way of existential interpretation, "generated a highly individualized and internalized understanding of the message of Jesus."

52. Similarly, Meyer, *Aims of Jesus.*

53. E. P. Sanders, "Jesus, Paul, and Judaism," *Aufstieg und Niedergang der römischen Weld* II.25.1 (1982): 425.

54. See esp. Sanders, *Historical Figure,* 196–204, discussing perfectionism.

55. Sanders, *Historical Figure,* 176, 179, 185. Sanders is far more willing than scholars such as Meier and Gnilka to admit that Jesus expected an imminent and dramatic transformation of the world *and was wrong* (see, ibid., 180, 183). He is also skeptical concerning the assertions that Jesus thought the kingdom to be especially connected with his own activities (*Jesus and Judaism,* 153; *Historical Figure,* 176–78).

56. Meier, *Marginal Jew,* 2: 331. Further, John P. Meier, "Reflection on Jesus-of-History Research Today," *Jesus' Jewishness: Exploring the Place of Jesus within Early Judaism,* ed. James H. Charlesworth (New York: Crossroad, 1991), 84–107, esp. 90–92.

57. Similarly, Witherington, *Jesus Quest,* 236.

58. Borg, *Jesus in Contemporary Scholarship,* 26–27; idem, *Conflict,* passim.

59. Marcus J. Borg, *Jesus, A New Vision: Spirit, Culture, and the Life of Discipleship* (San Francisco: Harper & Row, 1987), 180–84.
60. Richard A. Horsley, *Jesus and the Spiral of Violence: Popular Jewish Resistance in Roman Palestine* (San Francisco: Harper & Row, 1987), 160.
61. Horsley, *Spiral,* 285–317.
62. Horsley, *Spiral,* 192, 246–84.
63. Amy-Jill Levine, "Lilies of the Field and Wandering Jews: Biblical Scholarship, Women's Roles, and Social Location" (Plenary address to the Annual Meeting of the Catholic Biblical Association, University of Seattle, 1997).
64. See Harvey Falk, *Jesus the Pharisee: A New Look at the Jewishness of Jesus* (New York: Paulist Press, 1985), who makes the dubious proposal that Jesus was a Hillelite Pharisee with favorable attitudes toward Gentiles. He interprets the "Pharisaic" opposition that the Gospels report as conflicts between the dominant school of Shammai and an Essene branch of the Hillelite movement to which Jesus belonged. To call Jesus a Pharisee, however, broadens the scope of the term to the point of meaninglessness.
65. Sanders ("Jesus, Paul and Judaism," 411–18) insists that none of Jesus' Sabbath sayings represents a challenge to the sanctity of the Sabbath; the sayings on divorce do not challenge Deut. 24:1, since Jesus only makes the teachings on divorce more strict than the Torah; and Mark 7:15, which Mark takes as implying the abolition of the food laws (7:19b), is not authentic. Only Q 9:59–60 enjoins disobeying a commandment of the Torah. Vermès (*The Religion of Jesus the Jew,* 11–45) doubts that even Q 9:59–60 should be interpreted as a rejection of Torah commandments regarding the burial of the dead.
66. Crossan, *Historical Jesus,* 417–22; Mack, "Q and a Cynic-Like Jesus," 25–36. Strictly speaking, Mack does not write about the historical Jesus, but the character of the earliest Jesus movement. Yet he argues that "the Cynic-like data from Q and Mark are as close as we shall ever get to the real Jesus of history" (36).
67. Crossan (*Historical Jesus,* xii) speaks of Jesus' "ecstatic vision and social program [which] sought to rebuild a society upwards from its grass roots but on principles of religious and economic egalitarianism, with free healing brought directly to the peasant homes and free sharing of whatever they had in return." Mack ("Q and a Cynic-like Jesus," 34–35) argues that the Jesus movement "took a Cynic-like stance towards the world at large, but with respect to one another they were experimenting with a thoroughly social notion."
68. William E. Arnal, "Making and Re-Making the Jesus-Sign: Contemporary Markings on the Body of Christ," *Whose Historical Jesus?,* 309 (emphais original).
69. See Leif E. Vaage, "The Scholar as *Engagé,*" *Whose Historical Jesus?,* 186.

Chapter 3

The Gospel of Matthew

Donald A. Hagner

Those who study the Gospel of Matthew at the beginning of the twenty-first century will be in an advantageous position, thanks to the amount of scholarship devoted to this Gospel during the past few decades. After a relatively quiet period, Matthean studies have again become prominent. A monumental commentary, one of the largest and most important ever written, was finished in 1997: the new International Critical Commentary by W. D. Davies and Dale C. Allison, Jr.[1] In its scope and depth, this commentary is practically an encyclopedia of Matthew. A second major commentary, by the Swiss scholar Ulrich Luz, is currently in process and may well rival the Davies-Allison commentary for length.[2] A massive commentary on the Sermon on the Mount is now available from Hans Dieter Betz.[3] A fourth commentary, in two volumes, by the author of this chapter, has recently been published.[4] Many other commentaries have also appeared over the last fifteen years.[5] A volume of essays on Matthean subjects reflecting the work of the Matthew Group of the Society of Biblical Literature has recently appeared, edited by D. R. Bauer and M. A. Powell.[6] Monographs too numerous to list here have appeared and the number of articles published in journals has been significant. In the present essay, we do not intend to survey all of this literature. Instead, we aim to look at some of the key areas of interest that have emerged over the past twenty years or so, to determine trends and to assess the strength of some of the conclusions increasingly accepted by contemporary scholars.[7]

HISTORICAL QUESTIONS

The Date of the Gospel. The question of the date of Matthew would ordinarily not come into view in this type of an essay, except that it has recently gained considerable attention through the highly publicized claims of the German scholar Carsten P. Thiede. On Christmas eve of 1994 the "discovery" of evidence that could point to a new date for Matthew made front-page news in *The London Times* and was subsequently reported by other newspapers and leading news magazines. On the basis of a fresh examination of three papyrus fragments containing bits of Matthew 26—familiar to scholars as p64—Thiede came to the conclusion that these were to be dated not in the late second century as C. H. Roberts had originally suggested, but a full century earlier.[8] In another, coauthored publication, Thiede argued that comparison of the style of the letters of p64 with that of datable materials from the first century "yields a date of around A.D. 66, with a distinct tendency toward an even slightly earlier date."[9] The study refers to a need to reconsider the dating of a number of other papyrus manuscripts and to draw the conclusion that "the worldwide sensation arising out of the redating of the St. Matthew papyrus at Magdalen College, Oxford, is not an end in itself but merely a beginning."[10]

Thiede's argument has not won much support.[11] Critics have pointed out that he has really brought forward no new or persuasive arguments, either against the traditional dating of the fragments or in favor of his earlier dating. He does not show that Roberts's arguments were incorrect. His case rests entirely on the similarity of the shape of some letters to the same letters in five first-century manuscript sources, including four from Qumran. He ignores the *dis*similarity of other letters, however, and pays no attention to the more important issue of the manner in which the letters were formed. D. C. Parker, indeed, finds the shortcomings of Thiede's arguments "so fundamental as to render his paper worthless."[12]

As poorly founded as Thiede's conclusion is, however, a late first-century date for the writing of the Gospel is hardly something that can be taken for granted. We know very little indeed about the time of the writing of the Gospel. Not a few reputable scholars have argued for a relatively early date.[13] The important thing to remember is that we simply do not know enough to be dogmatic about the date of the Gospel. We are left to the various hypotheses and their relative strengths and weaknesses.

Matthew's Dependence upon Mark. One of the remarkable trends that has gained something of a following over the past few decades is the acceptance of the priority of Matthew over Mark. Since 1964, W. R. Farmer has tirelessly promoted the revival of the Griesbach hypothesis (i.e., that Mark is the abridgement of Matthew and Luke and the last Synoptic Gospel to be written).[14] Despite the amount of energy that has gone into this campaign, however, majority opinion continues to hold to the Two-Document Hypothesis (Mark and Q as the two main sources of Matthew and Luke). C. M. Tuckett has convincingly shown that the latter remains the superior way to account for the phenomena.[15] Both sides of the question have produced a sizable volume of literature and the debate continues,[16] but it is unlikely that the Griesbach hypothesis will win over the majority.

We may only add the point that it is not necessary to hold to Matthean priority to accept an early date (that is, pre-70) for the Gospel. The present author, for example, tentatively dates the Gospel in the late sixties, only a very short time after Mark, upon which Matthew remains dependent.[17]

Matthew's Community: Setting and Social History. One of the most active areas in Gospel studies in recent years has been the nature of Matthew's community. What was its makeup, its recent history, its present tensions? At least four important books deserve mention here. The first is a collection of essays originally presented at a symposium at Southern Methodist University in 1989,[18] and then three monographs, by A. J. Overman,[19] G. Stanton,[20] and A. J. Saldarini.[21]

In the symposium volume, several articles deal with the social setting of the Gospel. Attention is given to the possible urban location of Matthew's community since the Gospel can be seen to reflect the physical and social pressures of a typical Greco-Roman city such as Antioch.[22] Matthew's community represents "an embattled sect seeking to establish its self-definition on the margins of a Hellenistic-Jewish society," in effect having to maintain boundaries and manage crisis in relation to the Jewish community that was challenging it.[23]

Two symposium articles propose the idea that Matthew's community is best understood as a Jewish sect that has not yet made a clear break with the synagogue.[24] The view that Matthew represents a Christianity that is fully within Judaism has now been strengthened by the monographs of Overman and Saldarini. Against the traditional view that Matthew represents a strong *alternative* to Judaism, their hypothesis is that Matthew's group is to be understood as a sect within Judaism. Indeed, Overman talks of not Matthean Christianity, but Matthean *Judaism* and Saldarini not of Matthew's Jewish-Christian community, but of his Christian-*Jewish* community (my italics in both cases). The difference is not merely a semantic one, but one of substance that bears on the essence of Matthew. Both authors show beyond question the thorough Jewishness of the evangelist as reflected in the content of his Gospel. It cannot be doubted that there is much truth in this approach and that light is shed on many Matthean texts.

At the same time, however, this approach fails to account for the dramatically new things that Matthew brings out of his treasure box (see Matt. 13:52). A false dichotomy seems to underlie the work of Overman and Saldarini: Either Matthew is fully Jewish *or* fully Christian. They opt for the former to the neglect of the latter. But Matthew is both fully Jewish and fully Christian, and that is what makes this Gospel so complex and challenging.[25]

The work of Graham Stanton is more satisfying on this subject. He recognizes the thoroughly Jewish character of Matthew, but also that the tensions with Judaism in the Gospel and unique Christian aspects of the Gospel point to a separation that has taken place between the church and the synagogue. At the same time, however, debate with the Jewish community goes on for Matthew and his community. Yes, Matthew thinks of Christianity as the true form of Judaism. But the differences are so great that Matthew's community can hardly be regarded as a sect *within* a larger Judaism.

For the present author,[26] Matthew represents a group of Jewish Christians who find themselves in a particularly difficult situation—between the Jews on the one hand and the Gentile Christians on the other. They were well aware that their Christian faith had separated them from the Jews, and they faced the challenge of defining and defending their faith against continued Jewish unbelief and hostility. They believed that their Judaism alone was the true Judaism, which accounts for the considerable polemic in the Gospel. This hostility between Jews and Jewish Christians goes back almost to the very beginning and continues in a more or less steady crescendo over the decades.

These Jewish Christians had to think not only of their Jewish opponents, but also of the Gentile Christians with whom they shared their faith in Jesus. Now, ironically, they were in many ways closer to them than to their own people. The social dynamics of a situation such as this are well known, and categories referring to social conflict such as sectarian community, identity, boundaries, legitimation, deviance, and control have been used by Overman, Saldarini, and Stanton alike to understand the dynamics of Matthew's social situation. Many texts in Matthew gain illumination from this approach.[27]

The Integrity of the Tradition in Matthew. In the last two decades, the issue of the stability of the oral tradition underlying Matthew has attracted new attention. Following the lead of Birger Gerhardsson,[28] Rainer Riesner[29] and Samuel Byrskog[30] have shown the special character of the Jesus tradition. The fact that 80 percent of the sayings of Jesus are structured in parallel lines indicates that the material was designed to be easily memorized from the very beginning. Furthermore, memorization was fundamental to education in both the Jewish and Greco-Roman contexts, with the result that memories were more retentive then than they are in the modern world of printed texts. For the followers of Jesus who transmitted the material, in short, it was a sacred tradition that was handed on with a high degree of faithfulness. The fact that the disciples cherished Jesus as the unique Teacher brings with it a special care in the transmission of the tradition concerning him. It should not be inferred that the process of writing the Gospels was not a creative one, but only that the creativity did not fundamentally distort or misrepresent the tradition. Matthew in a double way presents a faithful account of Jesus and his teaching—an account that is both essentially reliable and that retrospectively reflects the faith of the post-resurrection church.

INTERPRETATION

Of the three main areas dealt with in this essay, interpretation is without doubt the one most in ferment. The ferment confronts all the Gospels and threatens to shake the very foundations of how we interpret them. At the root of the new interpretive methods is the multidisciplinary approach to New Testament interpretation that has so characterized the last quarter century. We will be wise to look for the contributions that can be gained from these and other new areas of study, and wise not to regard them as excluding the time-honored approaches of the past but as enriching them.

Literary Approaches. Literary aspects of the Bible have long been noted by scholars, and hence, literary criticism is not exactly a new thing. The contemporary approach to the Bible as literature, however, focuses upon literary features and employs the methods of modern literary criticism in such a way that it must be described as a "newer literary criticism," which has shown itself to be fruitful in a variety of ways.[31] The historical narratives of the Bible are stories, and the Gospels supremely so. That is, in the Gospels we confront all the things we are familiar with from other stories: for example, characters, plot, narrative flow, narrator, implied reader, and point of view. Close study of these matters has produced rich insight concerning the content and nature of the Gospels.

The Matthean scholar who has been making the most important contributions in this area is Jack Dean Kingsbury.[32] He has emphasized the necessity of dealing with the whole of the Gospel as a unified story and has produced illuminating studies concerning such things as plot[33] and character.[34] We cannot here summarize the results of the work done on Matthew thus far,[35] but must be content with the following generalization. It is clear that the evangelist has created a self-contained narrative world; filled it with a variety of contrasting characters; marked them with appropriate yet sometimes surprising traits; assembled a plot containing intrigue, drama, irony, and progression to a stunning climax; and has communicated his own perspective on the whole through his omniscient narrator. We have here what can be described from a literary point of view as the art of an author with considerable literary ability.[36]

Further study along these lines is much to be desired, and should prove to be rewarding. We may only add the importance of seeing this approach to Matthew as complementary to, and not a displacement of, historical studies. Ideally the two should work together.[37]

Structuralism. In view in this article is not surface structure, which has been studied often in the past, but the so-called deep structure that underlies human communication and indeed, according to the French structuralists, all forms of narrative. (The roots of structuralism as discussed here go back to the linguist Ferdinand de Saussure and the anthropologist Claude Lévi-Strauss.) Daniel Patte has provided two guides through the densely technical, sometimes esoteric, approach to texts known as structural exegesis.[38] In the second of these he proposes a method that focuses on the identification of "the explicit oppositions of actions," "the qualifications through which the opposed subjects . . . are contrasted," and "the effects upon the receivers . . . through which the opposed actions are contrasted."[39] Patte has written a commentary on Matthew using this method.[40] He finds the convictions of the evangelist particularly where Matthew sets up narrative oppositions, that is, where he says not only what he means, but also what he does not mean, and where he articulates tensions via themes that involve both old and new. A perusal of the commentary shows that some of the time these structural observations line up with what has been emphasized by traditional exegesis. Occasionally, however, the structuralist analysis produces unexpected and, to my view, questionable results.[41]

Social Approaches. Under this heading we do not return to the question of Matthew's own sociohistorical context discussed above but, rather, turn to contemporary readings of the Gospel that reflect modern social agendas. Generally in view here are the marginalized of society, whether for reasons of gender, poverty, race, or whatever. These readings of the Gospels are bound to increase because of their relevance to contemporary problems.

A key category here is the feminist reading of Matthew. Elaine Wainwright has provided us with a feminist perspective on the Gospel.[42] She, like others,[43] sees in Matthew a symbolic view of the world that is androcentric and patriarchal, where maleness is the norm and women are marginalized. She advocates a "revisioning" of the text wherein the male dominance of the text is unmasked for what it is, and the usually unnoticed significance of women in the text is given the attention it deserves. The goal is the perception of a forgotten story that concerns *both* women and men. Some scholars have been able to see some reason for hope in Matthew's treatment of women.[44] Though restricted by the hierarchical setting in which he found himself, the evangelist makes some attempt at liberating women by his references to them and by his inclusion of them among the disciples and crowds.

A number of scholars have focused on what Matthew has to say to the poor and underprivileged of society.[45] It cannot be denied that much in the Gospel is amenable to this concern. Although the ultimate solution to the problem of injustice for the evangelist is eschatological, his message also has decided implications for the present order. This approach to the text will continue to prove fruitful.

Reader Response Theory. This key area—one that affects the interpretation of all texts—continues to produce a growing malaise concerning traditional exegetical methods. At the heart of the issue is the inherent multivalency of texts and the unavoidable personal involvement of the interpreter in the construal of meaning. This reality not only legitimizes the special agenda readings referred to in the preceding section, but indeed requires a raising of consciousness concerning what interpreters do with texts.[46] The interpreter is required to recognize that all texts are multidimensional. Reader-response approaches affirm that fact and make the most of it.[47]

An increasing number of scholars have begun to exercise reader-response approaches to Matthew. Ulrich Luz, having devoted considerable energy to the study of the influence of Matthean passages in the history of the church (*Wirkungsgeschichte*), and thus facing the reality of the multivalency of Matthean passages, has moved closer to a reader-response position.[48] Luz tries to protect against the implied relativism of this approach, and he makes an important admission when he writes that "I feel that not every application and new interpretation of this text is 'true.' "[49] He aims toward an admirable, if elusive, "middle between 1) the domination of some people by others in the name of *their* absolute truth and 2) the complete relativity of truth, as if truth were a matter of personal liking only."[50]

Other Matthean scholars have been exploring reader-response approaches to the Gospel.[51] This area of Matthean study will undoubtedly continue, with rewarding results. The crucial involvement of the reader in interpreting the text will remain extremely important in the future discussion of how we arrive at meaning. Without ignoring the significance of this fact, the present author remains uneasy about moving to what would seem to be the logical conclusion of complete relativity in statements about the meaning of texts. To be sure, there can be no absolutely true interpretation. We deal necessarily with probabilities. And every author is inescapably the result of her or his background and works within a specific interpretive context. Nevertheless, with self-awareness of the interpreter's given perspective, the author's meaning can often be understood with a high degree of probability, and that meaning remains of determinative importance for the church.[52]

THEOLOGICAL QUESTIONS AND SPECIAL CONCERNS

The large number of specific theological subjects and other issues concerning Matthew can only be dealt with here briefly, but they at least deserve mention.

Structure. The structure of Matthew continues to be the subject of much study.[53] Because of the complexity of the Gospel, its varied and broken patterns, and its overlapping structures, no single analysis has proven satisfactory. The five discourses with their formulaic ending ("when Jesus finished these sayings") and the twofold "from that time" (4:17 and 16:21), dividing the Gospel into three main parts, are separate and overlapping markers. The most conspicuous feature of the total narrative is the alternation of blocks of narrative and teaching.

Anti-Semitism. Increasing sensitivity to the problem of anti-Semitism is evident in Matthean scholarship.[54] Since Matthew is a Jew writing to Jewish Christians, the intense polemic is to be understood as intra-Jewish. The opposition is mainly to the leaders, and the vitriolic language also reflects the conventions of contemporary rhetoric. The language is neither anti-Semitic nor, strictly speaking, anti-Judaic. It is clear, however, that the language can lead to anti-Semitism (for example, the notorious 27:25) and therefore every Christian teacher and preacher has the responsibility to make clear what these passages do *not* mean.

Discipleship. This obviously important concept in Matthew continues to receive much attention.[55] Many of the recent studies are enriched by the use of the latest methodologies. The disciples, in contrast to the crowds, are in the favored position of being with Jesus and are thereby enabled to understand the teaching of Jesus. They often serve as models for Matthew's community and today's readers.

Sermon on the Mount. Two large, important commentaries on the Sermon on the Mount have appeared, one by Robert Guelich,[56] and the other, already mentioned, by Hans Dieter Betz, along with a host of other studies.[57] The importance of the Sermon for Matthew can hardly be overstated, but at the same time, the Sermon continues to be one of the interpreter's greatest challenges. That challenge is basically a hermeneutical one that enables the Sermon to maintain its significance within the larger context of the whole Gospel—a point resisted by Betz—while at the same time articulating its relevance for contemporary society.

The Old Testament in Matthew. Another important subject for Matthean studies that continues to interest scholars is the evangelist's use of the Old Testament and particularly the famous formula quotations.[58] Recent emphasis has fallen on the source of the formula quotations—now generally thought to be Matthew's own creations—and especially upon the typological hermeneutic underlying the quotations, as well as how they can be seen to undergird Matthew's unique theological emphases.

The Law. Because the law receives such great emphasis in Matthew, it has naturally been the focus of much recent discussion.[59] In particular, scholars have been concerned with the relation between the law and righteousness, and between demand and gift in the Gospel's theology. Clearly the law remains of the highest significance for the evangelist and his community. Yet righteousness is defined not by the law *per se* but by the teaching of Jesus, or more precisely the law as definitively interpreted by Jesus. Moreover, the strong emphasis on ethical demand in the Gospel is counterbalanced by the kingdom as gift. The complexity of Matthew's theology will not yield to simplistic emphasis upon the law and ethical demand.

Christology. The high christology of Matthew continues to interest scholars.[60] Kingsbury has stressed the centrality of the title "Son of God" for Matthew. But

Matthew's other titles for Jesus are also important, as Kingsbury admits. One must go beyond the titles, however, to characterize Matthew's christology, for the Gospel is christological through and through. No single title, no single element of the tradition adequately conveys Matthew's christology. For Matthew, as Kupp has shown, Jesus is uniquely the manifestation of God's presence among his people.

Eschatology. Matthew's complicated eschatology will continue to be studied as it has been in recent years.[61] Like other New Testament writers, Matthew holds in tension an eschatology presently in the process of realization and an eschatology with a bold future expectation. Justice must be done to both sides of this tension. A number of puzzles continue to occupy scholars with regard to the future expectation of the evangelist. It may well be the case, as the present writer has argued, that the disciples including Matthew misconstrued some of the sayings of Jesus by their inability to separate the parousia from the destruction of Jerusalem. The Olivet Discourse will continue to fascinate scholars.

CONCLUSION

The Gospel of Matthew is an exceptionally complex document: multifaceted, rich with intertextuality, interrelated themes and motifs, reflecting a pressurized social context that involved the painful parting of two groups, both of which claimed loyalty to the Scriptures. At the center of the controversy and at the center of Matthew's narrative stands the mysterious and transcendent figure of Jesus, who announces the turning of the age by his words and deeds, whose magisterial teaching is presented in the five well-known discourses, and who at the climax of the narrative accomplishes redemption upon the cross and is vindicated by the resurrection. The popularity of this Gospel in the church over the centuries has often been noted, and the wealth of study of this Gospel over the last few decades indicates the challenges it continues to present. Much has been accomplished, but there is still much to do. From a historical point of view, Matthew's riddles are great. Its richness as a piece of literature is increasingly appreciated and will continue as a subject of exploration. Its theological contribution to the New Testament canon and to social issues facing the contemporary church will remain significant. As we move into the twenty-first century, the interest in Matthew is not likely to lessen. Indeed, with ongoing use of traditional methods, supplemented by the newer methods and perhaps methods yet unknown, the future study of this Gospel looks promising.

NOTES

1. W. D. Davies and D. C. Allison, Jr., *A Critical and Exegetical Commentary on the Gospel according to St. Matthew,* 3 vols., International Critical Commentary (Edinburgh: T. & T. Clark, 1988, 1991, 1997).

2. U. Luz, *Matthew 1—7: A Commentary* (Minneapolis: Augsburg, 1989). The second and third volumes of Luz's full work on Matthew exist at present only in German: *Das Evangelium nach Matthäus. 2 Teilband: Mt. 8—17* and *3 Teilband: Mt. 18—25,* Evangelisch-katholischer Kommentar zum Neuen Testament (Zurich and Braunschweig: Benzinger; and Neukirchen-Vluyn: Neukirchener Verlag, 1990, 1997). The commentary, however, is now being taken up in the Hermeneia series (Fortress Press), where we may expect to see the earlier volume in revised form as well as the future volumes that will complete it.

3. H. D. Betz, *The Sermon on the Mount: A Commentary on the Sermon on the Mount, Including the Sermon on the Plain (Matthew 5:3–7:27 and Luke 6:20–49).* Hermeneia (Minneapolis: Fortress Press, 1995).

4. D. A. Hagner, *Matthew 1—13,* WBC 33A, and *Matthew 14—28,* WBC 33B (Dallas: Word Inc., 1993, 1995).

5. R. Guelich (Sermon on the Mount), 1982; R. H. Gundry, 1984; R. T. France, Tyndale Commentary, 1985; J. D. Kingsbury, Proclamation (2nd ed.), 1986; A. Sand, Regensburg New Testament, 1986; R. Schnackenburg, Die neue echte Bibel, 2 vols., 1987; J. Gnilka, Herders, 1988; G. Strecker (Sermon on the Mount), 1988; R. H. Smith, Augsburg Commentary, 1989; D. J. Harrington, Sacra Pagina, 1991; R. H. Mounce, New International, 1991; C. Blomberg, New American Commentary, 1992; M. Davies, Readings, A New Biblical Commentary, 1992; A.-J. Levine, in C. A. Newsome and S. H. Ringe, eds., *The Women's Bible Commentary,* 1992; L. Morris, Pillar, 1992; D. Garland, 1993; D. R. A. Hare, Interpretation, 1993; J. A. Overman, New Testament in Context, 1996.

6. D. R. Bauer and M. A. Powell, eds. *Treasures New and Old: Recent Contributions to Matthean Studies.* Society of Biblical Literature Symposium Series 1. (Atlanta: Scholars Press, 1996).

7. For an especially helpful survey of Matthean studies before 1980, see Graham Stanton, "The Origin and Purpose of Matthew's Gospel: Matthean Scholarship from 1945 to 1980" in *Aufstieg und Niedergang der römischen Welt,* II.25.3, ed. W. Haase and H. Temporini (Berlin: Walter de Gruyter, 1985), 1889–951. For other, more recent treatments of Matthean studies, see J. C. Anderson, "Life on the Mississippi: New Currents in Matthean Scholarship 1983–1993," *Currents in Research: Biblical Studies* 3 (1995): 169–218; D. R. Bauer, "The Interpretation of Matthew's Gospel in the Twentieth Century," *ATLA Journal* (1988): 119–45; R. T. France, *Matthew: Evangelist and Teacher* (Grand Rapids: Zondervan Publishing House, 1989); A. Sand, *Das Matthäusevangelium,* Erträge der Forschung 275 (Darmstadt: Wissenschaftliche Buchgesellschaft, 1991); D. Senior, *What are they saying about Matthew?* (Rev. & expanded edition, Mahwah, N.J.: Paulist Press, 1996); and J. Riches, *Matthew,* New Testament Guides (Sheffield: Sheffield Academic Press, 1996). For the Sermon on the Mount, see W. Carter, *What Are They Saying About the Sermon on the Mount?* (Mahwah, N.J.: Paulist Press, 1994); idem, "Some Contemporary Scholarship on the Sermon on the Mount," *Currents in Research: Biblical Studies* 4 (1996): 183–215.

8. See Thiede's article, "Papyrus Magdalen Greek 17 (Gregory-Aland P64) A Reappraisal," *Zeitschrift für Papyrologie und Epigraphik* 105 (1995): 13–20; reprinted in *Tyndale Bulletin* 46 (1995): 29–42. Roberts's estimate was made in "An Early Papyrus of the First Gospel," *Harvard Theological Review* 46 (1953): 233–37.

9. Carsten Peter Thiede and Matthew D'Ancona, *Eyewitness to Jesus: Amazing New Manuscript Evidence About the Origin of the Gospels* (New York: Doubleday, 1996),

125. A new edition of the book has come out under the title *The Jesus Papyrus* (London: Orion, 1997).

10. Thiede and D'Ancona, *Eyewitness to Jesus,* 127.

11. For highly critical reviews, see P. M. Head, "The Date of the Magdalen Papyrus of Matthew (*P. MAGD. GR.* 17=P64): A Response to C. P. Thiede" *Tyndale Bulletin* 46 (1995): 251–85 (including photographs of the fragments); D. C. Parker, "Was Matthew Written before 50 CE? The Magdalen Papyrus of Matthew," *Expository Times* 107 (1995–96): 40–43; and G. Stanton, *Gospel Truth? New Light on Jesus and the Gospels* (London: HarperCollins, 1995), 11–19.

12. Parker, "Was Matthew Written before 50 CE?," 43.

13. See, for example: J. A. T. Robinson (40–60+), *Redating the New Testament* (London: SCM Press, 1976); B. Reicke (ca. 60), *The Roots of the Synoptic Gospels* (Philadelphia: Fortress Press, 1986); J. Wenham (ca. 40), *Redating Matthew, Mark & Luke: A Fresh Assault on the Synoptic Problem* (London: Hodder & Stoughton, 1991); R. H. Gundry (65–67), *Matthew. A Commentary on His Handbook for a Mixed Church Under Persecution,* 2nd ed. (Grand Rapids: Wm. B. Eerdmans Publishing Co., 1994).

14. W. R. Farmer, *The Synoptic Problem: A Critical Analysis* (New York: Macmillan Co., 1964). See also H.-H. Stoldt, *History and Criticism of the Marcan Hypothesis* (Macon: Mercer University Press, 1980); D. L. Dungan, ed., *The Interrelations of the Gospels* (Leuven: University Press, 1990).

15. C. M. Tuckett, *The Revival of the Griesbach Hypothesis: Analysis and Appraisal,* Society for New Testament Studies Monograph Series 44 (Cambridge: Cambridge University Press, 1983).

16. On one of the key difficulties for the two-source hypothesis, namely the so-called minor agreements, see A. Ennulat, *Die "Minor Agreements",* Wissenschaftliche Untersuchungen zum Neuen Testament 2.62 (Tübingen: Mohr, 1994), and G. Strecker, ed., *Minor Agreements. Symposium Göttingen 1991* (Göttingen: Vandenhoeck & Ruprecht, 1993).

17. See D. A. Hagner, *Matthew 1–13,* lxxiii–lxxv. Dependence upon Mark hardly requires that Matthew was written a decade later, as most scholars suppose. The interval between Mark and Matthew does not need to be more than a year or two, if that.

18. D. L. Balch, ed., *Social History of the Matthean Community. Cross-Disciplinary Approaches* (Minneapolis: Fortress Press, 1991).

19. A. J. Overman, *Matthew's Gospel and Formative Judaism: The Social World of the Matthean Community* (Minneapolis: Fortress Press, 1990). See also his commentary, *Church and Community in Crisis: The Gospel According to Matthew,* New Testament in Context (Valley Forge, Penn.: Trinity Press International, 1996).

20. G. Stanton, *A Gospel for a New People: Studies in Matthew* (Edinburgh: T. & T. Clark, 1992). See also his essay "The Communities of Matthew," *Interpretation* 46 (1992): 379–91.

21. A. J. Saldarini, *Matthew's Christian-Jewish Community* (Chicago: University of Chicago Press, 1994).

22. R. Stark, "Antioch as the Social Situation for Matthew's Gospel," in Balch, *Social History,* 189–210.

23. L. M. White, "Crisis Management and Boundary Maintenance: The Social Location of the Matthean Community," in Balch, *Social History,* 211–47.

24. A. F. Segal, "Matthew's Jewish Voice," in Balch, *Social History,* 3–37; A. J. Saldarini, "The Gospel of Matthew and Jewish-Christian Conflict," in Balch, *Social History,* 38–61.

25. For a penetrating critique, see R. H. Gundry, "A Responsive Evaluation of the Social History of the Matthean Community in Roman Syria," in Balch, *Social History of the Matthean Community,* 62–67, and his review of Saldarini in *Cross Currents* 44 (1994–95): 508–11.

26. Hagner, "The *Sitz im Leben* of the Gospel of Matthew," in Bauer and Powell, *Treasures New and Old,* 27–68.

27. A recent book edited by R. Bauckham, *The Gospels for All Christians* (Edinburgh: T

& T Clark, 1997), argues that the Gospels were not written for specific local communities but for general circulation in the churches; this argument threatens to do away with the problem we have been discussing in this section. There is without question a dimension of universality in these documents that makes them meaningful in a variety of contexts. But the realization that Matthew was written to Jewish Christians sheds light on so much of his redaction of Mark that at least this degree of specific addressees remains highly warranted.

28. See now the republication of his classic *Memory and Manuscript* (1961) together with his *Tradition and Transmission* (1964) in one volume in a new edition with a new introduction by the author and a new foreword by Jacob Neusner (Grand Rapids: Wm. B. Eerdmans Publishing Co., 1998). Also relevant are Gerhardsson's *The Origins of the Gospel Tradition* (Philadelphia: Fortress Press, 1979) and *The Gospel Tradition* (Lund: Gleerup, 1986).

29. *Jesus als Lehrer: eine Untersuchung zum Ursprung der Evangelien-Überlieferung* (Tübingen: Mohr, 1981), now in a 4th German edition.

30. *Jesus the Only Teacher: Didactic Authority and Transmission in Ancient Israel, Ancient Judaism and the Matthean Community,* Coniectanea biblica—New Testament 24 (Stockholm: Almqvist & Wiksell, 1994).

31. An excellent introduction is that of M. A. Powell, *What is Narrative Criticism?* (Minneapolis: Fortress Press, 1990). See, too, S. D. Moore, *Literary Criticism and the Gospels: The Theoretical Challenge* (New Haven, Conn.: Yale University Press, 1989), who describes the new literary approach in a rhetorically charged style.

32. J. D. Kingsbury, *Matthew as Story,* 2nd ed. (Philadelphia: Fortress Press, 1988). See also, on the importance of the implied reader, idem, "Reflections on the Reader of Matthew's Gospel," *New Testament Studies* 34 (1988): 442–60; R. A. Edwards, *Matthew's Story of Jesus* (Philadelphia: Fortress Press, 1985); D. B. Howell, *Matthew's Inclusive Story,* Journal for the Study of the New Testament Supplement Series 42 (Sheffield: JSOT Press, 1990); and W. Carter, *Matthew: Storyteller, Interpreter, Evangelist* (Peabody, Mass.: Hendrickson, 1996).

33. Kingsbury, "The Plot of Matthew's Story," *Interpretation* 46 (1992): 347–56. See also Powell, "The Plot and Subplots of Matthew's Gospel," *New Testament Studies* 38 (1992): 198–202; and F. J. Matera, "The Plot of Matthew's Gospel," *Catholic Biblical Quarterly* 49 (1987): 233–53.

34. Kingsbury, "The Figure of Jesus in Matthew's Story: A Literary-Critical Probe," *Journal for the Study of the New Testament* 21 (1984): 3–36; see, too, D. R. Bauer, "The Major Characters of Matthew's Story: Their Function and Significance," *Interpretation* 46 (1992): 357–67; and Powell, "Characterization on the Phraseological Plane in the Gospel of Matthew," in Bauer and Powell, *Treasures New and Old,* 161–77.

35. Further literary critical work on Matthew may be seen in J. C. Anderson, *Matthew's Narrative Web: Over, and Over, and Over Again,* Journal for the Study of the New Testament Supplement Series 91 (Sheffield: JSOT Press, 1994); and D. J. Weaver, *Matthew's Missionary Discourse: A Literary Critical Analysis,* Journal for the Study of the New Testament Supplement Series 38 (Sheffield: Sheffield Academic Press, 1990).

36. For commentaries that take their departure from a literary critical point of view, see M. Davies, *Matthew,* Readings: A New Biblical Commentary (Sheffield: JSOT Press, 1993); and D. E. Garland, *Reading Matthew: A Literary and Theological Commentary on the First Gospel* (New York: Crossroad, 1993).

37. The point must be made because of the unfortunate claim of some purists that literary analysis can only be properly done when historical (and theological) interests are ruled out as illegitimate.

38. D. Patte, *What is Structural Exegesis?* (Philadelphia: Fortress Press, 1976); and *Structural Exegesis for New Testament Critics* (Philadelphia: Fortress Press, 1990).

39. Patte, *Structural Exegesis for New Testament Critics,* 26.

40. D. Patte, *The Gospel According to Matthew: A Structural Commentary on Matthew's Faith* (Philadelphia: Fortress Press, 1987).
41. For similarly doubtful reviews of Patte's commentary from two leading Matthew specialists, see Kingsbury, *Journal of Biblical Literature* 107 (1988): 756–58; and G. Stanton, *Interpretation* 43 (1989): 184–86.
42. E. Wainwright, *Towards a Feminist Critical Reading of the Gospel According to Matthew,* Beihefte zur Zeitschrifte für die neutestamentliche Wisenschaft 60 (Berlin: Walter de Gruyter, 1991). See, too, her commentary on Matthew in *Searching the Scriptures: A Feminist Commentary,* 2 vols., ed. E. Schüssler Fiorenza (New York: Crossroad, 1994), 2.635–77.
43. For example, J. C. Anderson, "Matthew: Gender and Reading," *Semeia* 28 (1983): 3–28; A. C. Wire, "Gender Roles in a Scribal Community," in *Social History of the Matthean Community,* 87–126; E. Cheney, *She Can Read: Feminist Reading Strategies for Biblical Narrative* (Valley Forge, Penn.: Trinity Press International, 1996), which focuses on several Matthean texts. Compare Levine, "Matthew," in *The Women's Bible Commentary,* ed. C. Newsom and S. H. Ringe (Louisville, Ky.: Westminster/John Knox Press, 1992).
44. J. Kopas, "Jesus and Women in Matthew," *Theology Today* 47 (1990): 13–21; M. J. Selvidge, "Violence, Women, and the Future of the Matthean Community: A Redactional Critical Essay," *Union Seminary Quarterly Review* 39 (1984): 213–23. See, too, the work of S. L. Love, "The Household: A Major Social Component for Gender Analysis in the Gospel of Matthew," *Biblical Theology Bulletin* 23 (1993): 21–31; "The Place of Women in Public Settings in Matthew's Gospel: A Sociological Inquiry," *Biblical Theology Bulletin* 24 (1994): 52–65.
45. For example, Francis Watson, "Liberating the Reader: A Theological-Exegetical Study of the Parable of the Sheep and the Goats (Matt 25.31–46)" in *The Open Text: New Directions for Biblical Studies,* ed. F. Watson (London: SCM Press, 1993), 57–84. See also M. H. Crosby, *House of Disciples: Church, Economics, and Justice in Matthew* (New York: Orbis Books, 1988); D. J. Weaver, "Power and Powerlessness: Matthew's Use of Irony in the Portrayal of Political Leaders," in Bauer and Powell, *Treasures New and Old,* 179–96; and the chapter on "Social Justice" in M. A. Powell, *God With Us: A Pastoral Theology of Matthew's Gospel* (Minneapolis: Fortress Press, 1995), 113–48.
46. For a moving *cri de coeur* along these lines, see D. Patte, *Ethics of Biblical Interpretation: A Reevaluation* (Louisville, Ky.: Westminster/John Knox Press, 1995).
47. For an introduction, see J. P. Tompkins, ed., *Reader-Response Criticism: From Formalism to Post-Structuralism* (Baltimore: Johns Hopkins University Press, 1980). See, too, E. A. Castelli, S. D. Moore, G. A. Phillips, and R. M. Schwartz, eds., *The Postmodern Bible* (New Haven, Conn.: Yale University Press, 1995).
48. See especially his *Matthew in History: Interpretation, Influence, and Effects* (Minneapolis: Fortress Press, 1994), and his somewhat more pessimistic 1997 presidential address to the Society of New Testament Study: "Kann die Bibel heute noch die Grundlage einer Kirche sein? Über die Aufgabe der Exegese in einer pluralistischen Gesellschaft," in *New Testament Studies* 44(1998): 317–39.
49. Luz, *Matthew in History,* 81.
50. Ibid., 103. Patte's position would seem less satisfactory: "our multidimensional practice must make explicit that all the textual dimensions and all the legitimate readings have *equal authority*" (*Ethics of Biblical Interpretation,* 40, italics his).
51. For example, J. C. Anderson, "Matthew: Sermon and Story," in Bauer and Powell, *Treasures New and Old,* 233–50; and R. Pregeant, "The Wisdom Passages in Matthew's Story," in the same volume, pages 197–232.
52. For elaboration of this point of view, see Hagner, "Writing a Commentary on Matthew: Self-Conscious Ruminations of an Evangelical," in *Semeia* 72 (1995): 51–72. The article stands alone in this volume (which has as its theme, "Taking it Per-

sonally: Autobiographical Biblical Criticism") in its defense of the possibility of arriving at authorial intention and the importance of doing so.

53. The major contribution here remains that of Bauer, *The Structure of Matthew's Gospel: A Study in Literary Design,* Journal for the Study of the New Testament 31 (Sheffield: Almond, 1988). See, too, E. M. Boring, "The Convergence of Source Analysis, Social History, and Literary Structure in the Gospel of Matthew," *Society of Biblical Literature Seminar Papers* (1994): 587–611; Kingsbury, *Matthew: Structure, Christology, Kingdom* (Philadelphia: Fortress Press, 1975); F. Neirynck, "*Apo tote erxato* and the Structure of Matthew" in *Ephemerides theologicae lovanienses* 64 (1988): 21–59; and H. J. B. Combrink, "The Macrostructure of the Gospel of Matthew," *Neotestamentica* 16 (1982): 1–20; idem, "The Structure of the Gospel of Matthew as Narrative," *Tyndale Bulletin* 34 (1983): 61–90.

54. See S. McKnight, "A Loyal Critic: Matthew's Polemic with Judaism in Theological Perspective," in C. A. Evans and D. A. Hagner, eds., *Anti-Semitism and Early Christianity: Issues of Polemic and Faith* (Minneapolis: Fortress Press, 1993), 55–79; Luz, "Matthew's Anti-Judaism: Its Origin and Contemporary Significance," *Currents in Theology and Mission* 19 (1992): 405–14; E. A. Russell, "'Anti-Semitism' in the Gospel of Matthew," *Irish Biblical Studies* 8 (1986): 183–96; B. Przybylski, "The Setting of Matthean Anti-Judaism," in P. Richardson and D. Granskou, eds., *Anti-Judaism in Early Christianity,* vol. 1, Paul and the Gospels (Waterloo, Ont.: Wilfrid Laurier University Press, 1986), 181–200; G. Stanton, "The Gospel of Matthew and Judaism," in *A Gospel for a New People,* 146–68. Compare the treatments of Matthew 23 by Garland, *The Intention of Matthew 23,* Novum Testamentum Supplements 51 (Leiden: Brill, 1979); and K. G. C. Newport, *The Sources and Sitz im Leben of Matthew 23,* Journal for the Study of the New Testament Supplement Series 117 (Sheffield: JSOT Press, 1995).

55. M. J. Wilkins, *Discipleship in the Ancient World and Matthew's Gospel,* 2nd ed. (Grand Rapids: Baker Book House, 1995); W. Carter, *Households and Discipleship: A Study of Matthew 19—20,* Journal for the Study of the New Testament Supplement Series 103 (Sheffield: Sheffield Academic Press, 1994); S. C. Barton, *Discipleship and Family Ties in Mark and Matthew,* Society for New Testament Studies Monograph Series 80 (Cambridge: Cambridge University Press, 1994); Luz, "The Disciples in the Gospel According to Matthew," in G. N. Stanton, ed., *The Interpretation of Matthew,* 2nd ed. (Edinburgh: T & T Clark, 1995), 115–48; Patte, *Discipleship According to the Sermon on the Mount: Four Legitimate Readings, Four Plausible Views of Discipleship, and Their Relative Values* (Valley Forge, Penn.: Trinity Press International, 1996); R. T. France, "Matthew's Gospel and the Church," in *Matthew: Evangelist and Teacher,* 242–78; D. E. Orton, *The Understanding Scribe: Matthew and the Apocalyptic Ideal,* Journal for the Study of the New Testament Supplement Series 25 (Sheffield: JSOT Press, 1989).

56. R. A. Guelich, *The Sermon on the Mount: A Foundation for Understanding* (Waco: Word, Inc., 1982).

57. For example, C. Bauman, *The Sermon on the Mount: The Modern Quest for Its Meaning* (Macon, Ga.: Mercer University Press, 1985); Davies and Allison, "Reflections on the Sermon on the Mount," *Scottish Journal of Theology* 44 (1991): 283–309; J. Lambrecht, *The Sermon on the Mount: Proclamation and Exhortation* (Wilmington, Del.: Michael Glazier, 1985); Strecker, *The Sermon on the Mount: An Exegetical Commentary* (Edinburgh: T & T Clark, 1988); G. Stanton, "Interpreting the Sermon on the Mount" and "The Origin and Purpose of the Sermon on the Mount," in *A Gospel for a New People,* 285–325; Hagner, "The Ethics of the Sermon on the Mount," *Studia Theologica* 51 (1997): 44–59. See, too, W. Carter, *What Are They Saying About Matthew's Sermon on the Mount?* (Mahwah, N.J.: Paulist Press, 1994); and Luz, "The Discourse on the Mount (Matthew 5—7)," in his *The Theology of The Gospel of Matthew* (Cambridge: Cambridge University Press, 1993), 42–61.

58. France, "The Formula Quotations of Matthew 2 and the Problem of Communication," *New Testament Studies* 27 (1981): 233–51; idem, "Fulfillment," in *Matthew: Evangelist and Teacher,* 166–205; J. N. Neyrey, "The Thematic Use of Isa. 42.1–4 in Matthew 12," *Biblica* 63 (1982): 457–83; Stanton, "Matthew's Use of the Old Testament" in *A Gospel for a New People,* 346–63; D. J. Moo, *The Old Testament in the Gospel Passion Narratives* (Sheffield: Almond Press, 1983); G. M. Soares Prabhu, *The Formula Quotations in the Infancy Narratives of Matthew* (Rome: Biblical Institute, 1976); O. L. Cope, *Matthew: A Scribe Trained for the Kingdom of Heaven,* Catholic Biblical Quarterly Monograph Series 5 (Washington, D.C.: Catholic Biblical Association, 1976); L. Hartman, "Scriptural Exegesis in the Gospel of St. Matthew and the Problem of Communication," in M. Didier, ed., *L'Évangile selon Matthieu* (Gembloux: Duculot, 1972), 131–52.

59. K. Snodgrass, "Matthew's Understanding of the Law," *Interpretation* 46 (1992): 368–78; idem, "Matthew and the Law" in Bauer and Powell, *Treasures New and Old,* 99–128; Allison, *The New Moses: A Matthean Typology* (Minneapolis: Fortress Press, 1993); I. Broer, *Freiheit vom Gesetz und Radikalisierung des Gesetzes. Ein Beitrag zur Theologie des Evangelisten Matthäus,* Stuttgarter Bibelstudien 98 (Stuttgart: Katholisches Bibelwerk, 1980); M. Müller, "The Gospel of Matthew and the Mosaic Law," *Studia theologica* 46 (1992): 109–20; Hagner, "Balancing the Old and the New: The Law of Moses in Matthew and Paul," *Interpretation* 51 (1997): 20–30. On "righteousness," see B. Przybylski, *Righteousness in Matthew and his World of Thought,* Society for New Testament Studies Monograph Series 41 (Cambridge: Cambridge University Press, 1980); and, for a different view, Hagner, "Righteousness in Matthew's Theology," in M. J. Wilkins and T. Paige, eds., *Worship, Theology and Ministry in the Early Church* (Sheffield: JSOT Press, 1992): 101–20.

60. D. Kupp, *Matthew's Emmanuel: Divine Presence and God's People in the First Gospel,* Society for New Testament Studies Monograph Series 90 (Cambridge: Cambridge University Press, 1996); W. L. Kynes, *A Christology of Solidarity: Jesus as the Representative of His People in Matthew* (Lanham, Md.: University Press of America, 1991); Kingsbury, *Matthew: Structure, Christology, Kingdom* (Philadelphia: Fortress Press, 1975); idem, *Jesus Christ in Matthew, Mark, and Luke* (Philadelphia: Fortress Press, 1981); idem "The Title 'Son of David' in Matthew's Gospel," *Journal of Biblical Literature* 95 (1976): 591–602; Stanton, "Christology and the Parting of the Ways," in *A Gospel for a New People,* 169–91; Luz, "The Son of Man in Matthew: Heavenly Judge or Human Christ?" *Journal for the Study of the New Testament* 48 (1992): 3–21; France, "Matthew's Portrait of Jesus," in *Matthew: Evangelist and Teacher,* 279–317. See, too, B. Gerhardsson, *The Mighty Acts of Jesus According to Matthew* (Lund: Gleerup, 1979).

61. D. C. Sim, *Apocalyptic Eschatology in the Gospel of Matthew,* Society for New Testament Studies Monograph Series 88 (Cambridge: Cambridge University Press, 1996); Cope, "'To the Close of the Age': The Role of Apocalyptic Thought in the Gospel of Matthew," in J. Marcus and M. L. Soards, eds., *Apocalyptic and the New Testament: Essays in Honour of J. Louis Martyn,* Journal for the Study of the New Testament Supplement Series 24 (Sheffield: Sheffield Academic Press, 1989), 113–24; F. W. Burnett, *The Testament of Jesus-Sophia: A Redaction-Critical Study of the Eschatological Discourse in Matthew* (Washington, D.C.: University Press of America, 1981); F. Hahn, "Die eschatologische Rede Matthäus 24 und 25," in L. Schenke, ed., *Studien zum Matthäusevangelium* (Stuttgart: KBW, 1988), 107–26; Hagner, "Apocalyptic Motifs in the Gospel of Matthew: Continuity and Discontinuity," *Horizons in Biblical Theology* 7 (1985): 53–82; idem, "Imminence and Parousia in Matthew," in D. Hellholm and T. Fornberg, eds., *Texts and Contexts* (Oslo: Scandinavian University Press, 1995), 77–92; idem, "Matthew's Eschatology," in M. Silva and T. Schmidt, eds., *To Tell the Mystery* (Sheffield: JSOT Press, 1994), 49–71.

Chapter 4

The Gospel of Mark

Mary A. Tolbert

When St. Augustine, that immensely influential Christian leader of the late fourth and early fifth centuries, decided that the Gospel of Mark was an abbreviation of the longer, more detailed Gospel of Matthew, the result of that opinion was effectively to silence this politically and theologically disturbing early Christian writing for centuries to come. Indeed, from Augustine's period until the middle of the nineteenth century, Mark was tucked well out of the way as a "second" Gospel behind the much more important "first" Gospel, Matthew. Mark's apocalyptic message, while being preserved by its inclusion in the canon, was at the same time concealed by its assumed ancillary status. That message concerned an imminently returning Son of man, coming on clouds of glory to save those faithful followers who had rejected the human temptations of glory, honor, and power, and revealed themselves, by their anonymity, wholeness, and courageous endurance, to be the good earth of the coming kingdom of God. Such a message must have seemed increasingly incompatible with the influential Christian church of the fourth and fifth centuries, the new official religious arm of the Roman Empire. Even earlier, by the first half of the second century C.E. (if Eusebius's *Church History* is correct), the Christian leader Papias had to defend Mark's particular presentation of the message of Jesus by pointing out that the author was not an eyewitness to the events but rather a follower of Peter in Rome. Mark had written after Peter's death what he had heard from Peter but perhaps, as Papias himself was forced to conclude, the narrative was not in the best order.

Though it stood for close to fifteen hundred years, Augustine's view of Mark began to topple over a century and one-half ago through the historical investigations of modern scholarship. Many biblical scholars in the nineteenth century, while exploring the relationships among the canonical Gospels, began to argue that, contrary to Augustine's opinion, the Gospel of Mark was not the second but instead the first of the Gospels to be written, and it was not an abbreviation of the Gospel of Matthew, as the church had assumed for centuries, but instead one of Matthew's—and Luke's—most important sources. Thus, those Gospels may themselves serve as still earlier witnesses to dissatisfaction with Mark's version of the Christian *kerygma* (or proclamation). Their own fuller and longer versions of the story of Jesus might have been intended in part to correct and supplant what the author of Mark had written.

By identifying Mark as the earliest of the canonical narratives about Jesus, modern scholarship opened a Pandora's box of possibilities and conflicts over this most perplexing of the Gospels. This identification not only freed Mark from the controlling shadow of Matthew but also made it the center of debate about the genre of the Gospels and their purposes, as well as a major player in perennial quests of the historical Jesus. Besides long-standing questions about its genre, its ending, and the author, date, and place of its composition, new questions arose as the Gospel was scrutinized fully in its own right—questions related to the work's profoundly apocalyptic perspective or to its oddly negative portrayal of the disciples or of Jesus' ministry as a whole. For example, why does Jesus choose as his special twelve disciples those whose hearts are early hardened against his words (6:52) and who later flee from him or, worse, betray and deny him? Or, why would a story of a Jesus who dies at the hands of his enemies, abandoned by his twelve closest disciples, rejected by crowds that earlier followed him avidly, and whose announced resurrection is met with silence and fear, be in any sense "good news" (1:1)?

Once the Gospel of Mark stood again on its own and not as an appendage to the Gospel of Matthew, all of these issues and many more began to emerge. In the last two decades of research particularly, some of Mark's enigmatic character has finally begun to clear, yielding new, exciting insights into the Gospel itself and into the amazingly diverse and theologically creative world of earliest Christianity that it represents. However, before Mark's puzzling picture could start to come into focus, several important shifts in the way it was studied had to take place.

FROM HISTORY TO LITERATURE
AND LITERARY HISTORY

Mark's re-emergence on the center stage of scholarly debate had been prompted by the concern of many mid-nineteenth century scholars to counter the claims of David F. Strauss's massive 1835 study, *The Life of Jesus Critically Examined,* which had concluded that most of the material presented in the canonical Gospels was myth and not history.[1] In proposing that Mark was the earliest of the Gospels, these scholars also asserted that, as the earliest, Mark was the most historically accurate. Thus, for writing a life of Jesus at the turn of the twentieth century, Mark was understood to provide a simple history of the acts of Jesus' ministry. This "simple history" view of Mark was short-lived, being successfully challenged in the opening years of the new century by William Wrede's important 1901 study *The Messianic Secret.*[2] Although most biblical scholars were forced to accept Wrede's conclusion that Mark's material was a result of the work and concerns of the post-Easter community rather than a simple history of the ministry of Jesus, the evaluation of Mark as one of the primary sources for a life of the historical Jesus persisted—indeed, even to the present. Mark remained the earliest extant Christian document to present Jesus material at all[3] and, as such, the jumping-off point for many questers of the historical Jesus. Since Mark, however, was writing for the purposes and concerns of Christians living forty or more years after the death of Jesus, the only way to discover historical Jesus material in Mark was to dismantle the text into its possible oral traditions or hypothetical written sources. This task became the main work of historical criticism, and especially form criticism, which dominated the study of Mark throughout most of the twentieth century. Only in the last twenty or thirty years—since the early 1970s—has that dominant mode of study shifted decisively.

In the early 1970s, the study of Mark, along with the study of many other biblical texts, became the focus of the questions and concerns of literary critics. That Mark was a narrative, with narrator, characters, and plot, had long been recognized; indeed, Wrede himself had called for a program of research on the Gospel that would begin by trying to determine what the narrator was saying to the first readers as the foundation for all further historical study.[4] Still, the prominence of form-critical work on the supposed oral traditions behind Mark derailed that program for many decades. Furthermore, during the first half of the twentieth century, the author of Mark was no author at all but a mere compiler of community traditions, and often a rather bumbling compiler at that. In hindsight, it is quite obvious that searching in Mark for the presence and use of Jesus material *prior to* Mark was an approach that practically predetermined a negative assessment of the author's narrative (or theological) abilities.

Beginning in the late 1960s and early 1970s, especially in the United States, literary criticism became an increasingly popular way to examine biblical materials. In the study of the Gospels, literary criticism was an outgrowth of the German method of redaction criticism, the exploration of the editorial work of the evangelists as they used and incorporated their various sources. Especially for Mark, because its sources were unknown, redaction-critical studies turned into a more broadly based "composition criticism," which looked at the Gospel as a whole in trying to identify the particular hand of the evangelist. When some biblical scholars began drawing their orientation and analytical tools from the world of literary studies, the Gospel of Mark presented itself as an excellent place to begin. Formal studies of plot configuration, characterization, and sequencing, using the elaborate tools of continental narratology or the more familiar ones of American New Criticism, exploded into a scholarly world still mostly in the grip of historical criticism, receiving, as one might expect, a very mixed reception. While some scholars continued to see the newer literary methods as irrelevant to their historical task, many scholars recognized that some of the thorniest problems in Markan studies, like the genre and purpose of the Gospel, its negative depiction of the male disciples, and its anticlimactic ending, were problems with the way the narrative was structured—that is, *literary* problems that would perhaps be more amenable to literary solutions.

Moreover, as the general literary world turned to look more closely at the effects of literature on its reader or audience, Markan scholars in the early to mid-1980s followed along. Wrede's eighty-year-old question about what the narrator was trying to say to the readers finally began to be addressed, and in the process, the writer of the second Gospel was clearly shown to deserve the title of author. A good illustration of the new understandings of the Gospel that developed during this period can be seen in Robert Fowler's 1981 study of the two feeding stories in Mark, *Loaves and Fishes: The Function of the Feeding Stories in the Gospel of Mark*.[5] Form critics, judging Mark's two feeding of the multitudes stories in 6:33–44 and 8:1–10 as two slightly different accounts of the same event or tradition, had viewed Mark's incorporation of both versions of the story either as proof of his conservative editing practices or as further evidence of his incompetence as a compiler of tradition. Fowler asked a new question of the material: what might be the effect of these two stories on an audience? His answer was irony—and irony directed particularly at lampooning the male disciples. After hearing of Jesus' miraculous feeding of five thousand men with two loaves and five fish, an audience would be bound to find the disciples' question in the subsequent story concerning how they could feed a similar multitude (though actually one thousand fewer and with more food) to be ludicrous or simply stupid. The audience would expect Jesus to do exactly what he did before (which he does), while at the same time recognizing that their perception of Jesus is clearly superior to that of his own disciples. The author of Mark both confirms and sharpens this ironic treatment of the disciples in the very next episode (8:14–21), in which the disciples worry about having enough bread in the boat for the thirteen of them—since they have only one loaf! Rather than being the result of careless compiling, Fowler demonstrated that the two feeding stories were carefully located and purposely fashioned by the author to carry forward the negative evaluation of the disciples that builds throughout the Gospel.

Reader-response criticism, besides showing that Mark's narrative was thoughtfully and purposefully composed, also focused attention on the most important neglected "character" in the Gospel, its reader. The Gospel was written for the purpose of affecting readers in particular ways, and ignoring this goal of the text was responsible for much of the perplexity in its interpretation. However, when asking questions about the possible responses of a reader to a text, one soon realizes that the type of reader one is talking about makes a great deal of difference. Reader-response critics identified a mass of potential readerly types: the implied reader, the ideal reader, the critic as reader, the historical reader, the flesh-and-blood reader, etc. Two of these types of readers in particular have shaped the exploration of Mark in the last two decades, flesh-and-blood readers and historical readers.

One of the most important groups of flesh-and-blood readers of Mark in the 1980s and 1990s has been women, whose focus in reading the text has often been the feminist task of charting its gender dynamics. Some feminist readers, in noting Mark's sudden announcement in 15:40 of a group of women followers who had been with Jesus and had ministered to him in Galilee and who now, in the absence of his male disciples, become witnesses to his death, burial, and resurrection, see the Gospel reflecting a more central and important role for women than many of the other New Testament writings. Indeed, some of these readers, recognizing Mark's importance for early Christian history, argue that Mark's reference to this group of women followers indicates the more egalitarian organization of the early Jesus movement. Most feminists, then, acknowledge the fairly even-handed manner in which the author of Mark deals with men and women: his followers include both, those he heals include both, and those who act evilly include both (for instance, Herodias as well as Herod, in Mark 6:17–29). Many, however, still see the Gospel as basically supporting the subservient status of women by presenting most of them anonymously, by omitting any mention of their presence until the male disciples are removed from the story, and, most of all, by having them flee the empty tomb in fear, trembling, and silence. Gender analysis of Mark and indeed of other early Christian texts is still in its beginning stages and much work remains to be done as women read the Gospel of Mark as women.

While women are one of the major recent groups of flesh-and-blood readers to explore the narrative from their concrete historical and social perspectives, they are certainly not the only ones. Some third-world readers of the Gospel have also reflected on its story from the perspective of colonized or formerly colonized people, raising questions about the role of apocalyptic as a response of the powerless to the powerful, and other socially marginalized readers of Mark have investigated the theme of suffering in the Gospel as a way of understanding the dynamics of oppression and the misuse of power.

In addition to the increasing numbers of flesh-and-blood readers who are investigating Mark from their own particular social and cultural vantage points, the other readerly type that has become important in Markan studies is the historical reader. The recognition that any modern reader of Mark reads the text in ways that are different from the ancient audience led in the late 1980s and 1990s to a return to the historical milieu of the Gospel, this time in search of the literary history of Mark. What genres would an ancient Greek-speaking audience be able to understand and follow? What conventions of reading/hearing would an ancient audience expect? What constructions of gender and ethnicity shaped their view of reality? Since the vast majority of ancient Mediterranean people—and certainly early Christians as well—were nonliterate, what aural or oral compositional techniques would normally be present even in ancient writing? Asking these questions immersed some Markan literary critics in the other big turn in Markan studies during the past twenty or thirty years: the rising importance of understanding Greco-Roman culture.

FROM UNIQUE CHRISTIAN GOSPEL
TO CONVENTIONAL GRECO-ROMAN WRITING

From the perspective of the form critics, not only was the author of Mark a mere editor of community oral traditions, but the end result of that process was a genre of literature unique to the ancient world, the "Gospel." While, etymologically, the Greek term for *gospel* simply means an oral report of good news, form critics took the term as the descriptive title of a new, indeed, unique Christian genre of writing about Jesus begun by the editor of Mark. Evidence for this clearly chauvinistic claim about Mark was founded upon two bases, one negative and one positive. Negatively, Mark was assumed to be unique from the supposed lack of similar writings from extant Greco-Roman literature. Positively, theological arguments concerning the distinctiveness of Christianity as a religion were marshaled in support of the assertion of literary uniqueness for Mark. Midway through the twentieth century, the most influential of these theological affirmations were fashioned out of theories about language borrowed from the later philosophical work of Martin Heidegger. Heidegger had argued that language was the "house of Being"; so, some scholars reasoned, the new "Being" revealed in Jesus Christ naturally required a new language form for its expression. This rationale for the claim of uniqueness for the Gospel genre was put forward by scholars in the 1950s and 1960s who called their perspective the "New Hermeneutic," and it became the last in the long line of theological justifications used to secure the uniqueness of the Christian "Gospel." It was the last because the 1970s witnessed a sea change in the assumptions of biblical scholarship about the formative world of the Gospels.

Although all of the canonical Gospels were written in Greek—indeed, all of the New Testament documents as a whole are in Greek—the world of Greek education, literature, and culture had been judged to be mainly irrelevant to the study of Christian texts since early in the twentieth century. Because Christianity was profoundly connected to Judaism, beginning as a reform movement within Judaism, and because most early twentieth-century biblical scholars believed that Judaism remained distinct from the "pagan" religions of the Greek-speaking world, Greek culture and literature were only rarely consulted in the investigation of the Gospels. Research in the 1970s, secured mainly by the massive studies of Martin Hengel in *Judaism and Hellenism* and *Jews, Greeks, and Barbarians,*[6] proved beyond question the error of this pervasive assumption about the ancient Jews and Greeks. Hengel demonstrated conclusively that Judaism itself was profoundly hellenized by the third century B.C.E., centuries before the beginnings of Christianity. While hellenization may have proceeded at different rates and in different ways, provoking diverse responses among the many regions and peoples of the eastern Mediterranean Basin, all of the area, including the cities and towns of the Jews, were influenced in significant ways by Greek language, literature, cultural values, social institutions, and education. Christianity, like other Jewish sects in the first century C.E., was in all its various forms deeply indebted to Greek culture, although that debt might have contributed differently to the beliefs and practices of the Jerusalem Christian community than to the Christian communities founded in Asia Minor or Greece. Recognizing the importance of Greco-Roman forms of thought, speaking, and writing on the Gospels—and the whole of the New Testament—opened a wellspring of new insights into the historical situation and beliefs of earliest Christianity from which studies of Mark have already benefited and continue to benefit.

Some historical critics of Mark, who had not participated in the turn to literary studies but had instead enhanced their historical approaches in the late 1970s and early 1980s by the use of modern sociological and later anthropological methods, quickly took up the challenge to study the influence of Greco-Roman culture on the formation of the Gospel. For instance, in order to shed some light on Mark's peculiar portrayal of failed disciples, Vernon Robbins carefully investigated the patterns of teacher-disciple relations in both Greek and Jewish culture in his 1984 study *Jesus the Teacher: A Socio-Rhetorical Interpretation of Mark.*[7] Robbins emphasized the importance of recognizing the Gospel's presentation of the disciples as a form of rhetoric, and for him that meant that the depiction itself grew out of some concrete and socially defined rhetorical situation. So, his task was to explore the various socially defined types of teacher-disciple relations present in first-century Mediterranean culture. While this type of work on the Gospel of Mark by sociologists and, more recently, anthropologists has provided a broader and often improved understanding of the historical situation of the earliest Christians, some of their studies tend to ignore the textual or narrative nature of the Gospel. Thus, as with form criticism, this approach has not always supplied as much insight into the text of the Gospel itself as it might. However, by blending the interests of literary historians with those of sociologists and anthropologists, significant growth in our understanding of Mark and its world has occurred and even more is promised in the future.

Nevertheless, care must be taken in the application of all of these perspectives—sociological and literary alike—because of their general dependence on social or literary models developed either from modern industrialized or postindustrialized societies or from so-called "primitive" cultures within a larger, modern, postindustrial milieu. Although it is certainly possible to read Mark as a living text in the modern world without concern for its historical point of origin, when one is explicitly attempting to construct the beliefs and practices of early Christians or when one is trying to explore the Gospel's literary production, modern methods and viewpoints must be carefully scrutinized for their pertinence to antiquity. Thus, for example, the narrative theories of literary historians must be shaped to the special aural nature of ancient writing, which needs to be distinguished from the dynamics of stories produced either in a totally oral culture or in a predominantly writing culture; similarly, the social models of historical sociologists or anthropologists must be altered to fit the particularities of ancient Mediterranean society. Robbins's emphasis on rhetoric is a good example of this latter practice because ancient rhetoric is arguably one of the most influential social constructs in Greco-Roman society and as such has placed its stamp indelibly on the present literary structure of New Testament texts.

Rhetoric was the practice of speaking well and persuasively in all kinds of situations. The study and teaching of rhetoric began in the sixth century B.C.E., and because of the Greek custom of requiring every free adult male to defend himself in litigation, it quickly spread beyond the law courts to influence all forms of speaking and writing in Greek. Since the vast majority of people in antiquity were nonliterate, speaking persuasively was one of the most important routes to power and distinction. Well before the first century C.E., education in rhetoric was a basic part of the training of anyone who learned to write or read in the Greek language. The ancient rhetorical handbooks that have come down to the present from that time are compendiums of the rules and practices of persuasive speaking; by studying these texts, scholars have been able to understand the construction and conventions of ancient texts, including Mark, much more clearly. Indeed, all of this work has made clear the dependence of Mark on its hellenistic literary and social context. Far from being a unique genre of writing, the Gospel of Mark is a representative form of hellenistic popular rhetoric.

The force of these two major shifts in Markan research, the methodological one—from history to literature and literary history—and the contextual one—from unique text to Greco-Roman writing—can best be illustrated by sampling some of the hypotheses on traditional Markan problems generated by these newer perspectives.

GENRE AND PURPOSE

Although some attempt had been made in the early decades of the twentieth century to compare the Gospels to Greco-Roman forms of biography, that work had been attacked and dismissed by the form-critical majority. One problem encountered in comparing Mark to other extant ancient writing is that most writing that has survived from antiquity comes from the social and literary elite. Mark and most of the other New Testament documents appear to be shaped by an altogether different literary style and perspective, just as the earliest Christians themselves in the main ranked much lower on the social scale. Progress on this issue has finally come about by recognizing that ancient culture, just like modern culture, contained both elite and popular literature, including both elite and popular literary genres. Fortunately, examples of one genre of ancient popular literature can still be found in the texts of what is called the Greek "ancient novel." While only five complete ancient novels have survived, fragments of many others have been discovered from as early as the first century B.C.E. Two of the complete novels, Xenophon's "Ephesian Tale" and Chariton's "Chaereas and Callirhoe," display many stylistic similarities to the canonical Gospels. While these novels are shaped around romantic plots rather than the more biographical concerns of the Gospels, the simple narratives with brief dramatic episodes linked together by often rambling journeys—spiced by crucifixions and empty graves and supported by stereotypical minor characters—their use of central turning points, and elaborate final recognition scenes all demonstrate their affinity with the Gospels. Xenophon's "novel" in particular closely parallels the writing style of the Gospel of Mark in its rough paratactic Greek. What this comparison shows is not that the Gospels are necessarily ancient novels—though fragments of some more biographical novels that would be very close to the Gospels in form do exist—but, rather, that the Gospels are surely a type of ancient popular literature. Indeed, the genre of Mark might best be described as popular biography, drawing on the patterns and conventions of popular literature to fashion a moving biography of Jesus' last year. But why write such a text?

As Paul's letters witness, letter writing was probably the earliest and most popular Christian genre of writing. Many of the New Testament texts are configured as letters, even when their actual composition and use may have been for quite different ends than those of normal letters. The Gospels and Acts deviate profoundly from that generic option by fashioning narratives that purport to tell the story of the significant events in the life of Jesus or, in the case of Acts, early Christian "heros." Given its remarkably different generic formation, it seems unlikely that

Mark was written for the same general purpose as Paul's letters, that is, as intra-Christian polemic. Paul wrote to correct and persuade Christians of his position on many of the crucial issues facing the emerging community. Letters are an appropriate form for such an aim, as they can be fashioned with theses and proofs much like speeches. Narratives, however, are ill-suited to such purposes because one would often need to infer the "correct" position from the actions and reactions of various characters. Alternatively, what narratives do well is invite readers to identify with the hero and develop empathy with his or her position and fate.

For the author of Mark, the fate of Jesus was profoundly tied up with the fate of the world as a whole, for Jesus in Mark is portrayed as the final messenger of God announcing the beginning of the end times (13:7–8), the coming near of God's kingdom (1:14–15). Rather than responding to this message with repentance (1:15; 12:2–6), most of "this faithless generation" (9:19; see also 13:30) determine to reject Jesus and indeed collude in bringing about his death—and this collusion includes members of the Pharisees and Jerusalem's religious leaders, the crowds, the Romans, and even Jesus' own disciples. However, from the perspective of the author of Mark, death itself is redeeming—at least for the elect (13:27)—because it becomes the final provocation for God to act to bring an end to this profoundly evil world (12:7–11). This intensely apocalyptic message of the imminent end of the present evil world permeates the story of Jesus as Mark presents it.

By fashioning this story as a narrative with a hero, opponents, and other characters, the author of Mark invites readers—both ancient and modern—to identify with the plight of Jesus and align themselves with his actions and apocalyptic message. In other words, the very genre of the Gospel encourages readers/hearers to become believers in Jesus' way—at least at a narrative level. Such a generic choice makes good sense for a proselytizing text or a text written to encourage continued belief during difficult times—either or both of which may have been Mark's purpose. Historically, after the time of Paul, public preaching by Christians seems to have mainly come to an end, perhaps because of increasing Roman paranoia over the insurrectionist potential of religious cults. Whatever the reason, once such public activity ceased, how was the Christian message to be spread? A brief, easily readable tract of the story of Jesus that could be passed from extended household to extended household would have been an excellent solution to the problem. While literacy in antiquity was limited, more people could read at least minimally than could write. Mark's simple, nonsyntactic Greek would have been fully accessible even to such limited readers. Such a purpose seems more plausible than the earlier attempts by form and redaction critics to connect Mark to a particular Christian community as a christological corrective to false forms of belief, a situation constructed upon the model of Paul's letters. Moreover, such a proselytizing or exhortational purpose seems supported by a rhetorical understanding of the ending of Mark and the odd portrayal of the disciples.

THE ENDING AND THE DISCIPLES

The text of Mark probably ended at 16:8 when the women, having heard the words of the young man concerning Jesus' resurrection, leave the tomb in fear and trembling, saying nothing to anyone. Millennia of Christians, including the authors of Matthew and Luke, have found that ending inappropriate and anticlimactic, to say the least. The textual tradition of Mark is littered with attempts to rewrite the ending by adding more positive concluding material, as can be found in the so-called "Longer Ending" and "Shorter Ending" of Mark. Nevertheless, if Matthew and Luke used Mark as a source, as most modern scholars propose, then they are the earliest witnesses to Mark's ending, and they clearly had texts of Mark that ended at 16:8, since they follow Mark's version fairly faithfully up to the response of the women and then go off in totally different directions.

For the literary historian, the question raised by the ending is what rhetorical point is being made to the audience by recounting the fearful response of the women at the end of the story. In ancient writing, the endings of speeches, as well as stories, plays, and poems, were often fashioned as epilogues, with two main purposes: to review critical points made earlier in the text and to move the audience to accept the position of the author. Mark's ending fulfills these two traditional purposes. By presenting essentially new characters at the end of the story—the women, the young man, the guards, and Joseph of Arimathea—the author renews the audience's hope that some human followers of Jesus will prove faithful in ways that the twelve disciples (who fled at the arrest, betrayed Jesus to his enemies, and denied knowing him) did not. Moreover, the action of the women in leaving the tomb in silence and fear reiterates the response of fear and failure that many of those following Jesus in Mark eventually display in the face of possible persecution and suffering, reminding the audience of this most common human response to the coming near of God's kingdom.

While all of the Gospel is rhetorically crafted to affect an audience, the ending is especially designed to move them to action. Throughout most of the Gospel, the disciples of Jesus are depicted as hardened against his words and unable to understand his actions. As literary critics have pointed out, Mark uses irony to fashion much of the Twelve's presentation in the Gospel, creating a situation in which the audience is encouraged to feel themselves superior to the twelve male disciples in understanding and insight into Jesus' message. Indeed, Mark's manner of depicting the Twelve actually makes of the reader/hearer of the Gospel a better disciple than any of the Twelve turns out to be—one who understands about the feeding miracles, listens to Jesus' healing words, watches during his suffering prayer at Gethsemane, witnesses his trials and crucifixion, and hears the wonderful news of his resurrection. The rhetorical force of the narrative thus creates in the attentive reader or hearer of the Gospel the perfect disciple.

Since the women have already proved themselves more faithful than the disciples by remaining by Jesus in his crucifixion, burial, and death, generations of readers have hoped that at the tomb they would prove faithful again and bear the message of the resurrection to the waiting world. However, rather than fulfilling the expectations the narrative has built up, 16:8 dashes them completely. The power of that rhetorical move can be observed by the many ancient and modern attempts to deny or modify it. When the women at the end of the story fail (as the twelve male disciples did earlier) to tell the message of Jesus' resurrection, who else is available to take that message? The reader, of course, the perfect disciple created by the rhetoric of the story. Transforming the readerly perfect disciple into a real disciple is the point of the ending. Mark was, after all, not attempting to fashion a satisfying and perfectly fulfilling aesthetic experience by writing this story, but instead to convert the curious into believers and to galvanize believers into action in these end times. What the women fail to do now becomes the project of every hearer/reader of the Gospel, and the dramatically powerful rhetoric of the ending is the motivation for that transformation. Why Mark wanted to move readers to action is related both to his apocalyptic view of Christian faith and to the probable real situation in which he wrote.

DATE, AUTHOR, AND PLACE

Both the early Christian tradition and modern scholarship have placed the writing of the Gospel of Mark in times of persecution and death. The Christian tradition, as witnessed by Papias, at least, understood the Gospel to be written by a follower of Peter in Rome after Peter's death during the persecutions of Nero in the mid- to late 60s C.E. Many modern scholars, looking at the material in chapter 13 of Mark particularly, connect the writing to the destruction of the Temple in Jerusalem in 70 C.E. during the first Jewish-Roman war. Either way, the writer of the Gospel was facing a situation of persecution and tribulation, a situation in which many early Christians found their faith severely tried and hoped ardently that the promised return of Jesus was truly imminent.

While few contemporary scholars find the association of the author of this Gospel with Peter very probable, the author does seem to stand at some distance from the types of Judaism most closely connected to Jerusalem. Some have suggested that the author was a Gentile convert to Christianity, or, perhaps more likely, a diaspora Jew. The one thing we know for sure about the author was that he—or possibly she, for literacy among women went up slightly during this period—was able to write in Greek, a fairly rare ability in antiquity. Although the Greek style of Mark is quite simple from the standpoint of syntax, that simplicity may say more about the intended audience of the Gospel than about the ability of the writer.

Writing in antiquity took considerable financial support because of the materials involved and most of all because of the leisure time required to do it. So, wherever the Gospel was written, those materials and the opportunity for leisure time must be necessary components of the location. Modern scholars are divided on their view of a possible location for the writing of the Gospel. Some accept the church tradition locating the writer in Rome—or at least some other large urban area around the Mediterranean—while others see in the references to Galilee in 14:28 and 16:7 evidence that the author and/or the intended audience were to be found in the area of Galilee or Syria. More problematic is the hypothesis of some sociological critics, based on the settings actually mentioned in the story, that the Gospel comes from a very rural setting rather than an urban one. That hypothesis seems unlikely given the material requirements of writing and wide early circulation of the Gospel. The assumption that writing about rural settings requires one to be in a rural setting is precarious to say the least.

Consequently, what is now presumed about the Gospel of Mark is this: that around 70 C.E., an unknown Christian author in some urban area of the Mediterranean world wrote a story about Jesus' fate at the hands of mostly faithless human beings. The purpose of this story was to urge believers to endure the persecutions that raged around them and to preach the good news of Jesus' coming for the short interval that remained until the sun was darkened and the powers of heaven were shaken and the world became God's kingdom once again.

NOTES

1. David Friedrich Strauss, *The Life of Jesus Critically Examined,* Lives of Jesus Series, trans. G. Eliot (Philadelphia: Fortress Press, 1972; orig. pub. 1835–36).
2. William Wrede, *The Messianic Secret,* trans. J. C. Greig (Greenwood, S.C.: The Attic Press, 1971; orig. pub., 1901).
3. The so-called "Q" document, which along with Mark had been proposed by nineteenth century scholars as one of the other main sources of Matthew and Luke, was—and remains—a scholarly hypothesis, not an extant text, and the earliest Christian writings, Paul's letters, provide little to no information on the life, ministry, and teachings of the historical Jesus.
4. Wrede, *Messianic Secret,* 2–3.
5. Robert M. Fowler, *Loaves and Fishes: The Function of the Feeding Stories in the Gospel of Mark,* Society of Biblical Literature Dissertation Series 54 (Chico, Calif.: Scholars Press, 1981).
6. Martin Hengel, *Judaism and Hellenism: Studies in Their Encounter in Palestine During the Early Hellenistic Period,* 2 vols., trans. J. Bowden (Philadelphia: Fortress Press, 1974); idem, *Jews, Greeks, and Barbarians: Aspects of the Hellenization of Judaism in the Pre-Christian Period,* trans. J. Bowden (Philadelphia: Fortress Press, 1980).
7. Vernon K. Robbins, *Jesus the Teacher: A Socio-Rhetorical Interpretation of Mark* (Philadelphia: Fortress Press, 1984).

Chapter 5

Luke-Acts

John T. Carroll

The Gospel of Luke and the Acts of the Apostles, characterized a generation ago as a "storm center" in New Testament studies,[1] remain the focus of vigorous research activity.[2] While historical questions still claim attention,[3] they now compete with a wide range of theological, literary, and social-scientific approaches to Luke and Acts. This survey will point to some of the most important developments in Lukan scholarship today.[4]

UNITY AND GENRE OF LUKE-ACTS

Literary unity. The literary unity of Luke's two volumes, once axiomatic,[5] has recently been questioned by Parsons and Pervo.[6] They concede authorial unity but challenge the assumptions that Luke and Acts form one continuous narrative, express a consistent theological view, and conform to the conventions of a singular literary genre. A previous study by Wilson likewise distinguished the situations prompting Luke's two books—and their differing perspectives on such pivotal concerns as eschatology and the law.[7]

Nevertheless, most recent studies have emphasized the coherence of the two writings. Where redaction critics have interpreted Luke's Gospel through its revision of Mark, narrative critics have read Luke as the beginning of a story that achieves closure only in Acts.[8] Johnson, Tannehill, Tyson, and Kurz, among many others, offer subtle and perceptive readings of Luke-Acts as one unfolding narrative, and Darr adds nuance through his careful attention to the role of the reader.[9] O'Toole, also, employing composition criticism, argues that Luke-Acts articulates a coherent theological vision centering on God's provision of salvation to God's people.[10]

Is Acts the second half of one continuing story, or is it rather a sequel to the Gospel, perhaps even of a different genre and addressing a different audience? Would Luke's first readers have approached his second book with a different set of expectations? At present, discussions of genre, audience, setting, and purpose should leave the question open. At the same time, full weight must be given to the features linking the two writings, including their prefaces (Luke 1:1–4; Acts 1:1–2); shared themes, linguistic patterns,[11] and narrative strategies; and carefully spun webs of prophecy (promise) and fulfillment.[12] The Gospel's Easter narrative (chap. 24) points the reader ahead to the story narrated in Acts, where significant "narrative needs" established in the Gospel will be met.[13] The end of the Gospel, then, is not the end of the story. Conversely, the reader's experience of Acts is shaped by expectations and knowledge derived from hearing the Gospel. Whether originally conceived as one book in two parts or as an earlier book and its sequel, Luke and Acts should be read in tandem.[14] This does not mean that an artificial unity—literary, historical, or theological—is to be imposed on the text(s). The model of perfectly consistent texts, authors, and readers ought in any case to be abandoned, for the processes by which texts such as Luke and Acts are composed and read are both complex and dynamic: informed by various inherited traditions, one tells—and hears—the story, and the telling and the hearing expand knowledge and challenge perceptions, values, and commitments.

Genre. But what expectations would late first-century readers have brought to Luke and Acts? Although the question of genre is energetically debated in Lukan scholarship today, there is broad agreement that Luke-Acts, or at least Acts, is a historical work; such features as the prefaces, speeches, dramatic scenes, and the prominence of the motif of divine providence[15] reflect conventions of Hellenistic historiography. Aune classifies Luke-Acts as "general history," relating the origins and history of a particular group, while Plümacher and Palmer describe Acts as a "historical monograph," and Sterling terms Luke's work "apologetic historiography."[16] On the other hand, Kurz and Rosner prefer to assign Luke-Acts to the category of "biblical history"—that is, Luke's primary models were the historical books of the Jewish Bible.[17] To compel a choice between Hellenistic and Jewish historiography would be a mistake; Luke was influenced by literary models available to him in both Greco-Roman historiography (including Jewish history writing) and the Greek Bible.[18]

The genre of "history," however, has not won a unanimous verdict. Talbert and Burridge classify Luke's Gospel as biography (of the ancient Greco-Roman variety, of course), and Talbert even contends—though he has found few followers—that the pattern of Gospel (account of the teacher) + Acts (narrative of the teacher's successors) derives from the biographical genre.[19] The genre "biography" suggests that the focus of the narrative is Jesus; Green counters, however, that the narrative is theocentric (hence, historical in genre).[20]

Pervo, highlighting Luke's ability to entertain his readers, gives Acts a home among the ancient novels.[21] Luke and Acts are certainly entertaining as well as edifying narratives, but that quality also suits Greco-Roman and Jewish history writing of Luke's day. One should admit the probability that Luke borrowed and adapted elements of other literary genres, but his writings appear most at home in the world of Greco-Roman and Jewish historiography.

Context of Luke-Acts. The attempt to pinpoint the setting of Luke's work is notoriously precarious.[22] Even the most general description would provoke sharp dissent: Was the community primarily Jewish or Gentile? Was the target audience Christians or outsiders?[23] Which cultural context is more important in reading Luke-Acts—Greco-Roman or Jewish?

Until recently, the dominant paradigm in Lukan scholarship had Luke as a Gentile writing to Gentiles.[24] While this may remain the majority view, several scholars have turned it upside down. Jervell, Tiede, and Juel (to name only a few) all perceive Luke-Acts as a deeply Jewish work addressing the concerns of Jewish Christians in the closing decades of the first century.[25]

Jervell questions whether there is a Gentile mission in Acts at all. The church Luke profiles—even in narrating Paul's activity—remains predominantly Jewish. But that is the church within the narrative setting. Luke may be confronting a problem of legitimation, precisely because the churches he knows are not of Jewish pedigree like those within the narrative. Moreover, the direction of movement in the narrative is significant. Both Luke and Acts begin with scenes in Jerusalem, but the narrative ends in Rome, with Paul's assurance that the word of salvation will be heard among Gentiles (Acts 28:23–31). Luke appears not to have given up on the Jewish people,[26] but the churches known to him were likely composed more and more of Gentile converts. Still, if Luke was not an adherent of Judaism (was he perhaps a god-fearer himself?), he tapped the rich Jewish heritage in telling his story. Luke's relation to Jewish scripture warrants a closer look.

LITERARY QUESTIONS

Luke-Acts will continue to invite historical inquiry. It is a crucial source for any historical reconstruction of Christian origins, and knowledge of its own historical setting informs our reading of the narrative. Yet literary approaches occupy center stage as Lukan scholarship enters its third millennium.[27] Rhetorical-critical studies examine the way Luke's artful composition achieves its intended effects on readers (hearers).[28] Reader-response critics shift the focus to the reader and explore the ways in which readers seek to find coherent meaning in the text.[29] And narratological approaches are multiplying exponentially.[30] Especially valuable is the current work on characterization in Luke's narrative.[31] Brief notice can only be given here to one dimension of current literary study of Luke-Acts: intertextuality.

Intertextuality: Luke and Scripture. Echoes of the Jewish Bible resonate throughout Luke's writings.[32] Extensive quotations of scriptural passages appear at pivotal moments, notably the inaugural scene at Nazareth (Luke 4:16–30), the missionary discourses of Peter and Paul in Acts,[33] and Paul's final words addressed to Jews in Rome (Acts 28:25–28). There are also recitations of Israelite history, the most striking being Stephen's "defense" speech in Acts 7. The accused indicts his accusers, who by rejecting Jesus and his witnesses replicate the sins of their ancestors. By means of scripture citations but also in more subtle ways, Luke deploys scripture to present Jesus, despite his crucifixion, as the authentic messianic ruler, and to legitimate the incorporation of Gentiles within God's people (Acts 15:15–18). The Gospel prologue (1:5–2:52) is cast in biblical (Septuagintal) idiom, evoking memories of the classical faith and piety of ancient Israel. And biblical patterns—especially the prophetic paradigm—color the portrait of Jesus and his witnesses. The rich use of scripture in Luke-Acts advances the claim that the divine purpose in the history of the covenant people Israel is working itself out in the story Luke relates.

THEOLOGICAL QUESTIONS

Theological approaches to Luke-Acts do not predominate as in an earlier generation. Social-historical, sociological, anthropological, and literary approaches to the text have in recent decades often overriden explicit attention to theological questions. In accord with the strongly theological cast of Luke's literary project, however, Lukan scholarship is beginning to display renewed concern with theological vision.

Eschatology. Theological interest in Luke-Acts long focused on eschatology, due to the enormous influence of Conzelmann's pioneering redaction-critical study; his claim that Luke surrendered hope of an imminent eschatological fulfillment elicited a chorus of dissenting voices.[34] While Luke has made room for the reality of delay, the narrative retains clear signals of the approaching end of history. Still, the accent falls sharply on the note of present fulfillment in the activity of Jesus, whom Luke presents as the embodiment of salvation for God's people.

Christology. It is no surprise that the role and significance of Jesus in Luke's narrative are at the center of discussion today. Luke evokes the scriptural paradigm of prophet: Jesus discloses the character of God's realm and summons God's people to faithfulness, yet he experiences rejection. He is the definitive "prophet like Moses" whom the people must heed if they are to have a share in the covenant people of God—but true to form, the prophet meets resistance.[35] Although Jesus speaks, heals, and dies wearing the prophetic mantle, his anointing by the Spirit points at the same time to an even higher messianic vocation. Though repudiated by his people, he departs to a distant country—through resurrection and ascension—and receives acclamation as royal Messiah and universal Lord (Luke 19:11–27; Acts 2:36; 10:36).[36] So, with significant redefinition and much surprise (notably, crucifixion for the Messiah and a divine turn to the Gentiles), Jesus brings the promised redemption to Israel, fulfilling the hopes celebrated in the Gospel's prologue (1:5–2:52).[37] Moreover, the narrative offers a constellation of other images of Jesus. He is the "righteous one" who trusted in God and, though abused by the wicked, received vindication by God. He is the "savior" who healed the sick, extended forgiveness to the sinful, and welcomed into God's family persons living on the margins of the community. By his example of benefaction and through challenging words, he urged those of wealth and status to relinquish both of these prized commodities for the sake of the poor and lowly. Increasingly, scholars recognize that, important as specific designations ("titles") for Jesus are in Luke's story, one must draw from the entire, complex narrative (from Jesus' acts, speech, characterization by the narrator and by other characters, and so forth) in constructing the christological profile of Luke-Acts.

Interpreting the death of Jesus. Formerly, Luke was faulted for downplaying the saving significance of the cross.[38] To be sure, it is now seen that Luke ascribes saving significance to the whole of Jesus' life: his public ministry, death, and resurrection/exaltation. Nevertheless, the signal importance of the death of Jesus is evident in the care with which Luke relates the passion of Jesus—forcefully demonstrating his innocence in the sight of Roman authority, attributing his death to the hostility of the Jerusalem elite, using the cross to appeal for repentance on the part of the people of Jerusalem, displaying his unshakable loyalty to God, and having Jesus enact his role as forgiving savior at the very scene of his death.

Theology. The story Luke tells is first and foremost the story of God's way with Israel, and with all people.[39] God, the "neglected factor in New Testament theology,"[40] is beyond doubt the driving force in this narrative. The vehicles of God's activity are richly variegated—the "word" of God, the Holy Spirit, angels, prayers, visions, prophetic voices, portents, and of course Jesus himself (see, for example, Acts 10:36–38). With such a variety of instruments, Luke taps the repertoire of both (Hellenistic) Jewish and Greco-Roman cultures.[41] The narrative depicts and celebrates the realization of God's purpose to restore Israel and bring salvation "to the ends of the earth" (Acts 1:8).

QUESTIONS OF IDEOLOGY AND CULTURE

Luke and the Marginalized. Whatever the social level(s) of Luke's first community of readers, his narrative assigns a prominent role to matters of social status, honor, patronage, and wealth.[42] Here the application of cultural anthropology and sociology to the Lukan writings has been especially fruitful.[43] In Luke's narrative, the patron-client paradigm and the cultural norm of reciprocity are undermined. Jesus recruits patrons whose benefactions do not turn their beneficiaries into clients (Moxnes). At the considerable price of diminished honor, those of status and wealth are instructed to extend hospitality and share material resources precisely with persons who cannot reciprocate.[44] In fact, Jesus practices in Luke a policy of social inclusion so radical that he offends the "righteous" (Luke 7:33–34, 36–50). There is room within the company gathered around Jesus for those who find themselves on the margins of the community because of a wide range of circumstances: demonic oppression, age, gender, poverty, occupation (toll collectors), and moral and religious failure ("sinners"). The marginalized find honor in association with Jesus, while the status-conscious and the upright (usually Pharisees) express outrage at Jesus' lack of discretion. Both Jesus' words and his practices enact a thoroughgoing status reversal, programmatically announced in Mary's Magnificat (1:46–55) and Jesus' Nazareth discourse (4:16–30).

Wealth and Poverty. Especially prominent in Luke-Acts is the theme of poverty and wealth, which though not completely consistent is coherent.[45] At times, Jesus summons disciples to a life of complete renunciation (Luke 14:25–33; 18:18–25), yet the Gospel also affords hints that generous sharing of wealth with the needy will suffice (16:19–31; 19:1–10). Communal norms in Acts reflect this latter pattern, for Luke portrays a true "community of friends" whose generous spirit of sharing produces a fellowship where none are destitute (Acts 4:34). Proper use of wealth—the transfer of resources for the benefit of the poor—gives one friends and honor for eternity (Luke 16:1–13).

Women. Luke's handling of traditions concerning women continues to provoke intense debate. Everybody recognizes the prominence Luke-Acts gives to women, but modern readers have reacted in diametrically opposed ways. Some feminist scholars lament Luke's habit of confining women within traditional social roles and denying them tasks of witness and proclamation.[46] Even women who step onto the stage as inspired prophets (Anna in Luke 2:38 and the daughters of Philip in Acts 21:9) are given no voice by the narrator (unlike their co-prophets Simeon and Agabus). Karris counters that Luke, against the grain of his own cultural world, enhanced the place of women in the community.[47] Mary, the mother of Jesus, exemplifies true discipleship,[48] Martha's sister Mary receives permission from Jesus to assume the posture of a disciple, and while the male apostles refuse to believe the women's Easter testimony (reflecting the dominant cultural biases of the era), their faithful witness is consistent with a greater ministry than Luke actually assigns them. In fact, women such as Susanna, Joanna, and Mary Magdalene model for the whole community the appropriate stewardship of material goods in service of others (Luke 8:1–3). Seim argues that contemporary readers hear in Luke-Acts a "double message": women's voices as prophets and preachers are stifled but not entirely silenced.[49] Reflecting the cultural constraints of his own social location, Luke does not present women's ministry on a par with that of the (male) apostles and the other men authorized by them as witnesses and preachers in Acts. Yet the story Luke tells also hints that their full inclusion within the community of disciples must finally mean their empowerment as "eyewitnesses and ministers of the word" (Luke 1:2). We should observe, but not castigate the author for, the significant social and cultural constraints that have shaped this narrative.

The Jewish People. Without doubt, the most hotly debated issue in Lukan scholarship of the last two decades concerns the place of the Jewish people and Jewish religion in these writings. On this matter, too, the spectrum of opinions could not be broader. On the one hand, Jervell thinks it is the acceptance of the apostles' message by believing Jews (the nucleus of the restored Israel) that allows the incorporation of Gentiles within the people of God. And Tiede finds a place for Luke-Acts (as a theodicy) within Judaism in the aftermath of the failed Jewish rebellion against Rome.[50] Sanders, on the other hand, detects in the Lukan writings an implacable hostility toward Jews and everything Jewish.[51] Tyson finds a literary pattern whereby initial acceptance on the part of the Jewish people gives way to final rejection, and Tannehill's reading of Luke-Acts as a tragic story suggests that the narrative's final and discordant note of Jewish rejection cannot erase the reader's memory of the promise of salvation for Israel evoked at the outset.[52] Much depends on the scholar's decision to locate Luke inside or outside a Jewish milieu: prophetic critique from within or anti-Jewish polemic from without? Scholars today acknowledge that in a post-Holocaust context this issue is sensitive and potentially explosive. As in the case of Luke's treatment of women, responsible engagement with Luke's text requires attention to the full range and the complexity of the evidence in Luke-Acts; careful analysis of Luke's own social and cultural location and the way it has shaped his presentation of the theme; and self-awareness on the part of modern interpreters, who are likewise constrained by their own social and cultural location.

LUKAN STUDIES IN PROSPECT

Luke-Acts is an especially fertile field for scholarship on the threshold of the twenty-first century. In predicting that captivation with Luke's project will continue, I do not venture onto a limb. A happy coincidence finds prominent Lukan themes intersecting with vital religious concerns of contemporary readers. No other New Testament writing devotes so much space to the presence of women in the community of faith, or to the problem of wealth and poverty. And this narrative immerses the reader in the daunting and disturbing debate over the future of Israel and the problem of Jewish repudiation of Jesus the Messiah. These Lukan themes all touch on pressing concerns of our day.

It is perhaps the good fortune of scholars that Luke's story does not yield any clear or unambiguous answers to these questions, for readers encounter here intriguing tensions, complexity, and depth. Women, for all their prominence in the story, appear to be mainly passive and silent. Yet such women as Mary the mother of Jesus, Mary the sister of Martha, Mary Magdalene, Tabitha, Lydia, and Prisca assume roles that threaten to shatter the conventional mold. So the story points toward empowerment of both women and men for ministries of service and proclamation.

Luke's presentation of the activity of Jesus highlights his embrace of the socially marginalized. His vision of a divine realm marked by grand societal reversals requires the discarding of accepted cultural scripts of wealth, status, and honor. And yet Acts accents the high social status of many of the first generation of converts (16:37; 17:4, 34).

From beginning to end, Luke-Acts recalls God's ancient promises to Israel and raises expectations that the long-awaited salvation of the covenant people has now arrived. But what a surprising detour this path of salvation takes! The nation's "Savior" is scorned and killed, and by the end of the story Israel's hopes seem more and more to be deflected to the Gentile world.

Another tension is worth noting. On the one hand, the narrative goes to great lengths to underscore the political innocence and harmlessness of Jesus and his followers. On the other, Jesus' vision of God's realm *was* subversive, and so is the larger divine project to which this story points: not Caesar but Jesus is "Lord"; not Rome but the God of Israel is the author of peace and salvation. This is not the Book of Revelation, but such politically charged tensions course beneath the story, waiting to erupt. Readers in the twenty-first century, too, face difficult questions regarding the tensive interplay of religious and political institutions that appeal for loyalty and faithful service.

Finally, one should not underestimate the extraordinary literary qualities of Luke and Acts. Readers today are still drawn to Luke's compelling image of Jesus, and to a narrative replete with arresting parables and gripping dramatic tales of the early church—vulnerable, yet bold and confident—beginning to make its way across the Roman world. There is plenty here to entertain, instruct, challenge, and inspire generations of readers yet to come.

NOTES

1. The often-quoted phrase comes from W. C. van Unnik, "Luke-Acts, a Storm Center in Contemporary Scholarship," in *Studies in Luke-Acts*, ed. Leander E. Keck and J. Louis Martyn (Philadelphia: Fortress Press, 1980; orig. pub., 1966), 15–32.
2. Useful surveys of research on Luke-Acts include Mark Allan Powell, *What Are They Saying about Acts?* (Mahwah, N.J.: Paulist Press, 1991); idem, *What Are They Saying about Luke?* (Mahwah, N.J.: Paulist Press, 1989); W. Ward Gasque, *A History of the Interpretation of the Acts of the Apostles*, rev. ed. (Peabody, Mass.: Hendrickson, 1989); Charles H. Talbert, "Luke-Acts," in *The New Testament and Its Modern Interpreters*, ed. Eldon J. Epp and George W. MacRae (Atlanta: Scholars Press, 1989), 297–320; Francois Bovon, *Luke the Theologian: Thirty-Three Years of Research (1950–1983)*, trans. Ken McKinney (Allison Park, Penn.: Pickwick Publications, 1987); Earl Richard, "Luke — Writer, Theologian, Historian: Research and Orientation of the 1970s," *Biblical Theology Bulletin* 13 (1983): 3–15. See also *Cadbury, Knox, and Talbert: American Contributions to the Study of Acts*, ed. Mikeal C. Parsons and Joseph B. Tyson (Atlanta: Scholars Press, 1992).
3. Noteworthy is the six-volume series *The Book of Acts in Its First-Century Setting* (Grand Rapids: Wm. B. Eerdmans Publishing Co., 1993–97); see also *History, Literature, and Society in the Book of Acts*, ed. Ben Witherington III (Cambridge: Cambridge University Press, 1996).
4. We set aside such problems as the author's identity ("Luke"), the date and location of composition, and the delineation of sources. These are important questions, and every commentator on Luke and Acts must address them, but the remark of Joel B. Green illustrates the shift in concern of contemporary scholarship: "This commentary proceeds under the assumption that our ability to identify the author of the Third Gospel is unimportant to interpretation" (*The Gospel of Luke*, New International Commentary on the New Testament [Grand Rapids: Wm. B. Eerdmans Publishing Co., 1997], 20).
5. Thanks largely to the work of Henry Joel Cadbury; see especially *The Making of Luke-Acts* (London: SPCK, 1961; orig. pub., 1927).
6. Mikeal C. Parsons and Richard I. Pervo, *Rethinking the Unity of Luke and Acts* (Minneapolis: Fortress Press, 1993).
7. Stephen G. Wilson, *Luke and the Law*, New Testament Studies Monograph Series 50 (Cambridge: Cambridge University Press, 1983).
8. Though, to be sure, a closure that leaves many important questions unanswered, not least the fate of Paul. See William F. Brosend II, "The Means of Absent Ends," in Witherington, *History, Literature, and Society in the Book of Acts*, 348–62; compare also the important discussion of closure and narrative development in Mikeal C. Parsons, *The Departure of Jesus in Luke-Acts* Journal for the Study of the New Testament Supplement Series 21 (Sheffield: Sheffield Academic Press, 1987), 65–113.
9. Luke T. Johnson, *The Literary Function of Possessions in Luke-Acts*, Society of Biblical Literature Dissertation Series 39 (Missoula, Mont.: Scholars Press, 1977); Robert C. Tannehill, *The Narrative Unity of Luke-Acts*, 2 vols. (Philadelphia/Minneapolis: Fortress Press, 1986, 1990); Joseph B. Tyson, *The Death of Jesus in Luke-Acts* (Columbia, S.C.: University of South Carolina Press, 1986); idem, *Images of Judaism in Luke-Acts* (Columbia, S.C.: University of South Carolina Press, 1992); William S. Kurz, *Reading Luke-Acts: Dynamics of Biblical Narrative* (Louisville, Ky.: Westminster/John Knox Press, 1993); John A. Darr, *On Character Building: The Reader and the Rhetoric of Characterization in Luke-Acts* (Louisville, Ky.: Westminster/John Knox Press, 1992).
10. Robert O'Toole, *The Unity of Luke's Theology: An Analysis of Luke-Acts*, Good News Series 9 (Wilmington, Del.: Michael Glazier, 1984).
11. See the seminal study by Talbert, *Literary Patterns, Theological Themes and the*

Genre of Luke-Acts, Society of Biblical Literature Monograph Series 20 (Missoula, Mont.: Scholars Press, 1974).

12. See Johnson, *The Gospel of Luke,* Sacra Pagina 3 (Collegeville, Minn.: Liturgical Press, 1991), 15–17.

13. Compare Green, *Gospel of Luke,* 9–10. By reader, I mean here "implied reader," though the claim could be extended, by inference, to Luke's first real readers. Perhaps most significant among these narrative needs are the mission to the Jewish people, with its call to repentance and offer of forgiveness, and the incorporation of Gentiles within the people of God.

14. Both Green (*Gospel of Luke,* 6–10) and I. Howard Marshall ("Acts and the 'Former Treatise,'" in *The Book of Acts in Its First-Century Setting, Vol. 1: The Book of Acts in Its Ancient Literary Setting,* ed. Bruce W. Winter and Andrew D. Clarke [Grand Rapids: Wm. B. Eerdmans Publishing Co., 1993], 163–82) take account of the study by Parsons and Pervo but proceed to defend the literary unity of Luke-Acts.

15. See John T. Squires, *The Plan of God in Luke-Acts,* Society of New Testament Studies Monograph Series 76 (Cambridge: Cambridge University Press, 1993).

16. David E. Aune, *The New Testament in Its Literary Environment,* Library of Early Christianity 8 (Philadelphia: Westminster Press, 1987), 116–57; Darryl W. Palmer, "Acts and the Ancient Historical Monograph," in Winter and Clarke, *Acts in Its Ancient Literary Setting,* 1–29; Eckhard Plümacher, "Neues Testament und hellenistische Form. Zur literarischen Gattung der lukanischen Schriften," *Theologia Viatorum* 14 (1977–78): 109–23; Gregory E. Sterling, *Historiography and Self- Definition: Josephos, Luke-Acts and Apologetic Historiography* (Leiden: Brill, 1992).

17. Kurz, *Reading Luke-Acts;* Brian S. Rosner, "Acts and Biblical History," in Winter and Clarke, *Acts in Its Ancient Literary Setting,* 65–82.

18. The convergence of these two has been accented by Thomas L. Brodie, "Towards Unravelling Luke's Use of the Old Testament: Luke 7.11–17 as an Imitatio of 1 Kings 17.17–24," *New Testament Studies* 32 (1986): 247–67. Prompted by the prevalent Greco-Roman practice of imitatio, Luke found in the Jewish scriptures (specifically the cycle of Elijah and Elisha stories) the model for his own project.

19. See Talbert, *What Is a Gospel? The Genre of the Canonical Gospels* (Philadelphia: Fortress Press, 1977); idem, "The Acts of the Apostles: monograph or bios?" in Witherington, *History, Literature, and Society in the Acts of the Apostles,* 58–72; Richard A. Burridge, *What Are the Gospels? A Comparison with Graeco-Roman Biography,* Society for New Testament Studies Monograph Series 70 (Cambridge: Cambridge University Press, 1992).

20. Green, *Gospel of Luke,* 5–6. Robert L. Brawley, too, insists on the theocentric character of Luke's work. See *Centering on God: Method and Message in Luke-Acts* (Louisville, Ky.: Westminster/John Knox Press, 1990).

21. Richard I. Pervo, *Profit with Delight: The Literary Genre of the Acts of the Apostles* (Philadelphia: Fortress Press, 1987); see also S. P. and M. J. Schierling, "The Influence of the Ancient Romances on the Acts of the Apostles," *Classical Bulletin* 54 (1978): 81–88; Susan Marie Praeder, "Luke-Acts and the Ancient Novel," *Society of Biblical Literature Seminar Papers* (1981): 269–92.

22. See Johnson, "On Finding the Lukan Community: A Cautious Cautionary Essay," *Society of Biblical Literature Seminar Papers* (1979): 87–100.

23. Two recent studies attuned to Luke's Roman imperial context but perceiving his audience as insiders (Christians) rather than outsiders are Paul Walaskay, "And so we came to Rome": The Political Perspective of St. Luke, Society for New Testament Studies Monograph Series 49 (Cambridge: Cambridge University Press, 1983); and Philip Esler, *Community and Gospel in Luke-Acts: The Social and Political Motivations of Lucan Theology,* Society for New Testament Studies Monograph Series 57 (Cambridge: Cambridge University Press, 1987). By contrast, Tyson (*Images of Judaism*) sketches a portrait of Luke's implied reader as a literate god-fearer whom Luke

aims to attract to Christian rather than Jewish religion; compare Martinus C. de Boer, "God-Fearers in Luke-Acts," in *Luke's Literary Achievement: Collected Essays,* ed. Christopher M. Tuckett, Journal for the Study of the New Testament Supplement Series 116 (Sheffield: Sheffield Academic, 1995), 50–71.

24. Among those who regard Luke as a Gentile addressing a primarily Gentile audience, the spotlight does not always fall in the same place. Sharply accenting Jewish rejection of the gospel in Luke-Acts is Jack T. Sanders, *The Jews in Luke-Acts* (Philadelphia: Fortress Press, 1987). Robert Maddox holds in balance the theme of Jewish rejection and Luke's concern to show the legitimacy of Gentile churches. See *The Purpose of Luke-Acts* (Edinburgh: T. & T. Clark, 1985; orig. pub. 1982). Stephen G. Wilson stresses Luke's concern to ground the gentile mission in the divine purpose. See *The Gentiles and the Gentile Mission in Luke-Acts,* Society for New Testament Studies Monograph Series 23 (Cambridge: Cambridge University Press, 1973).

25. Jacob Jervell, *Luke and the People of God* (Minneapolis: Augsburg, 1972); idem, *The Theology of the Acts of the Apostles,* New Testament Theology (Cambridge: Cambridge University Press, 1996); David L. Tiede, *Prophecy and History in Luke-Acts* (Philadelphia: Fortress Press, 1980); Donald Juel, *Luke-Acts: The Promise of History* (Atlanta: John Knox Press, 1983).

26. See Tannehill, "Rejection by Jews and Turning to Gentiles: The Pattern of Paul's Mission in Acts," in *Luke-Acts and the Jewish People: Eight Critical Perspectives,* ed. Joseph B. Tyson (Minneapolis: Augsburg, 1988), 83–101; compare Brawley, *Luke-Acts and the Jews: Conflict, Apology, and Conciliation,* Society of Biblical Literature Monograph Series 33 (Atlanta: Scholars Press, 1987).

27. See the sketch of current literary methods in F. Scott Spencer, "Acts and Modern Literary Approaches," in Winter and Clarke, *Acts in Its Ancient Literary Setting,* 381–414.

28. For example, Willi Braun, *Feasting and Social Rhetoric in Luke 14,* Society for New Testament Studies Monograph Series 85 (Cambridge: Cambridge University Press, 1995); Philip E. Satterthwaite, "Acts Against the Background of Classical Rhetoric," in Winter and Clarke, *Acts in Its Ancient Literary Setting,* 337–79; and in the same volume, Bruce W. Winter, "Official Proceedings and the Forensic Speeches in Acts 24–26," 305–36; J. Ian H. McDonald, "Rhetorical Issue and Rhetorical Strategy in Luke 10.25–37 and Acts 10.1–11.18," in *Rhetoric and the New Testament,* ed. Stanley E. Porter and Thomas H. Olbricht, Journal for the Study of the New Testament Supplement Series 90 (Sheffield: Sheffield Academic Press, 1993), 59–73; and in the same volume, Daniel Marguerat, "The End of Acts (28.16–31) and the Rhetoric of Silence," 74–89.

29. For example, Darr, *Character Building;* Gerald Downing, "Theophilus's First Reading of Luke-Acts," in Tuckett, *Luke's Literary Achievement,* 91–109.

30. For example, Tannehill, *Narrative Unity;* Brawley, *Centering on God;* Kurz, *Reading Luke-Acts;* Parsons, *Departure of Jesus;* Tyson, *Death of Jesus;* idem, *Images of Judaism;* David B. Gowler, *Host, Guest, Enemy and Friend: Portraits of the Pharisees in Luke and Acts* (New York: Peter Lang, 1991); Jack D. Kingsbury, *Conflict in Luke* (Philadelphia: Fortress, 1991); Spencer, *The Portrait of Philip in Acts: A Study of Roles and Relations,* Journal for the Study of the New Testament Supplement Series 67 (Sheffield: Sheffield Academic Press, 1992); Steven M. Sheeley, *Narrative Asides in Luke-Acts,* Journal for the Study of the New Testament Supplement Series 72 (Sheffield: Sheffield Academic, 1992); William H. Shepherd, *The Narrative Function of the Holy Spirit as a Character in Luke-Acts,* Society of Biblical Literature Dissertation Series 147 (Atlanta: Scholars Press, 1994); Green, *The Theology of the Gospel of Luke,* New Testament Theology (Cambridge: Cambridge University Press, 1995); idem, *Gospel of Luke.*

31. Important work on characterization has been done by Tannehill, Brawley, Darr, Gowler, Spencer, and Shepherd (see notes 29 and 30).

32. See Traugott Holtz, *Untersuchungen über die alttestamentlichen Zitate bei Lukas,* Texte und Untersuchungen 104 (Berlin: Akademie, 1968); Martin Rese, *Alttestamentliche Motive in der Christologie des Lukas,* Studien zum Neuen Testament 1 (Gütersloh: Mohn, 1969); Darrell L. Bock, *Proclamation from Prophecy and Pattern: Lucan Old Testament Christology,* Journal for the Study of the New Testament Supplement Series 12 (Sheffield: Sheffield Academic Press, 1987); Charles A. Kimball, *Jesus' Exposition of the Old Testament in Luke's Gospel,* Journal for the Study of the New Testament Supplement Series 94 (Sheffield: Sheffield Academic Press 1994); Brawley, *Text to Text Pours Forth Speech: Voices of Scripture in Luke-Acts* (Bloomington, Ind.: Indiana University Press, 1995).

33. See Marion L. Soards, *The Speeches in Acts: Their Content, Context, and Concerns* (Louisville, Ky.: Westminster/John Knox Press, 1994).

34. Hans Conzelmann, *The Theology of St. Luke* (New York: Harper, 1961). To follow the subsequent debate, see E. Earle Ellis, *Eschatology in Luke,* Facet Books (Philadelphia: Fortress Press, 1972); Eric Franklin, *Christ the Lord: A Study in the Purpose and Theology of Luke-Acts* (Philadelphia: Westminster Press, 1975); A. J. Mattill, *Luke and the Last Things: A Perspective for the Understanding of Lukan Thought* (Dillsboro, N.C.: Western North Carolina Press, 1979); John T. Carroll, *Response to the End of History: Eschatology and Situation in Luke-Acts,* Society of Biblical Literature Dissertation Series 92 (Atlanta: Scholars Press, 1988); J. Bradley Chance, *Jerusalem, the Temple, and the New Age in Luke-Acts* (Macon, Ga.: Mercer University Press, 1988).

35. On Jesus as prophet, see Paul Minear, *To Heal and To Reveal: The Prophetic Vocation according to Luke* (New York: Seabury Press, 1976); Johnson, *Gospel of Luke;* idem, *Literary Function of Possessions;* David P. Moessner, *Lord of the Banquet: The Literary and Theological Significance of the Lukan Travel Narrative* (Minneapolis: Fortress Press, 1989).

36. Bock (*Proclamation*) argues that Luke presents Jesus as Messiah, yet the narrative's development privileges his status as Kyrios (Lord). Mark L. Strauss shows that Jesus' identity as the humble "servant of God" gives definitive shape to his role as the royal (Davidic) Messiah. The character of his life and death fulfills scriptural prophecies and patterns. See *The Davidic Messiah in Luke-Acts: The Promise and Its Fulfillment in Lukan Christology,* Journal for the Study of the New Testament Supplement Series 110 (Sheffield: Sheffield Academic Press, 1995). Other recent studies of Lukan christology include H. Douglas Buckwalter, *The Character and Purpose of Luke's Christology,* Society for New Testament Studies Monograph Series 89 (Cambridge: Cambridge University Press, 1996); David M. Crump, *Jesus the Intercessor: Prayer and Christology in Luke-Acts,* Wissenschaftliche Untersuchungen zum Neuen Testament 2/49 (Tübingen: Mohr, 1992); and Manfred Korn, *Die Geschichte Jesu in veränderter Zeit: Studien zur bleibendend Bedeutung Jesu im lukanischen Doppelwerk,* Wissenschaftliche Untersuchungen zum Neuen Testament 2/51 (Tübingen: Mohr, 1993).

37. Tannehill, by contrast, contends that the hopes kindled by the Gospel's opening chapters go unrealized in the tragic narrative that ensues. See "Israel in Luke-Acts: A Tragic Story," *Journal of Biblical Literature* 104 (1985): 69–85.

38. See Carroll, "Luke's Crucifixion Scene," in *Reimaging the Death of the Lukan Jesus,* ed. Dennis D. Sylva, Bonner biblische Beiträge 73 (Frankfurt am Main: Hahn, 1990) 108–24, 194–203. On the death of Jesus in Luke-Acts, see Jerome Neyrey, *The Passion according to Luke: A Redaction Study of Luke's Soteriology,* Theological Inquiries (Mahwah, N.J.: Paulist Press, 1985); Soards, *The Passion according to Luke: The Special Material of Luke 22,* Journal for the Study of the New Testament Supplement Series 14 (Sheffield: Sheffield Academic Press, 1987); Donald Senior, *The Passion of Jesus in the Gospel of Luke* (Wilmington, Del.: Michael Glazier, 1989); Jon A. Weatherly, *Jewish Responsibility for the Death of Jesus in Luke-Acts,* Journal for the Study of the New Testament Supplement Series 106 (Sheffield: Sheffield Academic

Press, 1994); John T. Carroll and Joel B. Green, et al., *The Death of Jesus in Early Christianity* (Peabody, Mass.: Hendrickson, 1995), 60–81; Peter Doble, *The Paradox of Salvation: Luke's Theology of the Cross,* Society for New Testament Studies Monograph Series 87 (Cambridge: Cambridge University Press, 1996).

39. For appreciation of the theocentric character of Luke-Acts, see Brawley, *Centering on God;* Green, *Theology of Luke;* idem, *Gospel of Luke.*

40. Nils A. Dahl, "The Neglected Factor in New Testament Theology," in idem, *Jesus the Christ,* ed. Donald H. Juel (Minneapolis: Fortress Press, 1991), 153–63.

41. See Squires, *Plan of God.*

42. See Green, *Theology of Luke;* idem, *Gospel of Luke;* compare, idem, "The Social Status of Mary in Luke 1,5—2,52: A Plea for Methodological Integration," *Biblica* 73 (1992): 457–72; Mary Ann Beavis, "'Expecting Nothing in Return': Luke's Picture of the Marginalized," *Interpretation* 48 (1994): 357–68; David L. Balch, "Rich and Poor, Proud and Humble in Luke-Acts," in *The Social World of the First Christians: Essays in Honor of Wayne A. Meeks,* ed. L. Michael White and O. Larry Yarbrough (Minneapolis: Fortress Press, 1995), 214–33.

43. See Halvor Moxnes, *The Economy of the Kingdom: Social Conflict and Economic Relations in Luke's Gospel,* Overtures to Biblical Theology (Philadelphia: Fortress Press, 1988); *The Social World of Luke-Acts: Models for Interpretation,* ed. Jerome H. Neyrey (Peabody, Mass.: Hendrickson Pubs., 1991).

44. Braun, *Feasting and Social Rhetoric.*

45. Johnson (*Literary Function of Possessions*) suggests that possessions have symbolic value in Luke-Acts; faithful use of wealth fashions the image of a community ordered under the leadership of the apostles. Other important treatments of the theme include Walter Pilgrim, *Good News to the Poor: Wealth and Poverty in Luke-Acts* (Minneapolis: Augsburg, 1981); David Seccombe, *Possessions and the Poor in Luke-Acts,* Studien zum Neuen Testament und seiner Umwelt 6 (Linz: Fuchs, 1982); Green, *Theology of Luke.*

46. See Mary Rose d'Angelo, "Women in Luke-Acts: A Redactional View," *Journal of Biblical Literature* 109 (1990): 441–61; Turid Karlsen Seim, *The Double Message: Patterns of Gender in Luke-Acts* (Nashville: Abingdon Press, 1994); Ivoni Richter Reimer, *Women in the Acts of the Apostles: A Feminist Liberation Perspective* (Minneapolis: Fortress Press, 1995); Barbara E. Reid, *Choosing the Better Part? Women in the Gospel of Luke* (Collegeville, Minn.: Liturgical Press, 1996); Robert M. Price, *The Widow Traditions in Luke-Acts: A Feminist-Critical Inquiry,* Society of Biblical Literature Dissertation Series 155 (Atlanta: Scholars Press, 1997); compare Powell, *What Are They Saying about Luke?,* 93–97.

47. Robert Karris, "Women and Discipleship in Luke," *Catholic Biblical Quarterly* 56 (1994): 1–20; compare Warren Carter, "Getting Martha out of the Kitchen: Luke 10:38–42 Again," *Catholic Biblical Quarterly* 58 (1996): 264–80.

48. Beverly Roberts Gaventa, *Mary: Glimpses of the Mother of Jesus* (Columbia, S.C.: University of South Carolina Press, 1995), 49–78.

49. Seim, *Double Message;* compare Reimer, *Women in the Acts of the Apostles;* d'Angelo, "Women in Luke-Acts."

50. Jervell, *Luke and the People of God;* Tiede, *Prophecy and History;* see also Brawley, *Luke-Acts and the Jews.* See notes 24–26 above.

51. Sanders, *Jews in Luke-Acts.*

52. Tyson, *Images of Judaism in Luke-Acts;* Tannehill, *Narrative Unity,* 2.344–57.

Chapter 6

Johannine Literature

Gail R. O'Day

From the days of its very first readers in the nascent Christian church, the Gospel of John has been seen as both delight and puzzle, as enlightening and confounding. It has generated mutually contradictory interpretations and been marshalled in support of radically diverse theological positions. In the second century C.E., for example, Gnostics appealed to the Gospel of John in support of their understanding of Jesus and the nature of Christian existence,[1] and Irenaeus (*Against Heresies*) made a similar appeal in his attacks on the Gnostics and defense of orthodoxy. Throughout the centuries, this Gospel has provided the impetus for some of the most significant developments in the study of the New Testament. Two of the most important European New Testament interpreters of the mid-twentieth century—Rudolf Bultmann in Germany and C. H. Dodd in Great Britain—produced what are now classic treatments of the Gospel of John, yet when one compares their interpretations, one is left wondering whether Bultmann and Dodd were reading the same Gospel![2]

The wide range of interpretations that this Gospel inspires may lead its readers to despair of ever penetrating the complexities of this text. It is possible, however, for the reader to view the rich interpretive history and the continuing generativity of this text as an advantage, not a hindrance. Given the diversity of approaches to the Gospel of John and the variety of questions interpreters put to this text, the Gospel provides the student of the Bible, at whatever level of contemplation, with a laboratory for most of the important methodological questions in contemporary New Testament studies.

In the last decades of the twentieth century, scholars have wrestled with the place of historical criticism in New Testament study. Prior to the 1960s, both the assumptions of historical criticism and the dominance of that method as the decisive method for New Testament scholarship were essentially unchallenged. Yet from the 1960s onward, the place of historical criticism in biblical scholarship has shifted. Historical criticism has not been abandoned, for it is an essential tool in trying to decipher ancient texts, but its limits have been recognized and other interpretive methods have entered the scholarly conversation (trends toward literary, cultural, and ideological modes of discourse are traced by Fernando Segovia in the first chapter of this book).[3] Three of the most important methods recently undertaken are social world criticism,[4] literary criticism,[5] and ideological criticism.[6]

There is a remarkable overlap between the methodological questions that shape the work of contemporary New Testament scholars in general and the particular questions that are important to the study of the Fourth Gospel. For example, some of the more important issues facing Johannine scholars are concrete instances of the more general methodological queries:

> Does John's portrait of Jesus have any contact with that found in the other Gospels or is it completely idiosyncratic and ahistorical? (historical criticism)
> What kind of reading experience does John create for the reader through its use of figurative language and extended discourses? (literary criticism)
> Is John anti-Jewish or thoroughly steeped in the Jewish religious life of its time? (social world criticism)
> Is John a positive resource for feminist readers of Scripture or irremediably patriarchal? (ideological criticism)

We will look at the way these different methodological issues and options shape Fourth Gospel study.

HISTORICAL CRITICISM

Under the rubric of historical criticism, I want to examine three interrelated issues in Johannine studies: the relationship of John to the other canonical Gospels, the place of John in the historical Jesus debate, and the interweaving of history and interpretation in the composition of the Gospel.

The relationship of John to the other Gospels. The common nomenclature used to speak of the canonical Gospels provides a useful beginning point for discussing their interrelationship. Matthew, Mark, and Luke are grouped together as the Synoptic Gospels, while the Gospel of John usually is positioned alone. Indeed, as if to emphasize further the perceived divide between John and the other Gospels, the Gospel of John is referred to most regularly as "the Fourth Gospel," while it is rare to hear the other Gospels referred to by number (for example, Luke as "the Third Gospel"). This distinction in nomenclature highlights how both the tradition of the Christian church and New Testament scholarship have tended to treat the Gospel of John as a special category and as a different kind of witness to the life of Jesus.

Clement of Alexandria made one of the earliest statements about John's relationship to the other Gospels: "Last of all John, perceiving that the external facts had been made plain in the gospel, being urged by his friends and inspired by the Spirit, composed a spiritual Gospel."[7] These words show that Clement assumed that the Gospel of John was the last Gospel to be written and that its author was dependent on the Synoptic Gospels for the "external facts" of Jesus' life. This understanding of Johannine dependence on the Synoptics remained the dominant view through the early decades of the twentieth century. The view was then challenged on the grounds that the Jesus traditions in John derived from a variety of oral traditions that circulated about Jesus in the early decades after his life and death, rather than from the written sources of the Synoptic Gospels.[8] In other words, the differences between John and the Synoptic Gospels were not due to John's alteration of the Synoptic Gospels, as Clement and centuries of interpreters after him had posited, but from John's separate access to independent Jesus traditions.

It is rather remarkable that within the span of fifty years, eighteen centuries of scholarly consensus about Johannine dependence on the Synoptics could shift to that of Johannine independence, but that is indeed the case.[9] While some scholars continue to make the case for John's dependence at least on Mark, if not on all the Synoptics,[10] the beginning point for most research into the Fourth Gospel is its independence from the Synoptics.

What difference does the disposition of this question make to readers of the Fourth Gospel? As shall be discussed more fully below, clarity about John's relationship to the other canonical Gospels has significant implications both for how John itself is read and for our understanding of the nature of Gospel literature and first-century Christianity. If, as the majority view holds, John constructed his Gospel narrative from an independent stream of Jesus traditions that may overlap with the traditions lying behind the Synoptic Gospels but are not dependent on them, then a much richer picture of religious formation in the first century emerges. Instead of the somewhat schematized picture of the way in which Jesus traditions moved from oral storytelling to written document that is often posited in Gospel criticism, Johannine independence from the Synoptics suggests a more multilayered process, in which stories and streams of tradition intersected at various points in the formation of Christian communities. It also allows for a fuller understanding of the nature of Gospels and the creativity of Gospel writers. A Gospel writer's decisions about how to incorporate and present Jesus traditions cannot be attributed simply to decisions made in relationship to other Gospels, but for the sake of the Gospel composition itself.

The place of John in the historical Jesus debate. The assessment of the relationship of John to the Synoptic Gospels is pertinent to the question of the place of the Fourth Gospel in debates about the historical Jesus. When one posits Johannine dependence on the Synoptics, then John has no value as a source of information about Jesus' life, because it only recycles and repackages what is found in the Synoptics. Among recent interpreters of John, Thomas Brodie argues this position.[11] Brodie, following wholly in the tradition of Clement, understands John's value to be principally spiritual, not historical.

The most extreme position taken in recent years on the historical worth of the Gospel of John in relationship to the Synoptic picture of Jesus is probably that articulated by Maurice Casey in his book *Is John's Gospel True?*.[12] Casey assumes that the Synoptic Gospels, especially Mark, present a reliable and easily recoverable picture of the historical Jesus, and that the Fourth Gospel's differences from the Synoptics are an intentional distortion of history. For Casey, John's Gospel is not true, because its portrait of Jesus differs so radically from that found in the Synoptics that it can only be regarded as nonhistorical.

It is interesting to observe how readily most historical Jesus scholars simply dismiss the Fourth Gospel from their conversations, without much acknowledgment of the presuppositions that underlie their moves.[13] That is, most historical Jesus scholars act as if the view of the Gospel articulated by Clement of Alexandria is incontrovertible fact: John has interest only as a "spiritual Gospel." Yet there is increasing recognition among many Johannine scholars that the Fourth Gospel may indeed contain reliable historical information, especially about the complex fabric of religious and political life under Roman rule in early first-century Palestine. David Rensberger, Raymond Brown, and Luise Schottroff, for example, all writing from quite distinct interpretive positions, have shown that the Gospel of John can be a source for reconstructing life in the time of Jesus and in the following decades.[14]

For there to be a full-bodied conversation about the historical Jesus—and about the nature of the Gospels as sources for historical information—then the Fourth Gospel must be included. If, as scholarly consensus now maintains, John is an independent witness to Jesus traditions, then it is a witness roughly contemporaneous with Matthew and Luke, and so cannot be so quickly discarded on the grounds that it is the "last." Moreover, by keeping the Fourth Gospel in conversation with the other Gospels, it enables the New Testament reader to see more clearly the ways in which the Jesus story was interpreted in the first decades of the church, and the ways in which twentieth-century assumptions about historiography color the contemporary quest for the historical Jesus.

History and Interpretation. The preceding discussion of John and the historical Jesus leads to a final topic under historical criticism, which—like the others in this section—was already signalled in Clement's remarks. According to Clement, John wrote a spiritual interpretation of the "facts" found in the other Gospels. That is, John was freer to recount Jesus' life in his own way, because the facts were already available in the other Gospel accounts. Clement correctly recognized that the Gospel of John brought the reader face to face with the tensive interrelationship of history, theology, and interpretation, but the tendency among New Testament scholars has been to resolve this tension through deemphasis of the question of history in relationship to John and to focus instead on Johannine "spiritualizing" of the Synoptics.[15] In so doing, a line between facts and interpretation is drawn that is not drawn in the Gospel itself. It is worth noting that Clement's own words do not themselves draw these lines, but rather describe the distinctive voice of the Gospel.

To try to separate what happened in the life of Jesus from its meaning is a false pursuit for this Gospel. That claim does not minimize or dismiss the possible historical value of the account of Jesus' life and ministry in John, but instead recognizes that for John, the value of the events of Jesus' life and ministry derives from the inseparable union of what happened and the meaning of those events. In each of the Gospels, the choices that the Evangelists make about what stories of Jesus to tell and what order in which to tell them are implicit acts of interpretation, but the

Fourth Gospel also contains explicit acts of interpretation that become part of the story's fabric. Perhaps the clearest illustration of this are instances in which the Fourth Evangelist incorporates explicit commentary about the post-resurrection perspective from which the Gospel is written into the story itself. John 2:13–22 and 12:12–16 narrate, respectively, the cleansing of the Temple and Jesus' triumphal entry into Jerusalem. The conclusions of these stories make direct mention of the disciples' remembering these events after Jesus' death and resurrection and only then are they able to understand their significance. The explicit hermeneutical move made here by the evangelist, through the voice of the narrator, is extraordinary; he has incorporated into the telling of the story directions on how to read the story. Two of the more well-known stories in the Jesus traditions thus are shown to have their meaning not in the facticity of the event itself, but in the way the event is appropriated later by those who "remember."

While most New Testament debates about history tend to be shaped solely by concerns with the historicity of any given account or portrait of Jesus, the Gospel of John pushes the interpreter beyond these traditional historical critical concerns to look instead at "the far more important, far more disturbing, problem of history itself and its meaning."[16] The Fourth Gospel thus has a crucial role to play in re-opening the question of the interrelationship of history, theology, and interpretation in early Christian documents.

LITERARY CRITICISM

The concluding paragraph in the historical criticism section above provides a smooth transition to a discussion of literary criticism and John, because it focuses attention on one of the central premises of a literary-critical approach to Gospel texts: that one cannot talk about *what* a Gospel text says without attending to *how* it is said. While reading strategies that are attentive to the literary dynamics of a biblical text have a crucial role to play in all biblical interpretation, they are essential for the interpretation of John precisely because of the Fourth Gospel's complex intertwining of event and interpretation, story and theology. This intertwining is maintained through the vehicle of the literary style and technique of the narrative, and so interpretive methods that help to identify these techniques and how they function in the Gospel narrative are a necessity.

To understand the perspective on the Fourth Gospel that literary-critical methods provide, it is helpful to review briefly the ways the meaning of the term "literary criticism" has shifted in New Testament studies in the twentieth century. In the late nineteenth and early twentieth centuries, when biblical scholars talked about looking at a biblical text from the perspective of "literary criticism," they meant studying a text to discover what one could learn about its literary prehistory. The purpose of literary criticism in its traditional sense was not to illuminate the literary features intrinsic to the text, as is the case in contemporary uses of the term, but to provide a coherent explanation for the history of the composition of the text.

In Johannine studies, traditional literary-critical explanations for the shape of the Fourth Gospel ranged from displacement theories (that is, the Fourth Gospel as we have it is the result of the displacement or rearrangement of certain sections of the manuscript)[17] to more developed source theories modeled on the work being done on the Pentateuch in Old Testament studies.[18] The most comprehensive and influential presentation of the literary history of the Fourth Gospel was that proposed by Bultmann, who appealed to displacements, a secondary editor, and an elaborate source theory to explain the composition of the Fourth Gospel.[19] One aspect of source theories that has continuing influence in Johannine studies is the proposal that the author of the Fourth Gospel had access to a written miracles source.[20] In all of these approaches to John, the Gospel text is simply one more piece of data in an historical inquiry.

The most significant shift in Johannine studies with regard to the redefinition of "literary criticism" was the work of R. Alan Culpepper, *Anatomy of the Fourth Gospel.*[21] Others had worked on literary aspects of John,[22] but Culpepper provided the first sustained study that focused, as the title suggests, on the literary elements that give shape to the Fourth Gospel story—for example, characters, plot, language use (symbolism, metaphor, irony). This book was essentially a work in what has come to be called "narrative criticism," as the emphasis was on the elements that go together to create the Gospel as story.[23] Literary criticism remains one of the primary approaches to Fourth Gospel study, employing a variety of reading strategies from new critical to deconstructionist.[24] There is not a complete break between the findings of the former "literary criticism" and its contemporary namesake, for many literary critics recognize that biblical texts are the product of a complex history, both oral and written. The most significant difference, however, is that questions of literary prehistory are not the decisive questions. Instead, contemporary literary critics read first with an eye toward the text and not what brought this text to them.

The benefit of this approach to Fourth Gospel study is that the story of Jesus in the Fourth Gospel can be read in and through the stylistic and narrative techniques that define it as a literary text. Study of the artistry and craftsmanship of the Gospel is recognized as an end in itself and not as a stepping stone to a greater goal. The stories in John, instead of being read first to see how they are *not* the Synoptic stories, are read first to see how they *are* the Fourth Gospel stories. Because of literary criticism's attention to the distinctive literary characteristics of the Fourth Gospel, the contemporary student of the New Testament is better equipped to recognize how the story of Jesus is told in John.

Yet not many literary-critical readers of John have put their reading strategies in the service of the broader question of the problem of history outlined above. If anything, an ahistorical assumption underlies much literary-critical work. This means that literary-critical studies can isolate history and story, just as do those interpretations that are concerned only with questions of historicity or that are intentionally "spiritual." That is, the focus of most literary-critical work simply brackets the question of the transformation of history in the literary account and focuses on questions of narrative and language use.

What often drops out in this construal of the interpretive question is attention to the theological content and assumptions that inform the Fourth Gospel's reshaping of the Jesus story. That dimension of the Gospel also drops out in historical criticism, when the goal is only to find out "what happened"—whether in the life of Jesus, the history of the church, or the formation of the document. Yet it also can disappear in literary-critical studies if the focus of attention becomes too formalist and the theological substance of the Gospel is not understood to be an integral part of its literary shape.[25] Attention to the ethical questions posed by the Fourth Gospel, especially the Gospel's language about "the Jews" (see below), also can disappear in a narrative-critical approach.[26]

The gains from literary-critical work on John are tremendous. The interpretive landscape of the Fourth Gospel looks completely different than it did only twenty-five to thirty years ago, and the necessary corrective to the disregard for literary art that characterized much of historical-critical work has been accomplished. But literary-critical work also introduces some problems of its own into Gospel study. First, the frequent piecemeal appropriation by biblical scholars of different elements of secular literary theory risks distorting both the original theories and the biblical texts. For example, most literary theories about characterization used by New Testament scholars derive from the study of nineteenth-century novels,[27] in which the notion of self-conscious human personality begins to emerge, and that is quite different from the approach to literary characters in first-century C.E. compositions. Also, while it might be possible, as New Critics claimed, to evaluate a piece of literature completely in the context of the world that the literature itself creates, that is not so clearly possible with a biblical text, and especially a Gospel. Each completed Gospel reflects years of a traditioning process, so that the stories in the Gospel are not strictly an individual author's creation, even if one wants to posit single authorship.

Second, form, content, and function must be interrelated in literary analysis. For the study of the Gospels in general and John in particular, function means more than the formal rhetorical function or the reading effect of particular literary features. The Gospels were not written only to give pleasure or to be artistically accomplished—although in places they are both those things—but there is a theological and pastoral function to the literary composition, and the Fourth Gospel's place in the life of a religious community is inseparably integrated into its literary effects.

As with historical criticism, the overlap of story and interpretation, history and theology in the Fourth Gospel again provides the New Testament interpreter with a unique perspective from which to assess the role of literary criticism in biblical study. The Fourth Gospel gives the literary critic a clearly self-conscious author, one who knows that he is using language to create particular effects, and who is also a self-conscious theologian and reinterpreter of tradition. The Fourth Gospel challenges the reader to push at the limits of literary-critical work and to discover new possibilities for articulating the irreducible interrelationship of story and theology in this New Testament text.

SOCIAL WORLD CRITICISM

For insight into the nexus of social, cultural, and economic factors that shaped first-century life, biblical studies has turned to the social sciences. Through the use of the resources of sociology and anthropology, as well as political science and economics, New Testament scholars try to create a picture of the social world in which the New Testament events took place and the documents were written. The goal is not so much historical reconstruction as the identification of the social dynamics of life in the ancient world.

The turn to social world questions is especially important in the case of the Fourth Gospel and has helped to establish a fuller context in which to interpret this book. The contributions of social world criticism to Johannine studies are most obvious in two areas of research: the Fourth Gospel's attitude toward "the Jews" and the synagogue, and the sectarian character of Johannine Christianity.

The Fourth Gospel and "the Jews." The Fourth Gospel's relationship to Judaism is a challenging and troubling question for both the general reader and the Johannine scholar. On the one hand, the Fourth Gospel seems to have been written by someone who was thoroughly immersed in the Jewish culture of first-century Palestine. Not only does the writer have a detailed knowledge of the practices of the major Jewish holidays, but he also is familiar with smaller ritual practices, like the availability of water for ritual handwashing (2:6). The Gospel is full of geographical details about Jerusalem and Palestine that suggest authorship by a resident of that area. And perhaps most noteworthy, the language of this Gospel is infused with vocabulary and imagery from the Jewish scriptures to a higher degree than any other New Testament document save Revelation. Yet, on the other hand, the Fourth Gospel seems to have at its heart an antagonistic relationship to Judaism. The clearest and most problematic example of this is the Gospel's language about "the Jews" (*hoi 'Ioudaioi*). Whereas in a few instances, "the Jews" seems to be used simply as an objective description of a particular social group (11:31), in most instances the term is disparaging at best, confrontational and vitriolic at worst (8:39–47). How is the reader to interpret these conflicting signals?

J. Louis Martyn's work on John and the synagogue is the foundation of all social world approaches to John and Judaism. In *History and Theology in the Fourth Gospel,* Martyn brought the question of John's relations with the synagogue world of the late first century squarely to the center of the concerns of the Johannine scholar.[28] Martyn's work hinged on the significance of the expulsion from the synagogue mentioned in John 9:22. Martyn proposed that this verse (like 12:42 and 16:2) refers to the Benediction Against Heretics that was introduced into the synagogue liturgy sometime after 70 C.E. and probably between 85 and 95 C.E. From this, Martyn concluded that the Fourth Gospel was written at the end of the first century C.E. in and to a community that was being expelled from the synagogue. This conflict and expulsion accounted for the antagonistic language about "the Jews."

All subsequent work on the question of John and the "Jews" was and continues to be framed in response to Martyn, whether building on Martyn's conclusions or disagreeing with them. Scholars who have based their social world investigations of John on Martyn's hypothesis include David Rensberger and Jerome Neyrey.[29] A comparison of the titles of Martyn's and Rensberger's books reflects the shift away from historical reconstruction (*History and Theology*) to concerns with the social factors that informed the life of the community (*Johannine Faith and Liberating Community*). Rensberger takes Martyn's historical emphasis about Johannine

Christianity and the synagogue and refocuses it on social world concerns in order to interpret Johannine theology in the light of the Johannine community's struggles with the synagogue. Neyrey uses the tools of social science to investigate how the Johannine community's relationship with its contemporary Jewish community influenced the formation of the Fourth Gospel narrative, and in particular, the development of its christology.

Yet the near-consensus acceptance of Martyn's hypothesis by Johannine scholars as the definitive answer for the social setting of the Fourth Gospel is also coming under increasing critical scrutiny. Among biblical scholars who study the relationship of Jews and Christians in the first century C.E., the impact and even the existence of the benediction posited by Martyn have been challenged.[30] Among Johannine scholars, Adele Reinhartz has questioned the exegetical basis upon which Martyn based his hypothesis and has proposed a more complex social situation for the interactions among Johannine Christians and Jews.[31] According to Reinhartz, the attitude of Johannine Christianity to Judaism reflects a situation in which Jewish Christians may not have been forcibly expelled from the synagogue but are nevertheless engaged in a process of self-redefinition that requires them to distance themselves from their Jewish heritage.

Reinhartz's work reflects a growing awareness among Johannine scholars (including those who accept Martyn's hypothesis) of the limitations of the synagogue expulsion model: it places responsibility for the vitriolic language against the Jews in John on the Jewish community that oppressed Johannine Christians by forcibly expelling them from the synagogue, not on the Johannine community itself. Reinhartz's view redresses this problem by returning responsibility for the anti-Jewish language to the Johannine community itself and its struggles to reconcile its faith in Jesus with its Jewish roots.[32]

The sectarian character of Johannine Christianity. The issue of the Johannine community's self-definition is echoed in another area studied by social-world critics: the extent to which Johannine Christianity is a sectarian movement. Working from the perspective of the sociology of knowledge, Wayne Meeks articulated a highly influential interpretation of Johannine Christianity as sectarian Christianity.[33] Meeks determined that the language of the Gospel, particularly the language about the relationship between heaven and earth and the descent of the Son of Man (for example, 3:13), suggested a community that understood itself to be alienated from the world in which it was located. Many Johannine scholars, taking their cue from Meeks's work, appealed to the work of sociologists to identify the way key characteristics of the Fourth Gospel—establishment of its own community in opposition to the world at large, dualism, exclusivism—fit the definition of sectarianism.[34]

Recent research in this area suggests that while social-scientific methods can be used to establish the contours of Johannine Christianity as a sect,[35] the implications of those findings for interpreting the theological substance of the Gospel is largely unexplored. Rensberger is one of the few Johannine scholars who explicitly puts the work of social world analysis in the context of theological investigation.[36] Just as with literary criticism, social world criticism is often oblivious to the inseparable interrelationship of social factors and theology in the Fourth

Gospel. Again, the study of the Fourth Gospel provides the reader with an opportunity to rethink the strict lines of interpretation imposed by methodological distinctions, because the Gospel narrative bears witness to the integration of historical context, the rhetoric of the text, social fabric, and theological substance in the creation of meaning.

IDEOLOGICAL CRITICISM

Social world criticism also faces a similar challenge to that faced by historical criticism, to avoid the assumption that one can determine an "objective" social reality. The responsible biblical critic must always attend to the different interests that are served by a particular social construction of reality.[37] Ideological criticism draws explicit attention to the values, belief systems, and power dynamics involved in the composition and interpretation of biblical texts. This method of criticism acknowledges that value-neutral interpretation is impossible, whether that interpretation occurred in the first century C.E.—with the choices New Testament writers made with regard to early Christian traditions—or in the twentieth century—with the choices modern interpreters make in their reading of a text. The goals of ideological criticism are multifaceted: to uncover the ideology that shapes a given text; to reread a biblical text in light of that ideology; to read a biblical text through the lens of contemporary ideologies—for example, feminist or liberation perspectives—to see what new interpretive possibilities can be found.

The overlap of interpretive methods is apparent when one looks at the way ideological criticism can shape the study of the "Jews" in John. The article by Reinhartz cited above is also an exercise in ideological criticism, because it examines the ways that the Johannine community's religious values clashed with those of its Jewish neighbors and the effect of that clash on the composition of the Gospel. It also engages in an ideological critique of Johannine scholars who have come to accept Martyn's hypothesis as fact, noting that such a view makes the anti-Jewish language less problematic for Christian interpreters who live in a post-Holocaust world. An even more pointed analysis of how the ideology of Johannine interpreters has allowed them to mute the harshness of the language about the "Jews" is offered by Werner Kelber, who shows how the ideological presuppositions of literary-critical readings make it possible to overlook this conflicted aspect of the Gospel.[38] Maurice Casey puts historical criticism at the service of ideological criticism to construct his critique of John's ideology in relationship to its Jewish contemporaries.[39]

Perhaps the most widely recognized type of ideological criticism is feminist biblical criticism. Feminist criticism draws on each of the three methods discussed in this essay in order to read for the ways that gender is a factor in the composition and the interpretation of biblical texts. Sometimes feminist criticism reads for the ways that the patriarchal culture—in which most, if not all, biblical texts were written—shapes the images of both men and women found in the texts. Feminist critics may reclaim a positive role for women, or call the bluff on patriarchal oppression that is masquerading as objective reality. Feminist critics also attend to the ways in which the assumptions of biblical scholarship have themselves repressed women's voices and interests.

Feminist criticism has made invaluable contributions to the study of John, because issues pertaining to gender are such an explicit part of the Fourth Gospel's fabric. John has more women characters in pivotal and active roles in relationship to Jesus than any other Gospel, and the study of women in John has proved a fruitful area of research.[40] Yet this Gospel's dominant language for God, "Father," also raises questions about the intersection of patriarchy, androcentrism, and theology in a way that no other New Testament document does. The feminist interpreter of John is thus drawn in two seemingly contradictory directions.[41] At the same time that the Gospel gives positive value to women and uses a nongendered image, "the Word," as a shaping christological category, it also gives the ultimate positive value to an inescapably male image of God and its attendant gendered image for Jesus as the Son. Feminist criticism has necessitated that readers of the Fourth Gospel recognize that gendered language and imagery are an inescapable part of the distinctive landscape of John.

Yet another form of ideological criticism takes as its starting point the job of naming the particular ideology of the modern interpreter. Attention to the contemporary reader's distinctive, even idiosyncratic, perspective is claimed as a positive and essential factor in interpreting the text. This form of ideological criticism is prominent in Johannine scholarship, because two of the main proponents of this type of biblical interpretation, Fernando Segovia and Jeffrey Staley, are Johannine scholars.[42] This approach to ideological criticism asserts that since the possibility of a reader's objective stance is only a scholarly fiction, it is incumbent upon the interpreter to name one's reading posture as an explicit part of one's interpretive act and to show the links between that posture and the interpretation of the biblical text that one produces. This particular form of ideological criticism usefully identifies the range of interpretive positions operative among readers of the Fourth Gospel, but one often wonders if in the process the interpreter's story becomes more important than the Gospel's story.

THE JOHANNINE EPISTLES

The methodological options discussed for the study of the Fourth Gospel also pertain to the study of the Johannine epistles,[43] but students of the New Testament have a far different interpretive task in front of them when reading the three Johannine epistles than when reading the Gospel. Indeed, the central challenge with regard to the epistles is to be able to speak with any degree of confidence about what these three documents actually are. Although they are referred to as epistles, the longest of the three, 1 John, bears no obvious marks of the epistolary form (for example, no opening or closing greetings). And even though they are called the "Johannine epistles," none of the three contains any explicit reference to the name of its author (2 John and 3 John are written by "the elder"). It is important to acknowledge that the three documents themselves establish no direct connection with the Gospel; the name John in the titles is a later addition. That the tradition was correct in linking the four documents together under the rubric "Johannine literature" has long been held to be true, as has the view that the epistles were written later than the Gospel and thus provide an example of intra-Christian controversies that arose as a result of debates over the proper interpretation of the Gospel of John.[44]

Another challenge to the interpreter of the Johannine epistles is their brevity. They provide such a slim database that it is difficult to know what to make of the answers one gets to one's questions and how to construct a framework in which to interpret them. Here the association of the epistles with the Gospel has been a great help to scholars, because it gives the scholar more data.

Recently, however, some scholars have begun to question the automatic linkage of the epistles with the Gospel and have argued the case for trying to interpret the epistles on their own terms and not always with reference to how they relate to the Gospel.[45] Reading the epistles on their own terms and apart from the Gospel would be in tune with the canonical location of these texts. They are placed with the "Catholic Epistles," that is, those documents addressed to the general church (in contrast to the specific named audiences of the Pauline epistles). This way of interpreting the epistles has important implications for one's understanding of the growth of early Christianity. When the epistles are read without a restrictive relationship to the Fourth Gospel, the picture that they paint of the struggles of a first-century C.E. Christian community does not have to be read as data about Johannine Christianity, but as yet one more theological option in the early stages of the church's life.

Continued scrutiny of the epistles may affirm the long-standing view that they belong to the Johannine tradition (as defined by the Gospel), but the question of the epistles' social and theological location is a more open question than one would have guessed would be the case twenty years ago.

NOTES

1. See the work of Elaine Pagels, *The Johannine Gospel in Gnostic Exegesis: Heracleon's Commentary on John* (Atlanta: Scholars Press, 1973).

2. Rudolf Bultmann, *The Gospel of John* (Philadelphia: Westminster Press, 1971); C. H. Dodd, *The Interpretation of the Fourth Gospel* (Cambridge: University Press, 1958). If Sir Edwin Hoskyns had not died before he finished his commentary on John (*The Fourth Gospel,* ed. by F. N. Davey [London: Faber and Faber, 1947]), he also would be included in this company.

3. For a thorough review of contemporary methods of interpreting the Bible and discussion of their relationship to historical criticism, see *To Each its Own Meaning: An Introduction to Biblical Criticisms and their Application,* ed. Steven L. McKenzie and Stephen R. Haynes (Louisville, Ky.: Westminster/John Knox Press, 1993); and Carl R. Holladay, "Contemporary Methods of Reading the Bible," in *The New Interpreter's Bible* (Nashville: Abingdon, 1994), I.125–49. Another interesting perspective on the shift in biblical study methods comes with the recognition that *Semeia,* a journal started to provide a publishing venue for experimental methods in biblical study, is approaching its twenty-fifth anniversary, and that many of its "experimental" methods now form part of the regular working vocabulary of biblical interpreters.

4. Social world criticism draws on the resources of the social sciences to understand the broader social and cultural dynamics in the ancient world. *Interpretation* 36 (1982) provides an overview of social world approaches to biblical studies.

5. Literary criticism moves beyond historical criticism's concern to identify the original form of the text or the different layers of composition in a biblical text, and instead focuses on the biblical texts as coherent literary creations. The term "literary criticism" is used as a blanket term here to include a wide variety of reading strategies that all take as their unifying perspective the presupposition that the biblical text is to be read as a completed, whole literary product, not one stage in a developmental model. More differentiated forms of literary criticism include rhetorical criticism, narrative criticism, structural criticism, and some forms of post-structuralism and deconstructionism.

6. Ideological criticism challenges the undergirding assumption of historical criticism— that it is possible to offer a value-free interpretation and thereby to reconstruct objective history—and focuses instead on the ideological interests that drive the composition and interpretation of biblical texts. For a discussion of the presuppositions of ideological criticism, see Elisabeth Schüssler Fiorenza, "The Ethics of Biblical Interpretation: Decentering Biblical Scholarship," *Journal of Biblical Literature* 107 (1988): 3–17; and Danna Nolan Fewell and David Gunn, *Narrative and the Hebrew Bible* (New York: Oxford University Press, 1993), 189–205.

7. Quoted in Eusebius, *Ecclesiastical History* VI.xiv.7.

8. The crucial study was Percival Gardner-Smith, *Saint John and the Synoptic Gospels* (Cambridge: Cambridge University Press, 1938). Gardner-Smith's findings were expanded and applied across the Fourth Gospel by Dodd, *Historical Tradition in the Fourth Gospel* (Cambridge: Cambridge University Press, 1963).

9. For a full discussion, see D. Moody Smith, *John Among the Gospels: The Relationship in Twentieth Century Research* (Minneapolis: Fortress Press, 1992).

10. C. K. Barrett works from a modified thesis of Johannine dependence on the Synoptics in his commentary, *The Gospel According to St. John,* 2nd ed. (Philadelphia: Westminster Press, 1978). The scholar most responsible for keeping the debate open is Frans Neirynck. See, for example, "John and the Synoptics: 1975–1990," in *John and the Synoptics,* ed. A. Deneaux (Leuven: Leuven University Press, 1992).

11. Thomas Brodie, *The Quest for the Origin of John's Gospel: A Source-Oriented Approach* (New York: Oxford University Press, 1992).

12. Maurice Casey, *Is John's Gospel True?* (London: Routledge, 1996).

13. For two contrasting perspectives on the relationship of John to the contemporary quest for the historical Jesus, see Marianne Meye Thompson, "The Historical Jesus and the Johannine Christ," in *Exploring the Gospel of John: In Honor of D. Moody Smith*, ed. R. Alan Culpepper and C. Clifton Black (Louisville, Ky.: Westminster John Knox Press, 1996), 21–42; and Stephen D. Moore, "Some Ugly Thoughts on the Fourth Gospel at the Threshold of the Third Millennium," in volume two of *What is John?*, ed. Fernando Segovia, 2 vols. (Atlanta: Scholars Press, 1996, 1998).

14. Raymond Brown, *The Death of the Messiah: From Gethesemane to the Grave: A Commentary on the Passion Narratives in the Four Gospels* (New York: Doubleday, 1994); David Rensberger, *Johannine Faith and Liberating Community* (Philadelphia: Westminster Press, 1988); Luise Schottroff, *Lydia's Impatient Sisters: A Feminist Social History of Early Christianity*, trans. Barbara and Martin Rumscheidt (Louisville, Ky.: Westminster/John Knox Press, 1995), 181–203.

15. For a striking example of this approach to John, see the recent commentary by Brodie, *The Gospel according to John: A Literary and Theological Commentary* (New York: Oxford University Press, 1993).

16. Hoskyns, *John,* 58.

17. F. Warburton Lewis, *Disarrangements in the Fourth Gospel* (Cambridge: University Press, 1910); B. W. Bacon, *The Fourth Gospel in Research and Debate* (New Haven, Conn.: Yale University Press, 1918).

18. Julius Wellhausen, *Erweiterungen und Anderungen in vierten Evangelium* (Berlin: Georg Reimer, 1907).

19. Unlike modern commentators who preface their work on the biblical texts with lengthy introductions, Bultmann provided no introduction in which he articulated his composition theories, but instead completely integrated his theories into the fabric of the commentary.

20. In recent times, Robert Fortna has been the most consistent advocate for the role of this "signs source" in the composition of the Fourth Gospel, *The Gospel of Signs: A Reconstruction of the Narrative Source Underlying the Fourth Gospel* (Cambridge: University Press, 1970); and *The Fourth Gospel and its Predecessor: from Narrative Source to Present Gospel* (Philadelphia: Fortress Press, 1988).

21. R. Alan Culpepper, *Anatomy of the Fourth Gospel: A Study in Literary Design* (Philadelphia: Fortress Press, 1983).

22. See, for example, Birger Olsson, *Structure and Meaning in the Fourth Gospel. A Text-Linguistic Analysis of John 2:1–11 and 4:1–42,* Coniectanea biblica — New Testament 6 (Lund: GWK Gleerup, 1974); and P. J. Cahill, "Narrative Art in John IV," *Religious Studies Bulletin* 2 (1982): 41–48.

23. For a thorough review of narrative criticism in biblical studies, see Powell, *What is Narrative Criticism?,* Guides to Biblical Scholarship (Minneapolis: Fortress Press, 1990).

24. For example, Paul D. Duke, *Irony in the Fourth Gospel* (Atlanta: John Knox Press, 1985); Gail R. O'Day, *Revelation in the Fourth Gospel: Narrative Mode and Theological Claim* (Philadelphia: Fortress Press, 1986); Jeffrey L. Staley, *The Print's First Kiss: the Implied Reader in the Fourth Gospel,* Society of Biblical Literature Dissertation Series 82 (Atlanta: Scholars Press, 1988); Mark W. G. Stibbe, *John as Storyteller: Narrative Criticism and the Fourth Gospel* (Cambridge: Cambridge University Press, 1992), and idem, *John's Gospel* (London: Routledge, 1994); Stephen D. Moore, "Are there Impurities in the Living Water that the Johannine Jesus Dispenses? Deconstruction, Feminism, and the Samaritan Woman," *Biblical Interpretation* 1 (1993): 207–27; Dorothy Lee, *The Symbolic Narratives of the Fourth Gospel: the Interplay of Form and Meaning,* Journal for the Study of the New Testament Supplement Series 95 (Sheffield: JSOT Press, 1994).

25. See the pointed criticism of Moore, *Literary Criticism and the Gospels: The Theoretical Challenge* (New Haven, Conn.: Yale University Press, 1989), 58. Moore's drive

in his own work, however, is not to close that gap as much as it is to challenge the presuppositions of much of the literary-critical work of contemporary New Testament scholars. The desire to link theology and narrative studies was one of the presuppositions of my earlier work, *Revelation in the Fourth Gospel.*

26. See the important article on this subject by Werner H. Kelber, "Metaphysics and Marginality in John," in Segovia, *What is John?,* 1.129–54.

27. The foundations for character study in literary criticism were laid by Henry James, *The Art of Criticism: Henry James on the Theory and Practice of Fiction,* ed. William Veeder and Susan Griffin (Chicago: University of Chicago Press, 1986); E. M. Forster, *Aspects of the Novel* (New York: Harcourt, Brace & World, 1962); W. J. Harvey, *Character and the Novel* (Ithaca, N.Y.: Cornell University Press, 1965); Robert Scholes and Robert Kellogg, *The Nature of Narrative* (London: Oxford University Press, 1966).

28. J. Louis Martyn, *History and Theology in the Fourth Gospel* (Nashville: Abingdon Press, 1968; 2nd ed., 1979).

29. Rensberger, *Johannine Faith and Liberating Community* (Philadelphia: Westminster Press, 1988); and Jerome H. Neyrey, *An Ideology of Revolt: John's Christology in Social-Science Perspective* (Philadelphia: Fortress Press, 1988).

30. Reuven Kimelman, "*Birkat Ha-Minim* and the Lack of Evidence for an Anti-Christian Jewish Prayer in Late Antiquity," in *Jewish and Christian Self-Definition,* vol. 2, ed. E. P. Sanders, et al. (Philadelphia: Westminster Press, 1981), 226–44; Stephen T. Katz, "Issues in the Separation of Judaism and Christianity After 70 CE: A Reconsideration," *Journal of Biblical Literature* 103 (1984): 69–74.

31. Adele Reinhartz, "The Johannine Community and its Jewish Neighbors: A Reappraisal," in Segovia, *What is John?,* vol. 2.

32. Casey *(Is John's Gospel True?)* also reads the language about "the Jews" in John from this perspective, but his goal is simply to engage in a diatribe against the Gospel of John, not to offer a new interpretive perspective from which to read the Gospel.

33. Meeks, "The Man from Heaven in Johannine Sectarianism," *Journal of Biblical Literature* 91 (1972): 44–72.

34. See, for example, Norman Petersen, *The Gospel of John and the Sociology of Light: Language and Characterization in the Fourth Gospel* (Valley Forge, Penn.: Trinity Press International, 1993). The interpretation of Johannine Christianity as a sectarian movement is far from settled. Raymond Brown, for example, using historical critical methods, not social world criticism, argues against a sectarian understanding of Johannine Christianity, *The Community of the Beloved Disciple* (New York: Paulist Press, 1979).

35. See, especially, Bruce Malina, *The Gospel of John in Sociolinguistic Perspective,* Protocol of the Colloquy of the Center for Hermeneutical Studies in Hellenistic and Modern Culture 48 (Berkeley, Calif.: The Center for Hermeneutical Studies in Hellenistic and Modern Culture, 1985).

36. See "Sectarianism and Theological Interpretation in John," in Segovia, *What is John?,* vol. 2, and "Oppression and Identity in the Gospel of John," in *The Recovery of Black Presence: An Interdisciplinary Exploration: Essays in honor of Dr. Charles B. Copher,* ed. Randall C. Bailey and Jacqueline Grant (Nashville: Abingdon Press, 1995), 77–94.

37. In Hebrew Bible studies, Norman Gottwald is an example of a scholar who has always been attentive to the interplay of social world criticism and ideology. See, for example, *The Tribes of Yahweh: a Sociology of the Religion of Liberated Israel, 1250–1050 BCE* (Maryknoll, N.Y.: Orbis Books, 1979). Note also the title of Gottwald's festschrift, *The Bible and the Politics of Exegesis: Essays in Honor of Norman K. Gottwald on his sixty-fifth birthday,* ed. David Jobling, Peggy L. Day, Gerald T. Sheppard (Cleveland: Pilgrim Press, 1991).

38. See Kelber, "Metaphysics and Marginality."

39. The irony of Casey's critique of John is that he seems completely unaware of the ways his own ideology informs his interpretation. That is, he attempts to present a highly tendentious reading of John as one that is objectively verifiable by data from the first century C.E.

40. Some representative studies include: Schüssler Fiorenza, "A Feminist Interpretation for Liberation: Mary and Martha: Luke 10:38–42," *Religion and Intellectual Life* 3 (1986): 21–36; Sandra Schneiders, *The Revelatory Text: Interpreting the New Testament as Sacred Scripture* (New York: Harper, 1991), 180–99; Gail R. O'Day, "John," in *The Women's Bible Commentary,* ed. Carol Newsom and Sharon Ringe (Louisville, Ky.: Westminster/John Knox Press, 1992), 293–304; Ingrid R. Kirzberger," Mary of Bethany and Mary of Magdala—Two Female Characters in the Johannine Passion Narrative: A Feminist Narrative-Critical Reader-Response," *New Testament Studies* 41 (1995): 564–85; Turid Karlsen Seim, "Roles of Women in the Gospel of John," in *Aspects of the Johannine Literature,* ed. L. Hartman and B. Olson, Coniectanea biblica—New Testament 18 (Uppsala: Almqvist & Wiksell, 1987): 56–73; Judith Lieu, "The Mother of the Son in the Fourth Gospel," *Journal of Biblical Literature* 117 (1998): 61–77.

41. See, for example, Reinhartz, "The Gospel of John," in *Searching the Scriptures, Volume 2: A Feminist Commentary,* ed. Elisabeth Schüssler Fiorenza (New York: Crossroad Publishing, 1994), 561–600, esp. 594–97; Judith Lieu, "Scripture and the Feminine in John," in *A Feminist Companion to the Hebrew Bible in the New Testament,* ed. A. Brenner, The Feminist Companion to the Bible 10 (Sheffield: Sheffield Academic Press, 1996), 225–40.

42. See Fernando Segovia and Mary Ann Tolbert, eds., *Reading from This Place* (Minneapolis: Fortress Press, 1994); Segovia, "Reading Readers of the Fourth Gospel and their Readings: An Exercise in Intercultural Criticism," in *What is John?,* 1. 237–77; and Staley, *Reading with a Passion: Rhetoric, Autobiography, and the American West in the Gospel of John* (New York: Continuum, 1995).

43. For a reading of the epistles from a perspective informed by historical criticism, see Brown, *The Community of the Beloved Disciple;* by literary criticism, Charles Talbert, *Reading John: A Literary and Theological Commentary on the Fourth Gospel and the Johannine Epistles* (New York: Crossroad, 1992); by social world criticism, Rensberger, *1 John, 2 John, 3 John,* Abingdon New Testament Commentaries (Nashville: Abingdon Press, 1997); by ideological criticism, O'Day, "1, 2, and 3 John," in *The Women's Bible Commentary,* 374–75; and Margaret D. Hutaff, "The Johannine Epistles," in *Searching the Scriptures, Volume 2,* 406–27.

44. The classic presentation of this view is found in Brown, *The Community of the Beloved Disciple.* The alternative view—that the epistles precede the Gospel—is advanced by Talbert, *Reading John: A Literary and Theological Commentary;* and Kenneth Grayston, *The Johannine Epistles: based on the Revised Standard Version,* New Century Bible Commentary (Grand Rapids: Wm. B. Eerdmans Publishing Co., 1984).

45. See Lieu, *The Theology of the Johannine Epistles* (Cambridge: Cambridge University Press, 1991).

Chapter 7

The Life and
Writings of Paul

Marion L. Soards

Paul was a first-century non-Palestinian Pharisaic Jew who changed from a persecutor of the earliest Christian church to one of the most effective and influential missionaries in all of Christian history. He called himself an "apostle of Jesus Christ" to "the Gentiles," and while it was primarily to non-Jews that he preached, his message had a significant impact even on the originally Jewish portion of early Christianity. The concrete residue of Paul's life and work is his letters to a variety of early Christian congregations around the Mediterranean either that he founded or with which he worked. These letters have exercised a profound influence on subsequent Christian thought and life in nearly every period of church history.

PAUL'S LETTERS

Since the epistles are what remain directly from Paul's efforts as an apostle, one should examine them in terms of their organization and style to see if they offer further insight into the character of their author. To perceive the genius of Paul's letters it is helpful to know something about letters and letter writing in antiquity.

Education, commerce, and travel in the Hellenistic era created a context for letter writing. There was even a semiprofessional class of letter writers called scribes or amanuenses. Letters moved surprising distances in Paul's day. The first letters in antiquity were official communications regarding governmental and military matters, but with improved conditions all sorts of letters were produced and sent to persons in distant locations. These included public decrees by rulers, official letters between authorities, business letters, friendly communications, and brief notes of all sorts. (One may consult the ancient letters in C. K. Barrett's *The New Testament Background: Selected Documents* in order to see examples of typical letters of Paul's age.) Careful study of the preserved written materials of antiquity demonstrates that in Paul's day, as in later periods of civilization, letters were written in standard forms. Normally, there were five sections to the letter: a *salutation* in three parts, naming the sender, identifying the addressee, and offering a greeting; a *thanksgiving;* the *body* of the letter; *final instructions* (*parenesis*); and the *closing* in two parts, which offer final greetings and the parting word. The letters are frequently dated and addressed at the very end of the correspondence.

Paul knew and used this format for composing his letters to congregations. Nevertheless, he clearly made modifications to the standard letter form. Thus, as an example of Paul's letter writing style, it is helpful to compare his briefest letter, Philemon, with the standard form of the Hellenistic letter. This comparison demonstrates how Paul's letter are similar to other letters of his day.

Salutation

Sender(s):	"Paul, a prisoner for Christ Jesus and Timothy our brother"
Recipient(s):	"to Philemon our beloved fellow worker and Apphia our sister and Archippus our fellow soldier and the church in your house"
Greeting:	"Grace to you and peace from God our Father and the Lord Jesus Christ"

Thanksgiving

"I thank my God always when I remember you (singular, indicating Philemon) in my prayers"

Body of the Letter

Paul discusses the return of Onesimus, a runaway slave.

Final Instructions (Parenesis)

Throughout the letter Paul has exhorted Philemon:
"receive him" (v. 17)
"charge that to my account" (v. 18)
"refresh my heart in Christ" (v. 20)

His final instructions are in v. 22,
"prepare a guest room for me."

Closing

Greetings:	"Epaphras, my fellow prisoner in Christ Jesus, greets you (singular) [and] Mark, Aristarchus, Demas, and Luke, my fellow workers"
Parting word:	"The grace of the Lord Jesus Christ be with your spirit."

Yet, as similar as the letters of Paul are to other Hellenistic letters, one should notice how Paul subtly altered the style of the standard letter for his own purposes.

These alterations reflect the peculiarly Christian character of Paul's letters and re-veal how thoroughly his relationship with Jesus Christ affected him. Indeed, God's revelation of the risen Christ gave Paul a new emphasis and left its stamp on every-thing he did, even the writing of letters. It is instructive to view the anatomy of some of Paul's changes of the form of a standard letter. For example, in the opening of his letters Paul identifies himself in relation to God and Christ. Moreover, he iden-tifies those to whom he writes in terms of their own roles as Christians. Further-more, he alters the language of the normal greeting and expands it into a lofty but practical wish for the recipients. The usual salutation in Hellenistic letters is the word "Greetings." But Paul does not send his readers "greetings"; he salutes them by saying, "grace and peace." The words *greetings* and *grace* resemble each other in Greek: "greetings" = *chairein* and "grace" = *charis*. Thus, Paul's salutation be-gins with a wordplay that reveals the effects of God's activity, and he develops his altered greeting by coupling a common Jewish greeting, "peace," with "grace."

Above all, one should recognize that Paul did not write letters casually. His epistles are often warm, passionate, and personal, but they are not just friendly communications. Paul wrote to address specific, problematic situations that ex-isted in particular churches. He sought through letters to extend his influence (of-ten in a deliberately authoritative fashion) in order to assure desired results, so that in every communication Paul always strives to build up the congregation ad-dressed. Thus, for Paul the letter was an instrument of work as an apostle. The ex-istence of the letters leads naturally to a consideration of the total practice of ministry of which the letters formed an important part.

PAUL'S MANNER OF MINISTRY

Toward the end of his ministry Paul wrote, "I have been able to bring to comple-tion the preaching of the gospel of Christ from Jerusalem around as far as Il-lyricum" (Rom. 15:19). In contemporary geographical terms he claims to have preached the "good news" from Israel through Asia Minor as far as portions of eastern Europe adjacent to the Adriatic. One wonders how Paul could have done this in twenty to twenty-five years of ministry. Thus, the usual image of Paul is of an impassioned preacher, but one should recognize that in fact Paul's missionary activity was teamwork. His letters reveal that he coordinated the activity of a sys-tematically organized band of missionaries and that his method was fairly consis-tent. Paul would move with a group of seasoned missionary colleagues to the capital city of a Roman province. Upon arrival he and his associates would ap-proach the local synagogue, and if possible set up a base for the proclamation of the gospel. If no synagogue existed, the team would seek out the "God-fearers," that is, Gentiles who were attracted to the theology and morality of Judaism but who had not become full converts. If there were no God-fearers, Paul and his com-panions would take the message to the local marketplace. In the process of mov-ing into a city, Paul would gather any Christians who already lived there and incorporate them into the missionary enterprise, thereby expanding his work. While Paul remained in the capital city and its immediate area, his fellow workers dispersed themselves throughout the other cities, towns, and villages of the region in order to establish satellite congregations. Paul would remain in one location until the job he set out to do was done (he was in Corinth a year and one-half and in Ephesus two years and three months) or, more often, until he became embroiled in a controversy that forced him to leave the region. Paul would then move on to repeat this process in a new location. Yet, he would not lose contact with the churches he founded; rather, he revisited the congregations when he deemed it necessary, and he used the writing of letters as a part of his missionary strategy, employing the written communication to influence and build up the congregations he addressed.

Some scholars attribute this method of organizing missionary work to the church at Antioch of which Paul was a representative, and which itself was extremely active in early Christian missionary work. This may be the case; or, if Paul was a Jewish missionary before he was a Christian, perhaps he adapted the technique from Jewish missionary activity. It may even be that Paul devised the strategy himself. Knowing the source of Paul's missionary style would be enlightening, but not knowing its origin does not detract from understanding Paul's work and appreciating its effectiveness. Discerning the particular features of Paul's life and work, however, is a major task of present and future New Testament scholarship.

RECONSTRUCTING PAUL'S LIFE

The New Testament and other early Christian literature seem to provide a wealth of sources for reconstructing the life of Paul. Over one-half of the book of Acts is an account of Paul's career from the time he was a persecutor of the church through his imprisonment in Rome toward the end of his life. Thirteen letters in the New Testament bear Paul's name as their author. Outside the canon of the New Testament, many volumes of early Christian literature present themselves as other "letters" by Paul or offer further accounts of his "acts."

Problems. When one turns to the early Christian literature to ascertain the life of Paul, one immediately encounters three serious problems.

First, extensive as the sources are, they provide *insufficient* data for writing a "life" of Paul. Little, if anything, is known about Paul's birth, childhood, and early manhood; indeed, we do not even know with absolute certainty when, where, and how Paul died. Much remains shrouded in mystery, for the sources for producing a Pauline biography are simply inadequate.

Second, one must establish the *authenticity* of the sources. For example, no contemporary scholar judges that Paul wrote any of the number of extrabiblical letters that are attributed to him, correspondences like "the Epistles of Paul and Seneca," "Paul's Letter to the Laodiceans," and "3 Corinthians." Clearly these were produced by others in the name of Paul. Moreover, because of matters of history, vocabulary, style, and theology, many scholars (frequently the majority) judge that as many as six of the thirteen letters in the New Testament attributed to Paul were written by his colleagues and students, not the apostle himself. The misattributed letters are 2 Thessalonians, Ephesians, Colossians, 1 Timothy, 2 Timothy, and Titus.

Only seven letters are judged without dispute to be authentic. Thus, many scholars conclude that all of the New Testament letters attributed to Paul are not of equal value for reconstructing the life of the apostle.

Third, it is sometimes impossible through harmonization to reconcile statements made in even the most reliable sources. For example, Acts 9 recounts that when Paul was struck down on the road to Damascus, he was "immediately" active there (in Damascus) preaching in the synagogues that Jesus was the Son of God. After "many days," Acts says, he went to Jerusalem in an effort to join the disciples; but they were afraid of him, because they doubted his sincerity, and so they avoided him. Then, one learns from Acts that Barnabas took Paul to the apostles, who accepted him. The result was that Paul preached, going in and out among the Jerusalem Christians and even down to Caesarea, so that "the church throughout Judea, Galilee, and Samaria had peace and was built up" (Acts 9:31). In contrast, Galatians 1:11–24 (especially verses 15–24) presents Paul declaring his independence as an apostle. He avers here that the gospel he preached did not come from any human; instead it came through a revelation by God of the risen Jesus Christ. Paul claims he was ordained by God, that he did not confer with "flesh and blood," that is, any human agent. He insists that when he was called by God he did not go up to Jerusalem to the apostles for their approval but went to Arabia and later returned to Damascus. He says that after three years he visited Cephas (Simon Peter) in Jerusalem for fifteen days; but he declares that he saw "none of the other apostles except James the Lord's brother" (Gal. 1:19). Indeed, Paul claims that he departed after this visit "still unknown by sight to the churches of Judea" (Gal. 1:22).

Frequently, accounts of early Christianity provide a harmonization of these passages. But such method is questionable. In historical work one cannot simply use a secondary source (here, Acts) to devise a framework into which a primary source (here, Galatians) is made to fit. The result of such harmonization is abusive of primary material and produces a distorted picture of early Christianity.

Methods. One can work through the difficulties in reconstructing Paul's life, but in order to do so, one must be guided by judicious reasoning. Briefly stated, the critical method that guides most contemporary Pauline studies is as follows:

First, the primary sources always have priority. Moreover, the soundest basis for understanding Paul is laid by using the seven undisputed letters of Paul: Romans, 1 Corinthians, 2 Corinthians, Galatians, Philippians, 1 Thessalonians, and Philemon. The other letters may be consulted in an ancillary capacity—though they add little if anything to one's knowledge of Paul's life.

Second, the secondary source, Acts, may be used cautiously as a supplement to the primary materials when it is not in conflict with the letters. Indeed, agreement of the primary and secondary materials gives one certainty, for the author of Acts shows no knowledge of Paul's letters or even that Paul wrote letters.

Third, other early Christian documents are almost useless for the purpose of reconstructing Paul's life. These works are highly legendary in character, but they do illustrate matters that are best regarded as debatable or unknown. For example, extrabiblical early Christian literature offers competing stories about Paul's death.

This diversity probably indicates that the exact manner of Paul's death was not widely known among subsequent Christians and that, because of their curiosity, these later Christians formulated a variety of accounts, using pious imagination to interpret freely the evidence that was available to them.

By taking the autobiographical material in Paul's letters, comparing that information with Acts, and then considering the extrabiblical sources, one distinguishes two kinds of material. On the one hand, some reliable information allows the composition of a brief narrative account of Paul's life and work. This account is nothing like a biography, since the sources do not provide extensive information. Nevertheless, one forms an impression of the man and develops a picture of his career as an apostle. In concise form, the story takes the following lines:

Paul, as a non-Palestinian Jew, also had an explicitly Jewish name, Saul, as was common for non-Palestinian Jews in the first century; still, he refers to himself in his letters by the Greek name, Paul. He was almost certainly born in Tarsus, a city in southeastern Asia Minor. He was from a family of Pharisees of the tribe of Benjamin and was named for the tribe's most illustrious member, King Saul. His letters show familiarity both with Jewish methods for interpretation of scripture and with popular Hellenistic philosophy, to a degree that makes it likely he had formal education in both areas. As an adult, Paul was most likely a resident of Damascus in Syria. He was an active persecutor of the early Christian movement—probably because he perceived it to be a threat to Torah obedience, and perhaps because the Christian mission made early inroads among the godfearing Gentiles who were associated with synagogue communities.

Paul became a Christian, an apostle, through a dramatic *revelation* of Jesus Christ. His first years as a Christian, spent in Arabia, are a mystery. Three years after his call, Paul went to Jerusalem to visit; he saw Peter and James. Later (after fourteen years), he returned to Jerusalem for a meeting often referred to as "the Jerusalem Conference" or "the Apostolic Council." Paul was a vigorous evangelist, traveling and preaching in Achaia, Arabia, Asia, Cilicia, Galatia, Judea, Illyricum, Macedonia, and Syria, and making plans for Italy and Spain. On the mission field he worked with a group of trusted colleagues (Aquila, Barnabas, Prisca, Silvanus, Sosthenes, Timothy, Titus, and others); he supported himself by practicing a trade, tent-making, which was a form of leather craftwork; he and his colleagues were often in danger and abused; and Paul himself suffered from a "thorn in the flesh." Along with evangelization, Paul worked among his non-Palestinian congregations on a major project, a collection for the poor Christians in Jerusalem that he hoped would reconcile the non-law-observant Christian givers and the law-observant Christian recipients. While actively engaged in evangelization of a region, Paul wrote to churches he had founded earlier in other areas to address problems experienced by those congregations. Paul's clear self-perception was that he was an "apostle of Jesus Christ to the Gentiles," that is, one sent to proclaim the good news of Jesus Christ among non-Jews.

The primary sources probably do not contain any information about Paul after he is imprisoned in Caesarea. Nevertheless, we may conclude almost certainly that while in prison (under the Roman officials Felix and, then, Festus), Paul somehow appealed to be tried before Caesar (Nero) and was sent to Rome for a hearing. Subsequently, he died there as a martyr.

Even in this material there is some uncertainty. For example, because of the am-
biguity of his statements, when Paul says "then after three years" (Gal. 1:18) and
"then after fourteen years" (Gal. 2:1), one cannot be sure exactly what he means.
He could be indicating two points in time, both dated from his call—to paraphrase,
"then three years after my call" and "then fourteen years after my call." But, he
could mean "then three years after my call" and "then fourteen years later"—in
other words, seventeen years.

This analysis and reconstruction (based on primary sources) omits information in
the secondary sources about which prudent interpreters of Paul must express reser-
vations. For example, Acts 22:3 informs the reader that Paul was brought up in
Jerusalem at the feet of Gamaliel—in other words, that Paul was a student in
Jerusalem of one of the most famous rabbis in Jewish history. But Paul himself never
mentions these credentials. This silence is striking, for there are places in his letters
where he lists his "Jewish" credentials at length. The mention of Gamaliel in these
listings would have amplified Paul's point concerning his former zeal for and status
in Judaism, but he does not mention the connection. It is possible that Paul studied
with Gamaliel in Jerusalem, but since he does not mention this himself, it is safest
to omit this item when reconstructing his life. Moreover, from Paul's own letters one
would not gather that he was a resident of Jerusalem. Paul himself says he did "go
up to Jerusalem to visit" and that he "returned to Damascus" (Gal. 1:18, 17). From
this manner of reference, serious students of Paul's life and work understand that he
was, as an adult, a resident of Damascus, not Jerusalem. Even more problematic is
the claim in Acts that Paul received an endorsement from the apostles in Jerusalem.
Not only does Paul not say this, he flatly denies it in Galatians.

In conclusion, by delineating and practicing a standard historical method for
the use of sources in the reconstruction of Paul's life, one achieves valuable results. On the one hand, one exposes information that allows a more sophisticated
reading of the New Testament documents in relation to one another. On the other,
one develops a picture of the life of Paul. This image may, through the conser-
vatism of the method, be a minimal one; but it is reliable, admitting no debatable
material. For more precise understanding of Paul's life and writings it is necessary
to consider evidence and elements of the sources that are related to the concrete
chronology of Paul's work.

CHRONOLOGY

Only a paucity of data exists to facilitate the attempt to map a Pauline chronology—that is, to locate times and places in the life of Paul. Moreover, there are
some uncertainties with regard to what is available. For example, how long was
Paul in Arabia (Gal. 1:17)? Or, where was he imprisoned when he wrote Philippians and Philemon?

Because of the lack of specific information and in light of the difficulties associated with using the materials that are available, many scholars argue that no more
than a relative dating of Paul's letters is possible. Even here there are problems,
for the preserved copies of Paul's letters are not dated. Moreover, the claims of
some scholars to recognize developments in Paul's thinking from one letter to an-

other are not persuasive, since they are based on the presuppositions that Paul's thought evolved and that he could not change his mind.

From these cautionary remarks one might gather that the prospect of working out a Pauline chronology is bleak. But these warnings should not completely deter an attempt at correlating dates and places for Paul's career. Indeed, one firm date for Paul's activity is ascertainable (though recent works by Jewett, Lüdemann, and Murphy-O'Connor draw conclusions that differ from the majority view). From Acts 18:12–18, one learns that Paul was in Corinth when Gallio was proconsul. An inscription found at Delphi (an ancient Greek town) permits dating of Gallio's term as proconsul from May of 51 C.E. to May of 52 C.E. By correlating Acts and the Delphic inscription, one learns when Paul could possibly have appeared before Gallio. At the earliest it was the summer of 51 and at the latest the spring of 52. Scholars mount arguments for both extremities. Since nothing in Acts 18:12 indicates that Gallio had taken office only recently, we will, for convenience, make use of the later date—recognizing that we could adjust the ensuing reconstruction by moving dates back almost one year.

The information concerning Paul's imprisonment in Caesarea under Felix and then Festus is another "definite" moment in Paul's life. Some scholars try to correlate the information in Acts 24–26 with other material from Roman history concerning the family of Felix, but this is quite complicated and fraught with difficulties. Thus, it is best to use the information in Paul's letters and Acts to work forward and backward from the dating of Gallio's term in office. Also to be considered are the conditions for travel in the ancient Greek world. For example, those who traveled on foot, as Paul no doubt did, could cover about twenty miles per day; few sea voyages took place during March, April, May, September, and October, and from November through February the Mediterranean was effectively closed for travel. When these factors are taken into consideration, one arrives at the following timetable:

35	Paul was called by God's revelation of Jesus Christ (or 32 C.E., depending on how one understands Paul's mentions of "three" and "fourteen" years)
35–38	Missionary activity in Arabia (Gal. 1:17) and Damascus (2 Cor. 11:32)
38	Paul visits with Peter (and James) in Jerusalem (Gal. 1: 18)
38–48	Missionary activity in Cilicia and Syria (Gal. 1:21)
48	"Apostolic Council" in Jerusalem (Gal. 2:1–10; Acts 15)
48 or 49	Incident with Peter and others in Antioch (Gal. 2:11–14)
49	Missionary activity in Galatia (Acts 16:6)
50	Missionary activity in Philippi, Thessalonica, and Beroea (Acts 16:11–17:14); travel to Corinth via Athens (Acts 17:15; 18:1); wrote 1 Thessalonians

Late 50 to May 52	Missionary activity in Corinth (Acts 18:11)
Summer 52	Travel to Caesarea; then Antioch; then passing through Asia Minor he paid a second visit to Galatia on the way to Ephesus (Gal. 4:13; Acts 18:18–23)
Late 52 to spring 55	Missionary activity in Ephesus (Acts 19:1, 8–10, 22); wrote Galatians; 1 Corinthians; perhaps portions of 2 Corinthians (possibly Philippians and Philemon)
54	Visit to Corinth (presupposed in 2 Cor. 13:1)
Late 54–55	Probably wrote portions of 2 Corinthians (10—13)
Summer 55	Travel through Macedonia to Corinth; wrote at least 2 Cor. 1:1–2:13; 7:5–16, perhaps 2 Corinthians 1—9
Late 55–early 56	Final stay in Corinth; wrote Romans
56	Travel to Jerusalem with the collection; arrest and imprisonment
56–58	Imprisonment in Caesarea; probably wrote Philippians and Philemon
58	Felix replaced by Festus; Paul appeals to Caesar and is sent to Rome
58–60	Imprisonment in Rome (Acts 28:30)
60+	Martyrdom

Obviously, the conclusion that Paul did not write the six disputed letters lies behind this particular reconstruction. The decisions concerning the authorship of these letters are not, however, related to chronology; as a result, persons who think that Paul did write the disputed letters can easily factor these letters into this account of Paul's life. 2 Thessalonians is located shortly after 1 Thessalonians, late in 50 or early in 51 from Corinth; Colossians, Ephesians, and the Pastoral Epistles are placed during the time of Paul's Roman imprisonment, in the period 58–60+.

PAUL'S RELIGIOUS BACKGROUND AND THOUGHT

Three related areas of ancient thought and life command attention for comprehending Paul's life and writings.

Judaism. Paul the Christian had once been Paul the Jew. It is clear from both his own letters and the story of his ministry in Acts that Paul was not merely a Jew but a Pharisee. He boasts from time to time in his letters of his Jewish past in rebuttal to other missionaries who caused problems in the churches that he had founded (see Phil. 3 and 2 Cor. 11). Thus, Paul shows that prior to being a Christian he was a zealous Pharisee. As noted above, Acts 22:3 preserves a tradition that associates Paul with Gamaliel I of Jerusalem, one of the most influential figures in first-century Judaism. While Paul does not mention this striking association when relating his Jewish credentials, independent from this memory the association of Paul with formal "rabbinic-style" education seems likely, for in his writings Paul manifests signs of what came to be called "rabbinic" style and logic (the designation "rabbinic" is actually anachronistic for Paul's time). Paul does midrashic exegesis of the Jewish scriptures; he demonstrates a clear perception of law observance as the heart of Judaism; and the contrast he draws between Christ and the law shows his disavowal of practicing the law's systemic righteousness, which he had once observed with confidence and contentment. These features of Paul's writings locate him within the stream of first-century Pharisaic Judaism; they do not, however, amount to evidence for the assertion that Paul was a rabbi—in fact, that office and title belong to a later period in Judaism. Yet, the scholarly discussion of Paul's writings during the past quarter century has focused in a particularly vigorous fashion on Paul's understanding and teaching concerning the law and its pertinence (or lack thereof) for Christianity.

Hellenism. As it is clear that Paul's past was in Pharisaic Judaism, it is also certain that Paul was a Hellenized Jew. According to Acts he was born outside Palestine in the Greco-Roman trade city of Tarsus. Indeed, Paul's own writings show signs of Hellenistic education. The basic mastery of the skills of reading, thinking, argumentation, and expression in writing are the hallmarks of Hellenistic education. Moreover, the letters are filled with telltale signs of Paul's Hellenistic heritage: From his quotation of Jewish scriptures one sees that Paul read the Bible in its Greek version, the Septuagint. Paul is thoroughly familiar with the conventions of popular Hellenistic philosophy and methods of literary interpretation. Moreover, he refers to himself with the Greek name, Paul, not the Jewish name, Saul; and the majority of his metaphors are drawn from the Greco-Roman world: households, sports, street life, and the military. Thus, during the past two decades, scholars have focused with steadily increasing energy on the relationship of Paul's letters to the style and devices of Greco-Roman rhetoric.

Apocalyptic. A third approach to Paul has designated apocalyptic Judaism as the determinative background for understanding his writings. Paul's language bespeaks an apocalyptic perspective in focusing on wrath, judgment, and the day of the Lord. He displays a yearning for the messianic age that characterized all apocalyptic writing. He shows an awareness of living on the boundary of two worlds, one dying and one being born. Further he has a sense of special urgency derived from the apocalyptic conviction that his generation is the last. The clearest sign of Paul's thoroughly apocalyptic perspective is the presence in his writings of the dualistic doctrine of Two Ages. This doctrine maintains that the age to come breaks into the current age through God's intervention and without human agency.

Twentieth-century Pauline scholarship has witnessed an ongoing debate as to which of these backgrounds best accounts for Paul's own understanding of what he did and said. Prior to the last two or three decades of study, scholars drew hard lines between the areas that were commonly accepted as having influenced Paul. For most, since Paul was certainly a Pharisee, "rabbinic" or, better, Palestinian Judaism was thought to provide the key to interpretation. Paul's use of apparently technical language in reference to tradition he had received and delivered (1 Cor. 15:3) to the churches he founded was taken to indicate his self-understanding and his attitude toward the tradition itself. Moreover, Paul's practice of midrashic exegesis (see Paul on Exodus in 1 Cor. 10 or on Abraham in Gal. 3) was thought to reveal his approach to the Old Testament, while his concern with the contrast between Christ and the law was determined by his past participation in Pharisaism.

Yet, other scholars argued that Hellenism was the most appropriate background for viewing and interpreting Paul. That Paul did allegorical exegesis was said to show still another attitude and approach toward the Jewish scriptures (see Paul on Sarah and Hagar in Gal. 4). Furthermore, the context of Hellenism was held to disclose the prerequisite clues for understanding such basic Pauline notions as the sacraments and christology. Since Paul was thoroughly Hellenistic in heritage, he would interpret baptism and the Lord's Supper in relation to the practices of Hellenistic mystery religions, and he would have understood Christ in terms of a general Hellenistic myth of a descending and ascending redeemer figure.

Scholars now recognize that the three backgrounds described above are not exclusive of one another and that each makes a contribution to a balanced reading of Paul, for Paul was influenced by and drew upon all of them. Nevertheless, it has become increasingly clear through the work of several contemporary scholars (Beker, Käsemann, and Martyn) that the apocalyptic element provided Paul with the basic framework of his thought and determined his comprehension of the world around him.

What is this apocalyptic perspective? When scholars are called upon for clarification, remarkably different understandings of "apocalyptic" come to the fore. *Apokalypsis* in Greek means "revelation." Paul uses this word to refer to his original encounter with the risen Jesus Christ (Gal. 1:13). That dramatic revelation was the occasion of Paul's call. Moreover, it was the time and means of Paul's being taught or given the basis of the gospel that he preached (Gal. 1:11–17). This disruptive intervention of God into Paul's life bespeaks the pattern of thought typical of first-century apocalyptic Judaism.

Apocalyptic is a special expression of Jewish eschatology that is characterized, as noted, by the dualistic doctrine of Two Ages. On the one hand there is "the present evil age," and on the other there is "the age to come." The "present evil age" is the world of mundane realities in which human beings live; the "age to come" is the supernatural realm of the power of God. There is no continuity between these ages. Indeed, apocalyptic Jewish thought held that at some future moment "the age to come" would break into the human realm by an act of God. In this moment of God's intervention the "present evil age" would pass away and "the age to come" would be established as a new reality, ordained and directed by God. Apocalyptic Judaism held that by this act of God, evil would be annihilated and those who were righteous would be redeemed. Thus "the age to come" was the hope of those who believed in God but found themselves oppressed by the forces of evil in the present world. In Jewish apocalyptic literature the authors usually claim to live in the last days of "the present evil age." Their message to readers is the joint promise and warning that the intervention of God is about to take place.

Throughout his letters Paul's language and patterns of thought reveal elements of this apocalyptic eschatology. For example, Paul frequently uses apocalyptic language: "destined . . . for wrath," "the wrath to come," "the wrath of God," "the day of wrath," "the day of the Lord Jesus Christ," "the day of salvation," "redeemed," "redemption," "this age," "the rulers of this age," "the present evil age," and "the ends of the ages." Moreover, Paul reveals in his letters the conviction that he and his readers are part of the last generation of humanity (1 Thes. 4:13–18, esp. v. 17; 1 Cor. 7:31; 15:51–57).

Paul does not use the phrase "the age to come," so some scholars deny the thoroughgoing apocalyptic character of his thought. Yet, he speaks in distinctively Christian phrases of the same idea when he speaks of "a new creation" and "the Kingdom of God." This difference in phrases indicates a slight, but fundamental, alteration on the part of Paul. He transforms the pattern of Jewish apocalyptic thought described above into a particularly Christian pattern of apocalyptic thinking that permeates all of his writings. In other words, *Paul articulates an apocalyptic perspective that has been modified in light of the Christ event.*

While Jewish apocalyptic eschatology thought in terms of two ages, the present (evil) age and the age to come, these periods were completely distinct; one age ended as the other began. Thus, reality was understood in terms of an absolute temporal (not metaphysical) dualism. As a Christian thinker, Paul has a similar, but remarkably distinct, view of time that stamps his entire thought process. He maintains the temporal dualism characteristic of Jewish apocalyptic, but he modifies the scheme in light of the Christ event so that *there are two distinct ages that are separated and joined by an interim period of time.*

For Paul the first temporal epoch is "the present evil age" (Gal. 1:4; 1 Cor. 2:6–8). This age is ruled by the god of this world (2 Cor. 4:4), namely Satan, and by the elemental spirits of the universe (Gal. 4:3; 1 Cor. 2:8). Under the influence of its rulers, this age is at odds with God (1 Cor. 15:24–28; Rom. 8:37–39). Nevertheless, this age is passing away (1 Cor. 7:31). The second epoch is the "new creation" (Gal. 6:14; 2 Cor. 5:17). This new age comes as God in Christ defeats the forces in opposition to him (Gal. 6:14; 1 Cor. 7:31; Rom. 5:21), and it is established as the reign of God, apparently an age of glory (1 Thes. 2:10–12; 1 Cor. 15:20–28; 2 Cor. 4:17; Rom. 5:2, 21).

According to Paul, the present exists as the juncture of the ages or as a mingling of the ages (1 Cor. 10:11; 2 Cor. 5:16). Here, 1 Cor. 10:11 is important. In this verse Paul describes himself and other humans in very striking terms that modern translations often obscure. For example, Paul's words as they were rendered in the Revised Standard Version read, "upon whom the end of the ages has come." This translation implies that Paul stands at the end of time and looks back at the ages (something like dispensations?) that have gone before—but, in fact, he does not. Paul's actual phrase literally says, "upon whom the ends of the ages have met," as the New Revised Standard Version now translates the words. Paul perceives that he and other humans live at the juncture of the ages. This juncture came about as a result of the cross of Christ (1 Cor. 1:17–18) and it will conclude, marking the absolute end of the present evil age, at the coming of Christ from heaven (1 Thes. 2:19; 3:13; 4:13–18; 1 Cor. 15:23–28). Thus, one sees that Paul was called and he thought, worked, and preached in this interim period. Much of Paul's message derives from his understanding of this juncture, for, as noted, it came about as a result of the cross of Christ (1 Cor. 1:17–18). In essence Paul thought and taught that sin has been defeated (Gal. 1:4; 1 Cor. 15:3; Rom. 4:25); that death has been condemned (1 Cor. 15:54–57; Rom. 8:31–39); that the Law has been exposed for what it is—powerless (Gal. 2:21; 3:24–25; Rom. 7:7–12); that Christ has discharged humanity from the curse of the Law (Gal. 3:13–14; Rom. 7:4–6); that although the battle goes on toward God's final victory, creation has been reclaimed by God (1 Cor. 15:20–28; Rom. 8:18–25); that God's sovereignty has been established (Rom. 8:31–39); that all creation presently awaits the grand assize (1 Thes. 5:2–11; 1 Cor. 6:2–3; 15:20–28; 16:21; Rom. 8:18–25); and while the Kingdom of God has not yet been fully established in glory, for Christians the present is effectively already the Messianic age in which, for now, everything is to be viewed from the vantage point of the cross (2 Cor. 5:16).

BIBLIOGRAPHY

Barrett, C. K. *The New Testament Background: Selected Documents*. London: SPCK, 1956.

Becker, J. *Paul: Apostle to the Gentiles*. Louisville, Ky.: Westminster/John Knox Press, 1993.

Beker, J. C. *Paul the Apostle: The Triumph of God in Life and Thought*. Philadelphia: Fortress Press, 1980.

Bornkamm, G. *Paul*. New York: Harper & Row, 1971.

Bousset, W. *Kyrios Christos*. Nashville: Abingdon Press, 1970; 2nd German ed., 1921.

Bruce, F. F. *Paul: Apostle of the Heart Set Free*. Grand Rapids: Wm. B. Eerdmans Publishing Co., 1977.

Bultmann, R. *Theology of the New Testament*. New York: Charles Scribner's Sons, 1951.

Davies, W. D. *Paul and Rabbinic Judaism,* 4th ed. Philadelphia: Fortress Press, 1980.

Doty, W. G. *Letters in Primitive Christianity*. Philadelphia: Fortress Press, 1973.

Dunn, J. D. G. *Jesus, Paul and the Law: Studies in Mark and Galatians*. Louisville, Ky.: Westminster/John Knox Press, 1990.

Ellis, E. E. *Paul and His Recent Interpreters*. Grand Rapids: Wm. B. Eerdmans Publishing Co., 1961.

Fitzmyer, J. A. *Paul and His Theology: A Brief Sketch,* 2nd ed., Englewood Cliffs, N.J.: Prentice Hall, 1989.

Hengel, M. and A. M. Schwemer. *Paul Between Damascus and Antioch: The Unknown Years*. Louisville, Ky.: Westminster John Knox Press, 1997.

Jewett, R. A. *Chronology of Paul's Life*. Philadelphia: Fortress Press, 1979.

Käsemann, E. *Perspective on Paul*. Philadelphia: Fortress Press, 1971.

Keck, L. E. *Paul and His Letters,* 2nd ed, Philadelphia: Fortress Press, 1988.

Knox, J. *Chapters in a Life of Paul.*, rev. ed. Macon, Ga.: Mercer University Press, 1987.

Lüdemann, G. *Paul, Apostle to the Gentiles: Studies in Chronology*. Philadelphia: Fortress Press, 1984.

Martyn, J. L. "Epistemology at the Turn of the Ages: 2 Corinthians 5:16," in *Christian History and Interpretation: Studies Presented to John Knox.*, pp. 269–87, ed. W. R. Farmer et al. Cambridge: Cambridge University Press, 1967.

Meeks, W. A. *The First Urban Christians: The Social Word of the Apostle Paul*. New Haven, Conn.: Yale University Press, 1983.

Meeks, W. A., ed. *The Writings of St. Paul*. New York: W. W. Norton, 1972.

Murphy-O'Connor, J. "On the Road and on the Sea with St. Paul," *Bible Review* 1 (Summer, 1985): 38–47.

Murphy-O'Connor, J. *Paul: A Critical Life*. Oxford: Clarendon Press, 1996.

Räisänen, H. *Paul and the Law*. Philadelphia: Fortress Press, 1986.

Sanders, E. P. *Paul and Palestinian Judaism: A Comparison of Patterns of Religion*. Philadelphia: Fortress Press, 1977.

———. *Paul, the Law, and the Jewish People*. Philadelphia: Fortress Press, 1983.

Schweitzer, A. *Paul and His Interpreters*. London: A. & C. Black, 1912.

Soards, M. L. *The Apostle Paul: An Introduction to His Writings and Teaching*. Mahwah, N.J.: Paulist Press, 1987.

Vielhauer, P. and G. Strecker. "Apocalypses and Related Subjects," in *New Testament Apocrypha: Writings Related to the Apostles; Apocalypses and Related Subjects,* ed. E. Hennecke and W. Schneemelcher, trans. R. McL. Wilson., 2 vols., 2.542–602. Louisville, Ky.: Westminster/John Knox Press, 1992.

Westerholm, S. *Israel's Law and the Church's Faith: Paul and His Recent Interpreters*. Grand Rapids: Wm. B. Eerdmans Publishing Co., 1988.

Chapter 8

Pauline Theology

James D. G. Dunn

Paul is the first and greatest Christian theologian. He is the only one who with his own voice clearly speaks to us from the first generation of Christianity. He is the first Christian we know of who wrestled at length and to good effect with a variety of theological and ethical issues. His letters quickly came to be recognized as of continuing authority for subsequent generations of churches; as part of the New Testament canon, they have served to define Christian theology as has no other set of documents. This last point remains true, even when later writers and confessions seemed more determinative, since they themselves acknowledged the prior authority of Paul. And even when Paul's theology has been subjected to severe critique, it has always been in the consciousness that he cannot be ignored and that alternative theological schemes must be justified by reference to Paul.

THE THEOLOGY OF PAUL
IN HISTORICAL RETROSPECT

The modern study of Pauline theology as a subdiscipline within biblical or New Testament theology dates from the work of F. C. Baur (1792–1860). It was Baur who first clearly exposed the dynamic of Paul's theologizing, that is, the theological process whereby a Palestinian Jewish sect became a universal Christian religion. It was precisely Paul's lot to shape that process and to determine the theological character of the emergent Christian church. And though biblical theology was initially conceived as a descriptive exercise, the power of Paul's theological reflections and teaching have been such that even the description of Pauline theology has been enough to generate contemporary theological controversy.

For Baur the process was marked by a lengthy confrontation between the Gentile Christianity of Paul and the Jewish Christianity of Peter, a confrontation that Paul initiated, paradigmatically, in the Antioch incident of Gal. 2.11–16, and which was reflected also in the tensions between the Cephas and Paul parties in Corinth (1 Cor. 1:12). In Baur's view, that confrontation lasted only for a century or so, before the triumph of the old Catholic church over surviving Jewish-Christian sects, yet it was Paul's stand against Peter that in effect justified the subsequent stand of Luther against the medieval Catholic church. In that sense Paul's theology of justification by faith, as originally expressed in opposition to the Jewish requirement of circumcision and the law, became the critically distinctive feature of Protestant theology.

After Baur, the focus shifted from the context from which Paul's theology emerged to investigation of the influences that shaped Paul's theology as it emerged into the wider Hellenistic world. This period of research (overlapping the end of the nineteenth and the beginning of the twentieth centuries) was typified by the concerns of what was called the History of Religions School. The goal was to understand Paul and his theology within the context of the other religions of the time. Initially, the primary issue was the extent to which Paul's teaching on baptism and the Lord's Supper (distinctive within the New Testament) had been determined by the equivalent rites of contemporary mystery cults. Influential also was the view of Wilhelm Bousset that Paul's christology had been decisively determined by the cultic veneration of Jesus as Lord. Most influential of all was the hypothesis of Rudolf Bultmann (1894–1976) that Paul's christology had been largely shaped by early gnosticism, in particular, by a pre-Christian gnostic Redeemer myth that Bultmann thought could be discerned within and behind Paul's christology. This Redeemer myth was the main focus of Pauline research throughout the middle decades of the twentieth century, with the gnostic documents from Nag Hammadi helping to sustain some of the earlier interest in the search for traces of this myth. But for an increasing majority the gnostic Redeemer myth has become a will o' the wisp. Underlying this activity, the common assumption was that the Hellenized theology of Paul was distant from the still Jewish teaching of Jesus.

For the most part, however, Pauline theology had become predictable and dully repetitive in this period. Catholic theology was only beginning to become liberated by the impact of the Second Vatican Council, and the Reformation paradigm for the most part reigned supreme and unchallenged in Protestant treatments of Paul's theology.

Two issues did excite some interest. One was the question of whether Paul's theology *developed* over the period of Paul's letter writing. The principal debating point was Paul's eschatology: in particular, did Paul significantly develop his theology between 1 Corinthians 15 and 2 Corinthians 5, and did his later theology reflect some disappointment and realignment consequent upon the delay of the parousia? The issue of development also embraced the question of Pauline authorship of the late members of the Pauline corpus: in particular, could Paul's theology and praxis have developed sufficiently within his lifetime to explain the different character (theology as well as vocabulary and style) of the Pastoral epistles? The other issue was whether it is possible to identify a *center* of Paul's theology, around which all the rest coheres. The issue was debated in relation to several alternatives, including "anthropology or christology" and "justification or participation in Christ or reconciliation." These two issues came together in debate as to whether the revelation given to Paul in his conversion on the Damascus road—more or less from the first—predetermined or possibly even already established the main emphases and outline of his theology. In the 1970s, however, the relative calm of Pauline studies was shattered by two major breakthroughs.

PAUL IN SOCIOLOGICAL AND RHETORICAL PERSPECTIVE

In the mid-1970s Gerd Theissen, now of Heidelberg, produced a series of incisive studies on 1 Corinthians. These brought to the fore the following question: To what extent had both the situation addressed by Paul and Paul's response to it been determined by social rather than theological factors? This question, in effect, reinvigorated the older concerns of the History of Religions School. But whereas the earlier members of that School had drawn on traditional classical scholarship to illuminate the possible influences of religious philosophy and practice (as seen preeminently in the commentary on 1 Corinthians by Johannes Weiss), Theissen brought to bear the newer discipline of sociology. In consequence, what had previously been assumed to be theological disputes between Paul and gnostic opponents about wisdom and the Lord's Supper, for example, suddenly became more luminous as clashes or tensions between rich and poor, socially powerful and powerless.

Theissen's work sparked a new round of research, each in turn bringing fresh insights into the factors that shaped Paul's practical theology. For example, Ronald Hock drew out the implications of the fact that Paul supported himself as a tentmaker ("theology while you work"). Scott Bartchy and Dale Martin illuminated not simply the reality of slavery but also Paul's advice to slaves and his use of slave metaphors. Bengt Holmberg clarified the language and reality of power and authority in Paul's ministry. Bruce Malina has shown how relevant to exegesis were the typical ancient concerns with honor and shame. Peter Marshall analyzed Paul's financial relationships with the Corinthians in terms of friendship. John Chow demonstrated how much of Paul's advice makes sense against the background of a social system structured on patron-client relationships. The work of anthropologist Mary Douglas brought out the extent to which purity concerns determined social relations. The single most important study in the field, though, has undoubtedly been that of Wayne Meeks, *The First Urban Christians,* which serves as a mature synthesis and paradigmatic statement of what can usefully be said about Paul (including his theology) from this perspective.

Almost as vigorous through this period has been the somewhat complementary approach to Paul through ancient rhetoric. In this case Hans Dieter Betz of Chicago filled the role equivalent to that of Theissen. Betz's analysis of Galatians (1979) in terms of rhetorical structure opened a new door in Pauline studies. Since then the ancient rhetorical handbooks have become familiar tools for many Pauline commentators, engendering considerable debate as to which categories of rhetorical composition best apply to Paul's letters: judicial (to persuade in relation to the past), deliberative (to persuade in relation to the future), or epideictic (usually in praise or blame of someone).

R. D. Anderson has recently pointed out the dangers of this approach—particularly the assumption that there was a uniform rhetorical system in antiquity, and the danger of applying any particular rhetorical model too rigidly. Betz himself did not know what to make of the paraenetical section in Galatians, since there was no place for exhortation in what he took to be an example of judicial rhetoric. In actual practice, Anderson notes, ancient rhetoric was supple. The interplay of *topoi* or motifs is much more significant for understanding the dynamic of Paul's theologizing than the possibility of giving the letter a particular rhetorical label. The most effective treatment of 1 Corinthians, given this more realistic objective, has undoubtedly been that of Margaret Mitchell. She sees the letter primarily as an appeal for unity—with Paul seeking to persuade the Corinthians to end their factionalism and to be reconciled to each other, and making regular use of terms and phrases such as one might expect to find in an ancient discussion of factionalism and concord.

One value of these approaches and individual studies has been to earth Paul's theologizing in the grittiness of social relations as they must actually have been and to enable the twentieth-century reader to appreciate something of Paul's persuasive power as a preacher and pastor as well as a theologian. Whatever the particular contributions of the individual studies, together they should help prevent any relapse into understanding Paul's theology as a merely dogmatic or idealistic system.

THE NEW PERSPECTIVE ON PAUL

In 1977 E. P. Sanders, now of Duke University, threw an apple of discord on to the aimless roundabout of discussions on Pauline theology. For centuries the effective key to Paul's theology had been the antithesis between law and gospel—Paul's doctrine of justification by faith (gospel) confronted by and defined in antithesis to justification by works (law). The almost inevitable extension of this was the characterizing of Paul's theology as a whole as an antithesis between Christianity (gospel) and Judaism (law); its distinctive features had first emerged in Paul's own reaction against his Jewish past, and the sustained opposition of the Judaizers to his mission determined his theology's maturing shape.

Sanders, however, demonstrated convincingly that the traditional Protestant view of ancient Judaism was seriously flawed, a stereotype that owed more to Reformation polemics than to a critical study of the Jewish texts. Such a study underlined, in contrast, the degree to which ancient Judaism had been from the first a religion of grace, not of self achievement. This character of grace pervaded the whole, from the first choice of a slave people in Egypt with nothing to commend them (Deuteronomy), through the provision of daily and annual sacrifices to deal with the problem of sin and transgression. Within this pattern of religion, the role of the law was not to enable individuals to achieve acceptance by God and membership in the covenant, but to guide those who were already God's people in the way they should live. The view that Judaism was a religion that condemned anything short of perfection is still maintained by some, but the work of Sanders and those who have taken up his insights leaves less and less room for this view.

The debate set in motion by Sanders has been vigorous and at times bad-tempered (presumably because it touched on matters of personal faith and cherished tradition). It has largely focused on Paul and the law and the internal coherence of Paul's theology. Some, notably Heikki Raisanen, have concluded that Paul's teaching on the law is basically incoherent. Stephen Westerholm and others have argued that for Paul to be consistent, there must have been a legalistic form of Judaism against which he was reacting. Hans Hübner suggests that his views significantly developed in the course of his letter writing. Others (particularly James Dunn) have claimed that Paul's view of the law is more differentiated, that what he objected to was the law maintained as guarantee and assurance of Israel's set-apartness to God and requiring sustained set-apartness from all other nations; in Paul's perspective this attitude and the proselytizing policies that it encouraged were as much evidence of sin's abuse of the law as any sequence of individual transgressions. This third response has probably the best chance of providing a new large-scale consensus, since it takes seriously the character of the Judaism of the period, and sets in coherent context both Paul's more negative and his more positive statements about the law.

One of the important corollaries to this discussion might be called the rescue of the traditional doctrine of justification by faith from too narrow a focus on the individual's personal salvation. From a study of the contexts in which Paul formulates his teaching on justification (particularly Galatians and Romans) it is evident that the teaching emerged as a way of answering the question: How is it that Gentiles can be acceptable to the God of Israel, to share in Israel's covenant righteousness? Do Gentiles have to proselytize in order to experience the blessing that God promised through Abraham to the nations? In other words, the issue was of religious versus national or racial identity as well as of personal salvation. Rediscovery of this dimension frees up one of Paul's most important motifs to speak with greater power than ever: God's grace pays no attention to race and ethnicity and the rules by which societies protect their identities and sacred traditions. Paul's gospel is for all who believe.

THE IMPACT OF THE HOLOCAUST
ON CHRISTIAN SELF-UNDERSTANDING

A major contributory factor in the reassessment of Paul's attitude to his native Judaism has been the Holocaust. Over the past generation it has been a progressively more sobering experience for many Christians to realize to what extent the traditional theological antithesis between Christianity and Judaism depended on the traditional reading of Paul. From the epistle of Barnabas, Melito, and Chrysostom to the Holocaust is a very long road, with many twists and turns, but it is, sad to confess, a direct route. And, regrettably, readings of Paul have provided text and confirmation for most of the way. Fortunately, however, Christian revulsion at the Holocaust has combined with the new perspective on Paul to begin, but still only begin, to build a new and more accurate picture of Paul's theological understanding of Israel.

Critical here has been the recognition that Paul's conversion was not a conversion from first-century "Judaism" as we today would define the term. Rather, it was a conversion within Judaism, or, more accurately, a conversion from one sect of Judaism to another, from Pharisaic Judaism to a conception of Israel more open to Gentiles as Gentiles. The fact that Paul the apostle did not think of himself as an apostate, but rather as carrying forward Israel's task to be a blessing to the nations and a light to the Gentiles, tells us much about his understanding of his new faith. For him, Christianity was defined not by opposition to Israel but by reference to Israel's heritage and missionary task. The related fact that Paul's key discussion on the subject (Rom. 9–11) is not about "Israel and the Church" (as has traditionally been asserted), but simply about Israel (God's faithfulness to Israel) makes the same point. Paul's hope was not for a Christianity distinct from Israel, but for an Israel defined by the grace and call of God within which Gentiles had an integral place. Paul's focus on Israel even while redefining Israel calls for a redefining of a Christianity that has usually understood itself in antithesis to historic Israel.

The consequences of this repositioning on Paul's theology can be far-reaching. First, the old play-off between Jewish particularism and Christian universalism is largely turned upside down. Paul drew his universalism from the universalism of the Jewish scriptures—which began with Adam and continued with Abraham before Moses ever appeared on the scene. And it was Christian particularism that allowed the thought that pogrom and genocide could conceivably be justified. Second, the propriety and use of Jewish scriptures within a Christian Bible can be given a much better theological rationale than hitherto; only as part of Israel can Christianity claim Israel's scriptures. And, not least, the continuing relationship of Christian and Jew can be transformed from one of evangelism to one of ecumenism—the mutuality of Jew and Christian within the one people of God affirmed as Paul envisaged it.

WHAT IS "THE THEOLOGY OF PAUL"?

If Christian identity as traditionally conceived has come in for some questioning in the light of the current reassessment of Paul's theology, we should not be surprised if the concept of "Paul's theology" itself has undergone a similar crisis in identity. For the last twenty years, it has also been marked by a crisis in confidence in the larger hermeneutical process: How are such ancient texts to be read? What does the reader contribute to the meaning of such a text? How should we expect them to speak to the end of the twentieth century? The crisis has been more serious in regard to the Gospels and Jesus. The fact that Paul's theology was expressed in letters directed to particular situations and churches has made the problem of recovering or uncovering meaning that much easier. But even so, the concept of Paul's theology suddenly became a good deal more slippery than it had always seemed. Was his theology what he actually said in the individual letters, or a larger reservoir of coherent thought on which the different letters drew, or even the impact they made on his readers? When a theology of Paul is written, should it even pretend to be some kind of objective description of what Paul said, or would have said, or still says? Or is it rather the product of a sort of interrogation of the first-century writer by a modern reader, as much, if not more, determined by the questions and the way they have been posed than by the text itself?

It is a significant easing of this problem to recognize that Paul's writing itself was a kind of dialogue, a dialogue at different levels. At the deepest level we have to speak of his inherited faith, much of which remained as powerful as ever when he became a Christian, without ceasing to be a Jew. At middle level was the impact of the gospel on him and in particular his encounter with the risen Christ in his conversion, which certainly transformed his theology as well as his life. At the most accessible level we can speak of his dialogue with the churches to which he wrote, the themes of the letters themselves, the issues and concerns which arose in the churches and out of Paul's relations with them and which he sought to address in his letters.

The value of such an awareness is the recognition that a theology of Paul that remains only at the most accessible level is bound to be superficial. As in all dialogues, it is the allusion, the echo, the taken-for-granted—what can be assumed between the dialogue partners and therefore need not be explicitly stated—that gives the dialogue its richness, its relevance and its "bite." In Paul's case, for example, it is evident that he constantly assumed his traditional Jewish faith in God as one, as creator and judge, and as God of Israel. He never developed a doctrine of God as such, and any attempt to construct such a doctrine solely from Paul's explicit statements would be at best very patchy. And yet it can hardly be doubted that Paul's belief in God was absolutely foundational for his theology. To bring this fact out, however, requires filling out Paul's references to God and the often bare allusions to God's functions that pepper his writing, and to do so by reference to Paul's inherited faith. Only when the scope of his inherited monotheism has been grasped can the nuances of Paul's christology of Jesus as Lord be properly appreciated.

The same applies to the use Paul makes both of his ancestral scriptures (the Old Testament) and of earlier Christian tradition. As the long lists at the end of almost all modern Greek New Testaments make clear, allusions to the Old Testament are far more extensive than explicit quotations. The scriptures that pervade so much of Paul's language and conceptuality certainly shaped his theology. The recent work of Richard Hays has marked a new stage in sensitivity to such echoes and allusions and to their formative influence on Paul's writing. Only in this manner can the reader fully appreciate the full character and scope of Paul's use of Adam and Wisdom motifs to spell out his appreciation of Christ.

As with the Old Testament so also with the earlier Christian tradition. The fact that so many of Paul's statements of the Christian gospel are probably quotations of earlier credal formulas should have alerted us to this key fact. In quoting such formulas Paul was able to assume a fuller statement of the gospel as a common grid with his readers. In consequence, any restatement of Paul's gospel (including, not least, his theology of the cross) has to unpack these briefer forms by reference outside of Paul.

This also holds for Paul's allusions to Jesus' teaching and ministry. The paucity of explicit references to Jesus' words has always caused some surprise. But when the ear is alerted to hear what need not be said because the first readers did not need to be explicitly reminded, then many more allusions can be recognized and their function within and as part of Paul's theology acknowledged. Such recognition would go a long way to clarifying another old debate in Pauline theology: whether and to what extent his theology was dependent on or valued the teaching of Jesus prior to Jesus' death.

Helpful as all this is, however, in assessing the complexity and the realism of Paul's theology in its historical context, it is only of partial help in resolving the hermeneutical issues that continue to trouble the use and perceived relevance of Paul's theology in contemporary theology and church life. The issue of the ministry of women and the issue of homosexuality need only be mentioned for this point to be appreciated. The ongoing dialogue about and with Paul's theology on such points is far from ended.

REDISCOVERING THE SPIRIT

Debate on the center of Paul's theology is often reduced to a choice between "justification by faith" and "participation in Christ." The latter recognizes that one of the most pervasive motifs in Paul's letters is expressed in the often-used phrases, "in Christ" and "through Christ," not to mention "into Christ," "with Christ," and "the body of Christ." This latter theme has not been given so much attention in the last few years, the interest having been sidetracked by debate about pre-Christian gnosticism, or absorbed into the theology of baptism and of the body of Christ sacramentally conceived.

However, another outside factor influencing reassessment of Paul's theology has been the charismatic renewal movement within and apart from traditional Christian denominations. This movement has brought fresh attention to a number of largely overshadowed features of Paul's theology. One is the gift of the Spirit as a factor evidently much more crucial than baptism and much more frequently in view than justification in Paul's theology of conversion and initiation. Somewhat curiously, this feature seems to have made little impact on the way Paul's teaching is used in contemporary ecumenical discussion.

Another hitherto neglected feature brought to the fore by this movement is the importance of Paul's own religious experience in shaping so much of his principal and most distinctive vocabulary, including key terms like "grace" and "love" and motifs like "in Christ" and "Christ in me." The fact that an experiential theology is easily abused (as history readily illustrates) has resulted in this aspect of Paul's theology being downplayed, but has also limited the value of Paul's theology in providing the checks and balances (theological and organizational) that Paul himself found to be necessary and counseled to his churches.

A third feature is closely related to the first two: the fact that Paul understood his chief image for church (the body of Christ) in terms of charismatic community. The charisms of the Spirit as the diverse functions of the body are what constitutes oneness as a body. The influence of this feature of Paul's theology on contemporary ecumenical ecclesiology is well illustrated by the earlier work of Hans Küng; however, the late twentieth-century reality remains a spectrum of ecclesial practice that overlaps to some extent in hymnody but rarely in polity. Not least of importance is the degree to which a Pauline theology of the Spirit continues to put in question traditional concept and practice of sacrament and priesthood.

In short, the last quarter of the twentieth century has seen a revitalization of debate such as few could have envisaged earlier about Paul's theology and its continuing relevance. It is as a vigorous contributor to several ongoing theological, ecclesiastical and ethical issues that the letters of Paul enter upon the twenty-first century.

Titles referred to above:

Anderson, R. D. *Ancient Rhetorical Theory and Paul*. Kampen: Kok Pharos, 1996.
Bartchy, S. S. *First-Century Slavery and 1 Corinthians 7.21,* Society of Biblical Literature Dissertation Series 11. Missoula, Mont.: Scholars Press, 1973.
Baur, F. C. *Paul: the Apostle of Jesus Christ,* 2 vols. London: Williams & Norgate, 1873, 1875 (original, 1845).
Betz, H. D. *Galatians,* Hermeneia (Philadelphia: Fortress Press, 1979).
Bousset, W. *Kyrios Christos*. Nashville: Abingdon, 1970 (original, 1921).
Bultmann, R. *Theology of the New Testament*. London: SCM Press, 1952.
Chow, J. K. *Patronage and Power: A Study of Social Networks in Corinth,* Journal for the Society of the New Testament Supplement Series 75. Sheffield: JSOT, 1992.
Dunn, J. D. G. *Jesus, Paul and the Law: Studies in Mark and Galatians*. Louisville, Ky.: Westminster/John Knox Press, 1990.
Hays, R. B. *Echoes of Scripture in the Letters of Paul*. New Haven, Conn.: Yale University Press, 1989.
Hock, R. F. *The Social Context of Paul's Ministry: Tentmaking and Apostleship*. Philadelphia: Fortress Press, 1980.
Holmberg, B. *Paul and Power: The Structure of Authority in the Primitive Churches as Reflected in the Pauline Epistles*. Lund: Gleerup, 1978.
Hübner, H. *Law in Paul's Thought*. Edinburgh: T. & T. Clark, 1984.
Kung, H. *The Church*. London: Burns & Oates, 1968.
Malina, B. J. *The New Testament World: Insights from Cultural Anthropology*. London: SCM Press, 1983.
Marshall, P. *Enmity in Corinth: Social Conventions in Paul's Relations with the Corinthians,* Wissenschaftliche Untersuchungen zum Neuen Testament 2.23. Tübingen: Mohr, 1987.
Martin, D. B. *Slavery as Salvation: The Metaphor of Slavery in Pauline Christianity*. New Haven, Conn.: Yale University Press, 1990.
Meeks, W. A. *The First Urban Christians: The Social World of the Apostle Paul* . New Haven, Conn.: Yale University Press, 1983.
Mitchell, M. M. *Paul and the Rhetoric of Reconciliation: An Exegetical Investigation of the Language and Composition of 1 Corinthians*. Louisville, Ky.: Westminster/John Knox Press, 1993.
Raisanen, H. *Paul and the Law,* Wissenschaftliche zum Neuen Testament 29. Tübingen: Mohr, 1983.
Sanders, E. P. *Paul and Palestinian Judaism*. London: SCM Press, 1977.
Theissen, G. *The Social Setting of Pauline Christianity*. Philadelphia: Fortress Press, 1982.
Weiss, J. *Der erste Korintherbrief*. Kritisch-exegetischer Kommentar. Göttingen: Vandenhoeck, 1910.
Westerholm, S. *Israel's Law and the Church's Faith: Paul and His Recent Interpreters*. Grand Rapids: Wm. B. Eerdmans Publishing Co., 1988.

For further reading:

Barrett, C. K. *Paul: An Introduction to His Thought*. Louisville, Ky.: Westminster John Knox Press, 1994.
Bassler, J. M., ed. *Pauline Theology, Vol. 1: Thessalonians, Philippians, Galatians, Philemon*. Minneapolis: Fortress Press, 1991.
Becker, J. *Paul: Apostle to the Gentiles*. Louisville, Ky.: Westminster/John Knox Press, 1993.
Beker, J. C. *Paul the Apostle: The Triumph of God in Life and Thought*. Philadelphia: Fortress Press, 1980.
Davies, W. D. *Paul and Rabbinic Judaism,* 4th ed. London: SPCK, 1981 (original, 1948).

Donaldson, T. L. *Paul and the Gentiles: Remapping the Apostle's Convictional World*. Minneapolis: Fortress Press, 1997.

Dunn, J. D. G. *The Theology of Paul the Apostle*. Grand Rapids: Wm. B. Eerdmans Publishing Co., 1998.

Fitzmyer, J. A. *Paul and His Theology: A Brief Sketch,* 2nd ed. Englewood Cliffs N.J.: Prentice Hall, 1989.

Hay, D. M. ed. *Pauline Theology Vol. 2: 1 & 2 Corinthians*. Minneapolis: Fortress Press, 1993.

Hay, D. M., and E. E. Johnson, eds. *Pauline Theology Vol. 3: Romans*. Minneapolis: Fortress Press, 1995.

Hengel, M. *The Pre-Christian Paul*. London: SCM Press, 1991.

Hengel, M., and A. M. Schwemer. *Paul Between Damascus and Antioch*. London: SCM Press, 1997.

Johnson, E. E., and D. M. Hay, eds. *Pauline Theology Vol. 4: Looking Back, Pressing On*. Atlanta: Scholars Press, 1997.

Käsemann, E. *Perspectives on Paul*. London: SCM Press, 1971.

Keck, L. E. *Paul and His Letters*. Philadelphia: Fortress Press, 1982.

Murphy-O'Connor, J. *Paul: A Critical Life*. Oxford: Clarendon Press, 1996.

Ridderbos, H. *Paul: An Outline of His Theology*. Grand Rapids: Wm. B. Eerdmans Publishing Co., 1975.

Roetzel, C. J. *The Letters of Paul: Conversations in Context,* 2nd ed. Atlanta: John Knox Press, 1975.

Sanders, E. P. *Paul*. Oxford: Oxford University Press, 1991.

Segal, A. F. *Paul the Convert: The Apostolate and Apostasy of Saul the Pharisee*. New Haven, Conn.: Yale University Press, 1990.

Stendahl, K. *Paul Among Jews and Gentiles*. Philadelphia: Fortress Press, 1976.

Chapter 9

The Disputed
Letters of Paul

Richard P. Carlson

"But as for you, teach what is consistent with sound doctrine" (Titus 2:1). This nineteen-hundred-year-old admonition in many ways sums up a number of the concerns expressed in the six epistles that scholars have labeled the Disputed Letters of Paul (Ephesians, Colossians, 2 Thessalonians, 1 Timothy, 2 Timothy, and Titus). In these letters, Paul is presented as the great apostle who now stands at a distance from the audience. He writes to instruct and admonish the next generation of Christians and their leaders so that they would hold onto the sound doctrines, teachings, and traditions they have received. Such persistence in the true faith is especially needed in light of the false teachings that threaten the doctrinal integrity of the church (see Eph. 4:14–24; Col. 1:28; 2:7–8, 20–23; 3:16; 2 Thess. 2:1–15; 1 Tim. 1:9–11, 18–20; 4:1–16; 5:17–22; 6:1–3; 2 Tim. 1:11–15; 3:10–17; 4:1–5; Titus 1:9–16). Thus the ongoing stability of the Christian church and household is at stake and needs to be protected through the implementation of the structured life envisioned in these epistles.

Yet precisely because the Pauline authorship of these six letters is in serious dispute within scholarly circles, a host of issues arise that are pertinent not only to the admonition of Titus 2:1 but also to all of the Disputed Letters. If Paul did not write them, who did and to whom were they written? What constitutes "sound doctrine"? What reality does such sound doctrine seek to construe? What may be the social and historical realities it seeks to quell or supplant? What authority undergirds such admonitions and is that authority valid for twenty-first century readers? In wrestling with such issues (and also with each other), scholars have recently opened new vistas for understanding the Disputed Letters—vistas that will continue to be explored over the course of the new century. Our survey will include considerations of literary, social, historical, theological, and hermeneutical issues involved in reading the Disputed Letters.

LITERARY ISSUES AND INSIGHTS

Literary issues involve such matters as authorship, rhetorical type, and genre.

Authorship. Disputes among scholars over the authorship of the six letters are nothing new. Indeed, the dispute over Paul's authorship of Ephesians goes back to the sixteenth century. Significant research in this area has been carried out for over a century and one-half as many scholars have sought to establish just what these letters are not, namely, letters penned by the Apostle Paul. Methodologically, scholars have continuously compared the language, syntax, theology, and historical or social factors at work in or behind each of the Disputed Letters with similar factors evidenced in the Undisputed Letters (Romans, 1 Corinthians, 2 Corinthians, Galatians, Philippians, 1 Thessalonians, and Philemon). So, for example, it has long been demonstrated that over one-third of the words that make up the Pastoral Epistles (1 Timothy, 2 Timothy, Titus) are not found in the Undisputed Letters; that the sentence structures of Ephesians are decidedly more complex and elongated than the constructions normally employed in the Undisputed Letters; and that the eschatology of Colossians and 2 Thessalonians is markedly different from the eschatology of the Undisputed Letters. Taken together, these arguments and a wide range of other pieces of internal and external evidence amassed through 150 years of scholarship have convinced a majority of Pauline scholars that Paul did not write any of the Disputed Letters. Rather, at a time subsequent to Paul's death four different authors wrote these six letters (assuming the common authorship of the Pastoral Epistles). Not only did they attribute their works to Paul, they also made intentional use of Pauline letters, traditions, and claims to authority in the composition of their own letters.

This broad scholarly consensus at the end of the twentieth century indicates that in the twenty-first century the issue of Paul's authorship of the Disputed Epistles will probably not be at the forefront of scholarly endeavors. The authorship issue, however, will not completely disappear. The burden of proof does seem to have shifted now to those who regard Paul as author of the Disputed Letters. Because of this, new studies may well be generated to challenge the broad evidence establishing non-Pauline authorship. The significant issue confronting those who wish to mount such a challenge will be consequent interpretation of the Undisputed Letters. Simply put, to claim and offer plausible arguments in support of the Pauline authorship of a letter such as Ephesians is not a closed affair. If one claims that the person who wrote Ephesians also wrote Romans and 1 Corinthians, then that claim affects any interpretation of Romans and 1 Corinthians. If Paul did indeed write Ephesians, then the theological shifts evidenced in that letter's christology, ecclesiology, and eschatology work backwards to color how one understands the christology, ecclesiology, and eschatology displayed in the Undisputed Letters. Hence the issue of authorship continues to matter. Whenever one claims Pauline authorship for any or all of the six Disputed Letters, there will be a subsequent need to reinterpret the seven Undisputed Letters in order to harmonize all thirteen letters of the Pauline corpus.

On the other side of the coin, questions of authorship remain at issue for those who reject the Pauline authorship of the Disputed Letters. If Paul did not write these letters, who did and why? Here scholars are not necessarily focusing on the historical identity of the authors (which may be impossible to establish) but on the historical, social, and theological exigencies that motivated different authors to compose these letters and to ascribe them to Paul. For example, what are the historical factors motivating a Christian theologian in the last quarter of the first century to pen 2 Thessalonians? Is this author rejecting a letter ascribed to Paul or an oral tradition that claims that the Day of the Lord has already arrived? Is the real author writing to the Christian community in Thessalonica because he is rejecting the eschatology of a genuine letter such as 1 Thessalonians? Or might this disputed letter have been penned as a rejection of another disputed letter such as Colossians in which it is claimed that Christians have been raised with Christ (Col. 2:12–13; 3:1–4)?[1]

Rhetorical type. While over 150 years of scholarship have focused on what the Disputed Letters are not (that is, written by Paul), scholarship in the past two decades has tended to focus more on what rhetorical features these letters contain. For example, recent rhetorical analyses of 2 Thessalonians have shown it to be a letter employing deliberative rhetoric.[2] In deliberative rhetoric, an author or speaker seeks to persuade the audience to take certain actions or adopt appropriate attitudes that will set them on a particular course in the future. On the one hand, such an understanding of 2 Thessalonians immediately sets it apart from 1 Thessalonians. In that letter Paul was employing epideictic rhetoric (that is, rhetoric in which the author seeks to persuade the audience to hold or reaffirm certain positions in the present via the use of praise or blame). Though they share several literary features, the letters of the Thessalonian correspondence have very different goals. On the other hand, this understanding of the 2 Thessalonians' rhetoric allows those goals to come to the forefront. Through the argumentation of this letter, the author seeks to persuade the audience to reject the advancement of a purported Pauline position which claims that the Day of the Lord has already arrived (2 Thess 2:1–2). In contradistinction to such a false claim, the author seeks to establish what he considers to be the true timetable of events leading up to that eschatological Day. In service of this rhetorical goal, the author also issues exhortations for appropriate, steadfast behavior in anticipation of that Day and presents Christ as the cosmic avenger who will vindicate the vigilant and wreak eschatological doom on the unbelievers (1:5–10; 2:11–12; 3:1–5).

Thus in understanding this letter's rhetorical type, we come to understand what the letter seeks to do and how it goes about accomplishing that task. This, in turn, helps readers understand in a new way the literary relationship between 1 Thessalonians and 2 Thessalonians. The literary parallelism between these two letters has long been noted, and has often held up as proof that Paul wrote the second letter to the same audience after a short interval and so was consciously utilizing the same literary framework. Glenn Holland, however, has shown that there is much more to this literary relationship than the reduplication of a prior letter's framework. While the author of 2 Thessalonians has intentionally copied the structure of 1 Thessalonians as well as borrowed particular phrases or formulae, the content of this letter is clearly his own and serves the particular rhetorical goals noted above. Thus neither proximity in time nor the same author writing to the same audience explains the literary relationship between Thessalonian letters. Rather the pseudonymous author of 2 Thessalonians used the Pauline letter known as 1 Thessalonians to promote his version of Pauline eschatology, authenticate his authority, and legitimize his particular rhetorical goals.[3]

The work of Andrew Lincoln on the literary issues surrounding Ephesians is another important example of how scholarship has moved beyond traditional issues such as authorship to pay serious attention to rhetoric and the impact it has for understanding this disputed epistle.[4] Scholars have long noted that Ephesians is structured into two distinct sections, chapters 1—3 and chapters 4—6, and that the former section addresses doctrinal issues while the latter deals with ethical issues. Lincoln's analyses, however, go much further. He has shown that chapters 1—3 employ the epideictic rhetoric common in congratulatory letters to engage the readers in a celebration of the common identity and status they share in and with Christ as participants in God's salvific plan. The second half of the letter, chapters 4—6, is a deliberative argumentation in which the readers are exhorted to display their God-given reality through appropriate behavior and relationships. The letter closes (indeed climaxes) with the *peroratio* of 6:10–20. The *peroratio* of an ancient speech or letter seeks to recapitulate the discourse's main points and arouse the emotions of the audience. In the *peroratio* of Ephesians the letter's argument is summarized by rallying the audience as vigilant participants in a cosmic war. Armed with God's battle attire and praying constantly in the Sprit, they are reminded that they fight on the victorious side because of the identity and status they share in and with Christ.

Genre. The work of Benjamin Fiore on the Pastoral Epistles is an example of how scholarly attention to epistolary genre enhances our reading of a section of the Disputed Letters.[5] Fiore has argued that the Pastoral Epistles are hortatory rather than doctrinal in nature and scope. As such they move in the stream of the epistolary paraenetic tradition especially evident in the popular philosophical schools of the Greco-Roman world. Through the use of both paraenetic and Pauline traditions as well as the employment of personal example, the author of the Pastorals seeks to promote his vision of proper moral standards, behavioral patterns, leadership structures, and communal attitudes while also refuting what he considers to be heretical deviations in these areas. Thus the strong personal tone of the Pastorals is not evidence of Pauline authorship but represents the intentional use of a particular rhetorical strategy and epistolary genre for the sake of achieving overarching hortatory purposes.

Rhetorical analyses such as these are helping modern readers better understand the intents, emphases, strategies, and structures at work in the Disputed Letters. Similarly, recent literary analyses have gone beyond noting where these later letters used Pauline passages or categories. Instead, they help show how these authors have intentionally crafted the Pauline material in order to achieve their own particular purposes. Although issues regarding authorship remain pertinent (though not prominent), the Disputed Letters are finally being approached as part of the New Testament worthy of investigation in their own right rather than simply as material that has deviated from Paul.

SOCIOLOGICAL AND HISTORICAL ISSUES AND INSIGHTS

In the last quarter of the twentieth century, various studies have been produced that deal with sociological and historical issues in and behind the Disputed Letters. Such studies have significantly broadened our understanding of these six epistles.

They have also provided readers with tools for classifying and tracing institutional and leadership development at a time when the first generation of church leaders was dying out. These studies help modern readers recognize, understand, and perhaps even critique the ways in which Christianity near the close of the first century chose to draw on social models from the Greco-Roman world to order and normalize the social reality of Christian households and communities.

With regard to institutional development of the Undisputed Letters in the churches, the work of Margaret MacDonald is insightful.[6] Building upon previous studies on social theories of institutionalization, MacDonald argues that Colossians, Ephesians, and the Pastoral Epistles do not simply represent the dawn of institutionalization in early Christian social development. In point of fact, institutionalization occurred early on as Christian communities acted to typify their social interactions and patterns of ritual. The goals and forms of institutionalization depicted in the Disputed Letters, however, differ significantly from those evidenced in the Undisputed Letters. The Undisputed Letters depict community-building institutionalization whereas an institutional effort toward stabilization is at work in Colossians and Ephesians. The church's place not only in society but also in the cosmos is explained in these two epistles through the symbol of the Church as the Body of Christ with Christ as the head (Eph. 1:22–23; 4:15–16; 5:23; Col 1:18, 24; 2:10, 19). This christologically defined reality serves to stabilize the status and roles of church members. Knowing that one belongs to the Body of Christ allows one to map where one belongs in the cosmic structure of reality, in Greco-Roman society, in the Church, and in one's household.

The Pastoral Epistles engage in institutional *protection* more than community building or stabilization. On the one hand, the author of the Pastorals has concluded that the community needs protection from certain false teachers who are a threat not only to right doctrine but also to the proper behavioral patterns and social structures of the institution. In fact, the latter is of greater concern in these three letters. On the other hand, protection for the community is found in the recognition of its legitimate leaders and the appropriate patterns of behavior for all strata of the community. Whereas the Church as the Body of Christ with Christ as the Head stands as the stabilizing image for the institution in Colossians and Ephesians, the church as "household of God" becomes the protecting image for the community in the Pastoral Epistles. By adopting the household image from Greco-Roman society and the leadership patterns evidenced therein, an air of social respectability within the dominant culture is provided for the Christian community. Likewise, deviant behavior is more readily controlled in such a household structure (be it the individual household or the church as household) so that the Christian patriarch and his values "protect" subordinates from the dangerous allures of false teachings and attendant behavioral patterns. Thus twenty-first-century readers are better able to understand how patriarchal societal structures became normative through the institutionalization patterns established at the end of the first century.

The imagery and function of the household and household codes (or *Haustafeln*) in the Disputed Letters have been the focus of a number of studies by David Balch and others over the past twenty-five years.[7] In Greco-Roman culture the household was understood to be a microcosm of, and the bedrock for, society. The codes themselves go back to Aristotle and depict what is by nature the social order and attendant conduct within the household and so within society as a whole. The household codes (Ephesians 5:21–6:9; Colossians 3:18–4:1; 1 Timothy 2:8–15; 5:12; 6:1–2; Titus 2:1–10; 3:1) reflect a Christian acculturation of the basic societal structures, norms, behaviors, and leadership patterns for Christian marital, parental, and master-slave relationships. In many ways such an adaptation of household standards reflects a move toward "political correctness" on the part of the authors of the Disputed Letters. As noted above, this move has the external benefit of social respectability and the internal benefit of social control over deviant teachings and behaviors.

In terms of a conceptual framework, it is also important to note that while both Ephesians and the Pastoral Epistles theologize the household and the church, they do so in converse ways. In Ephesians, the reality of the Church as the Body with Christ as the Head is used as a model for the household. Hence human marriage is interpreted via the model of the celestial marriage between Christ and his bride, the church (5:21–33). An important implication of this view is that an inherent power differential always exists between both sets of partners. The superior (Christ, the husband) exudes love toward the inferior (the Church, the wife), and the inferior is to subordinate herself to the superior. Nevertheless, there can be no allowance for equality between human marital partners because that relationship remains a reflection of the eternal marital relationship between Christ and the church in which an equality between the partners is impossible. In the Pastoral Epistles the lines of conceptualization are reversed so that the Greco-Roman household becomes the model for the church as household of God (1 Tim. 3:14–15). Thus the job description of bishop as head of the church fits/reflects a description of a good household head in that society (1 Tim. 3:1–7).

Other recent studies have attempted to delve into the historical circumstances at work behind the adaptation of such societal norms in the Pastoral Epistles. Independent of one another, Dennis MacDonald and David Verner conclude that the author of the Pastorals was seeking to combat the social and theological stances later evidenced in the second-century work, *The Acts of Paul and Thecla*.[8] There, the heroine breaks out of the expected social position of subordinate wife and child-bearer in order to assume the role of itinerate Christian preacher, teacher, and baptizer whose ministry is blessed by Paul. While celebrated in the extracanonical tradition, this behavior and pattern for ministry are considered a threat to the correct political structures of the church by the author of the Pastorals. There, Paul is depicted as abjectly rejecting such actions or roles for women. Instead, he commands that women are to remain silent in church, are forbidden to teach, must seek enlightenment from males, need to remain within the proper social boundaries of the household, should seek marriage (unless old age precludes it), and are to have children. Normative leadership is the same for both the household and the church. The respectable, wealthy male is the one best suited for the noble office of bishop, for the one who manages his own household in accord with society's norms is best equipped to manage God's household. Lewis Donelson has shown that in the second century the conservative, nonspeculative, socially acceptable vision of

Christianity set forth in the Pastoral Epistles was embraced by (so-called) orthodox Christianity.[9] Hence the Paul of these letters surpassed both the Paul of the Undisputed Letters and the Paul of the extracanonical traditions in undergirding patriarchy, ecclesiological authority, proper offices for ministry, and socially acceptable behavioral norms for centuries to come.

The Disputed Letters do not represent the first attempt to subordinate the role/place of women or slaves in the Christian community. Nonetheless, in many ways they have stood as the final word about the role/place of such social subordinates for subsequent centuries. The first-century Greco-Roman patriarchy embedded in these texts will still confront the twenty-first-century reader. By understanding the Greco-Roman conception of the household that the Disputed Letters accepted as natural and normative, one is better equipped to interpret such culturally conditioned texts in a non-Greco-Roman society where egalitarian relationships are held up as normative.

THEOLOGICAL AND HERMENEUTICAL ISSUES AND INSIGHTS

For much of the twentieth century, the work done on the theology of the Disputed Letters centered on the issue of authorship. For those who judged Paul to be the author of these six letters, the theology found therein was merged (or at times crammed) into the theological picture and patterns of the Undisputed Letters. Thus the theology of an epistle such as Colossians was interpreted in harmony with and expanded by the rest of the Pauline corpus. For those who rejected Pauline authorship of the six letters, the difference between Paul's "real" theology and deutero-Pauline theology were highlighted. In these cases, the focus of the theology of Colossians was on how it was not Pauline. Interestingly enough, in both instances the theology of a given disputed letter was not really allowed to stand in its own right, but was investigated and established in comparison (either positively or negatively) to the Undisputed Letters.

More recent attempts have been made to investigate the theology of the Disputed Letters apart from such comparisons. Yet there have been some methodological problems. In commentaries on these epistles, the tendency is to discuss theology on a pericope-by-pericope basis so that the resultant picture is more the theologies of the various pericopes than the coherent theology of the whole letter. Is it possible to establish *the* coherent theological core of a given disputed epistle? What qualifies as a letter's core? How does one determine it? Even more important, whose theology is being sought: the theology of an author or the theology of the text? Can a text's theology exist apart from a given author or must it be considered a partial expression of that given author's theology?[10] Questions such as these will continue to confront theological analyses of the Disputed Letters in the twenty-first century.

As the twenty-first century dawns, perhaps the most fruitful theological investigations into the theologies of the Disputed Letters will focus not on the author behind the text but on the text and its implied author. Thus a core question would not simply be, "Who wrote this letter and what is that author's theology?" but, "How is reality construed in and through the symbolic universe constructed in a given letter by its implied author?"[11] With this approach, Paul the Apostle stands as the implied (though not necessarily the real) author of a text that constructs its own social and theological reality for the implied reader through the discourse and rhetoric of the text itself. A seminal example of such an approach to the theology of an undisputed epistle is found in Lincoln's presentation on the theology of Ephesians.[12] While investigating the core symbols and themes of Ephesians, Lincoln never loses sight of the letter's central concern to present/promote the reader's God-established identity, and he is continually cognizant of the rhetorical strategies and language employed by the implied author to achieve that goal. Through such an approach, Lincoln is able to trace the symbolic universe constructed in Ephesians. This symbolic universe consists of two main parts, heaven and earth, which have been restored to cosmic harmony in Christ and in which the readers have been given a particular status, identity, and norms for behavior because of their relationship with Christ. Understanding the symbolic universe and their place in it allows the readers to understand where they have been and where they are going.

Lincoln's approach demonstrates the possibility of understanding a text's theology not as something abstracted from its various passages but as something embedded in the symbolic universe constructed in and through the text by the implied author's use of rhetoric. With such an understanding, future explorations into the theology of the Disputed Letters have the potential to be more holistic as they seek to intertwine theological, social, and rhetorical elements at work in a letter's text. Thus, new avenues of theological exploration are being opened for twenty-first-century readers. For example, how do the goals of the deliberative rhetoric in 2 Thessalonians interrelate with a symbolic universe in which demonic entities have assigned periods and roles in God's eschatological time frame, which will climax with the revelation of the Lord Jesus as cosmic avenger and vindicator? With regard to Colossians, studies have long focused on the heresy being attacked through the letter's christological claims. More recently it has been noted that the letter's hierarchical christology (manifested most clearly in the Christ-hymn of 1:15–20) clearly supports the letter's use of household codes to structure social life.[13] But how do these items fit together within the symbolic universe constructed by the implied author? Colossians actually presents the clash of two symbolic universes: the one perpetrated by the letter's targeted opponents in which the *stoicheia* (2:8, 20) threaten human lives, and the other supported by the implied author in which the triumphant Christ serves as the glue of the cosmos in whom believers' lives are now hidden and ecclesiological and sociological reality is structured.

In addition to such theological issues, a number of interrelated hermeneutical issues face any reading of the Disputed Letters. A prominent one involves canonicity. The assumption of Pauline authorship of these epistles helped bring about their acceptance into mainstream Christian tradition and into the canon. What becomes of their place in the canon when they are regarded as pseudepigraphical works from a post-Pauline generation? While their theological claims should certainly be analyzed and understood in their own right, what happens to the authority they hold since their authorship rests not with the Apostle Paul but someone assuming Paul's name and asserting his authority? Are these letters as normative for the life, faith, and theology of the Christian community as Undisputed Letters such as Romans or Galatians? If one holds to a notion of canon based on apostolic authorship, then the pseudepigraphic nature of the Disputed Letters looms as a major issue. Similarly, for readers who believe that all Scripture is equally valid and authoritative, passages such as 1 Timothy 2:8–15 and Ephesians 5:21–33 will continue to be employed to subordinate women and deny them significant leadership roles in the third millennium.

Hermeneutical issues of relevancy and authority come particularly to the forefront in the matter of the household codes. It has been shown that an Aristotelian understanding of reality based on patriarchal subordination was incorporated into Christian communities through the adoption of the household codes by the authors of the Disputed Letters. Is such an Aristotelian conception of social reality relevant in the twenty-first century, when Aristotelian conceptions of physical and biological reality have long been rejected? Do codes that subordinate select classes of human beings in the name of Christ still hold authority in the Body of Christ? Can texts whose views on slavery have been rejected for over a century still have their views of women's subordination accepted in the twenty-first century?[14]

In considering the hermeneutical issues of canonicity, relevancy, and authority for the Disputed Letters in the twenty-first century, perhaps it would be helpful to return to the admonition of Titus 2:1. To teach what is consistent with sound doctrine may mean the rejection of certain teachings in the Disputed Letters as readers seek consistency with the sound gospel vision of liberation as presented in Galatians 3:27–28 or the Spirit's empowerment of the whole body of Christ as visioned in 1 Corinthians 12:3–26. As the Disputed Letters retheologized the Undisputed Letters to make Paul relevant for a post-Pauline age, so might readers of the Disputed Letters need to retheologize *these* letters in an effort to make the Pauline corpus relevant for a post-modern age. Indeed, the very existence of the Disputed Letters shows that theological reflection on the gospel and its social, ethical, and doctrinal implications did not stop with the death of the first generation of Christians. Thus theological reflections should not stop with the production of the Disputed Letters at the close of the first century but should be continued by readers of the New Testament at the dawn of the twenty-first century.

NOTES

1. The former scenario is proposed by Gerhard Krodel, "2 Thessalonians," in *The Deutero-Pauline Letters,* ed. Gerhard Krodel, Proclamation Commentaries, rev. ed. (Minneapolis: Fortress Press, 1993), pp. 56–57. The latter is given serious consideration by Frank Hughes, *Early Christian Rhetoric and 2 Thessalonians,* Journal for the Study of the New Testament Supplement Series 30 (Sheffield: JSOT Press, 1989): 97–104.

2. Glenn Holland, *The Tradition that You Received from Us: 2 Thessalonians in the Pauline Tradition,* Hermeneutische Untersuchungen zur Theologie 24 (Tübingen: Mohr, 1988), 1–58; Hughes, *2 Thessalonians,* 51–74; and Robert Jewett, *The Thessalonian Correspondence: Pauline Rhetoric and Millenarian Piety,* Foundation and Facets (Philadelphia: Fortress Press, 1986), 61–87. It should be noted that through their examinations of the letter's rhetoric Holland and Hughes reject Pauline authorship while Jewett accepts it.

3. Holland, *2 Thessalonians,* 59–90.

4. See the following studies by Andrew Lincoln: " 'Stand, Therefore . . . ': Ephesians 6:10–20 as *Peroratio,*" *Biblical Interpretation* III (March 1995): 99–114; "The Church and Israel in Ephesians 2," *Catholic Biblical Quarterly* 49 (1987): 605–24; *Ephesians,* Word Biblical Commentary 42 (Dallas: Word, Inc., 1990); and "The Theology of Ephesians," in *The Theology of the Latter Pauline Letters,* New Testament Theology (Cambridge: Cambridge University Press, 1993), 75–166.

5. Benjamin Fiore, *The Function of Personal Example in the Socratic and Pastoral Epistles,* Analecta Biblica 105 (Rome: Biblical Institute Press, 1986).

6. Margaret MacDonald, *The Pauline Churches: A Socio-historical Study of Institutionalization in the Pauline and Deutero-Pauline Writings,* Society for New Testament Studies Monograph Series 60 (Cambridge: Cambridge University Press, 1988).

7. For bibliographic citations, succinct overviews, and brief reviews of these studies, see David Balch, "Household Codes," *Anchor Bible Dictionary,* 3.318–20.

8. Dennis MacDonald, *The Legend and the Apostle: The Battle for Paul in Story and Canon* (Philadelphia: Westminster Press, 1983), and David Verner, *The Household of God: The Social World of the Pastoral Letters,* Society of Biblical Literature Dissertation Series 71 (Chico, Calif.: Scholars Press, 1983).

9. Lewis Donelson, *Pseudepigraphy and Ethical Argumentation in the Pastoral Epistles,* Hermeneutische Untersuchungen zur Theologie 22 (Tübingen: Mohr, 1986).

10. Many of these questions were insightfully posed by Margaret Mitchell during the 1995 inaugural meeting of the Society of Biblical Literature's Theology of the Disputed Paulines Group through her paper, " 'Speaking of God as He was Able': Three Accounts of the Theology of 1 Timothy Compared (A Response to L. T. Johnson, J. L. Sumney, and B. Fiore)."

11. On the construction of a symbolic universe see Margaret MacDonald, *Pauline Churches,* 10–18, and Norman Petersen, *Rediscovering Paul: Philemon and the Sociology of Paul's Narrative World* (Philadelphia: Fortress Press, 1985), 200–302.

12. Lincoln, "Theology of Ephesians."

13. For reviews of five basic schools of interpretation regarding the Colossian heresy, see Richard DeMaris, *The Colossian Controversy: Wisdom in Dispute at Colossae,* Journal for the Study of the New Testament Supplement Series 96 (Sheffield: JSOT Press, 1994), 11–40. On Christological hierarchy and the household codes, see Carolyn Osiek and David Balch, *Families in the New Testament World: Households and House Churches,* Family, Religion, and Culture (Louisville, Ky.: Westminster John Knox Press, 1997), 182–85.

14. For examples of a feminist hermeneutic of suspicion as it involves readings and critiques of the Disputed Letters see Clarice Martin, "The *Haustafeln* (Household Codes)

in African American Biblical Interpretation: 'Free Slaves' and 'Subordinate Women,'" in *Stony the Road We Trod: African American Biblical Interpretation,* ed. Cain Hope Felder (Minneapolis: Fortress Press, 1991), 206–31, as well as the pertinent articles in *The Women's Bible Commentary,* ed. Carol Newsom and Sharon Ringe (Louisville, Ky.: Westminister/John Knox Press, 1992) and *Searching the Scriptures, Vol. Two: A Feminist Commentary,* ed. Elisabeth Schüssler Fiorenza (New York: Crossroad, 1994).

Chapter 10

Hebrews and the
Catholic Epistles

Pheme Perkins

HEBREWS

Hebrews contains several passages that are familiar to Christians, such as the opening description of God's Son (1:1–4), the portrayal of Christ as the merciful High Priest (4:14–5:10), and the definition of faith as the proof of things unseen (11:1). Yet these familiar phrases are embedded in a complex sequence of interlocking images that are foreign to modern readers. Much of the argument is drawn from passages in the Old Testament that refer to the cultic practices in ancient Israel. Readers today find it difficult to conceive the importance of blood sacrifices and rituals in bringing believers close to God. Consequently, the argument in the central section of Hebrews, that the blood of Christ is the true sacrifice for which the others were mere preliminary foreshadowing (7:1–10:18) often seems trivial.

In a third-century papyrus, Hebrews was located directly after Paul's epistle to the Romans. The concluding reference to Timothy's impending release (implying association of Timothy with the author) contributed to the suggestion that Paul was the author of this letter. But the theological emphasis on the cultic implications of Christ's death is very different from Paul's theology of the cross. So is the ornate Greek style in which the letter is written. Were Paul the author, one would expect him to identify himself and to appeal to his apostolic authority. Instead, the author of Hebrews speaks as one of that larger group of leaders who are responsible for guarding the faith of the community (13:17–19). From antiquity until the present, scholars have sought to resolve the authorship problem by suggesting that some other person connected with the Pauline mission wrote the epistle. Barnabas, Luke, and Apollos have been favorite candidates, but there is not enough evidence to reach any conclusion.

The style of argument shows that its author was well-versed in the Greek translation of the Old Testament and in the techniques of ornate Greek prose composition. Many of the verbal echoes that would have pleased an ancient audience cannot be retrieved in English translations (see Attridge 1989, 21–23). This rhetorical flavor is responsible for the interweaving of themes throughout the letter. The author says that he has written a "word of exhortation" (13:22). Some scholars suggest that Hebrews should be understood as a piece of epideictic oratory more than as a letter aimed to address immediate, practical concerns. Such speeches aimed to celebrate and reinforce communal values by praising famous persons. In this instance Hebrews celebrates God's final and decisive word of salvation in Christ. The communal values to which the author returns again and again are associated with faithful endurance in the practice of one's faith (10:36–12:13). There is some danger that believers will fall away from the enthusiasm they showed at first (10:32–34). They should have progressed to a more mature faith but appear to be somewhat sluggish or stagnated (6:1–12).

The great images of Christ's saving work developed in the doctrinal sections of Hebrews serve as examples to motivate the audience, depicted as the pilgrim people of Israel on a journey to the promised land, the "resting place" in the heavens with Christ (2:1–4:13). The contrast between what is earthly and what is heavenly runs throughout the epistle. Perfection can only be found in heaven where God's eternal permanence and holiness are found. Jesus' death on the cross was also his entry into a heavenly sanctuary where that sacrificial blood remains able to cleanse the conscience of believers (9:14; 10:2, 22). External rituals cannot bring about the interior transformation that purifies the heart. Everything in the Old Testament story of Israel's wanderings or her cultic sacrifices is merely an earthly copy. The preliminary first covenant had to be replaced by the new one with its promise of salvation (8:1–13). But if the new covenant offers nothing less than salvation in the heavenly rest, the consequences of turning aside from God's gift in Christ is also more severe. Hence, Hebrews alternates its striking images of salvation with stern warnings against apostasy from the faith its readers have embraced (10:35–39; 12:18–29).

Does the emphasis on Old Testament sacrificial rites indicate that the addressees faced challenges to their faith other than the lack of progress and waning of earlier enthusiasm? Both Jews and pagans associated priesthood and animal sacrifices with worship of god(s). At the very least, Christians might need to explain the lack of any earthly sanctuary, sacrifice, or priesthood (see Pfitzner 1997, 203). Or, the emphasis on joining Christ who died "outside the camp" (13:11, 13) may indicate that the addressees seek to retain ties to the local Jewish community at the expense of confessing that God's Son died to effect the new covenant promised by God (so Lindars 1991, 4–11). All proposals of that sort go beyond the explicit statements in the hortatory sections of the epistle. The text itself refers to two difficulties, waning commitment and external pressure (Attridge 1989, 10–13). Yet severe persecution lies in the community's past (10:32–34). Unlike Christ, who is the model of faith for those who follow him, these Christians have not been asked to die for the faith (12:1–11). This exhortation to follow Christ, the "pioneer and perfecter" of faith, depicts Christian life as an athletic competition. Like runners, the mature believer will strip off everything that makes it difficult to follow Christ. At the same time, believers may find themselves subject to shame and dishonor when they are judged by earthly standards. Hence the author has used epideictic oratory to transform shame into honor (see DeSilva, 1996). The catalogue of heroes of faith that follows the famous definition in chapter 11 provides legitimacy for the despised Christian community by providing it with a distinguished genealogy of ancestors from Abel through the entire span of Old Testament history (see Eisenbaum, 1997). They all had confidence in God's promise of a better covenant (11:39–40). Thus Christians not only follow the example of Christ but are challenged to live up to a distinguished ancestry that embraces the entire story of salvation.

THE CATHOLIC EPISTLES

1 Peter, 2 Peter, James, and Jude have been designated "catholic" or "general" epistles (Eusebius, *History of the Church*, 2.23.25). This term indicates that these writings differ from the familiar Pauline model. Paul's letters refer to specific churches and often name others along with the apostle in the opening. Some scholars suggest that these persons also served as co-authors (Murphy-O'Connor, 1995). In the catholic epistles, one only finds a stylized identification of the sender: "Peter, apostle of Jesus Christ" (1 Peter 1:1); "James, a servant of God and of the Lord Jesus Christ" (James 1:1); "Jude, a servant of Jesus Christ and brother of James" (Jude 1); and "Simeon Peter, a servant and apostle of Jesus Christ," (2 Peter 1:1). 1 Peter does give a general address, Roman provinces in Asia Minor (Pontus, Galatia, Cappadocia, Asia, and Bithynia). It also names two associates in the conclusion ("Silvanus, a faithful brother" and "my son Mark," 1 Pet. 5:12–13). The other letters provide no references to particular places or persons in the address or final greeting. James even omits the conclusion characteristic of a letter. Of course, if these writings are "catholic"—that is, addressed to churches everywhere—then such localized information would not be anticipated.

The relationship between this group of writings and others in the canon provides another set of puzzles:

1 Peter's closest literary parallels are to Pauline epistles. Both Silvanus (2 Cor. 1:19; 1 Thes. 1:1; 2 Thes. 1:1; perhaps identical with the Silas of Acts 15:22, 40; 16:19, 25, 29; 17:4, 10, 14; 18:5) and Mark (Acts 12:25; 13:5, 13; 15:37–39; Col. 4:10; 2 Tim. 4:11; Philemon 24) are familiar figures in the Pauline mission. The content of 1 Peter also shares traditions of ethical exhortation with Romans (1 Peter 1:14//Rom. 12:2; 1 Peter 2:6–8//Rom. 9:32–33; 1 Peter 2:13–17//Rom. 13:1–7; 1 Peter 3:8–9//Rom. 12:16–17; 1 Peter 4:10–11//Rom. 12:6).

The "Peter" who is the authorial voice in 2 Peter is the disciple who witnessed the resurrection and transfiguration (2 Peter 1:16–18), not the author of 1 Peter (Paulsen 1992, 93–99). Its content does not draw on the Pauline writings but incorporates much of Jude. Still, 2 Peter 3:15–16 enlists the authority of Paul's letters for its theological views in contrast to misunderstandings being advanced by others. Thus, 1 Peter and 2 Peter both appeal indirectly to the authority of Pauline models. The territory of 1 Peter 1:1 lies outside the Pauline mission area (if Paul's Galatia refers to the southern towns of Lystra and Iconium). It would appear that 1 Peter seeks to extend apostolic authority to churches without such a founder while 2 Peter aims to establish the unity of apostolic teaching.

Some scholars connect the Jewish traditions found in James and Jude with composition in Palestine by James, the brother of the Lord (Acts 15:13; 21:18; 1 Cor. 15:7; Gal. 1:19; 2:9, 12; so Martin 1988, xxxiii–xli; Johnson 1995, 92–98; 118–21) and the less well-known brother, Jude (Matt. 13:55; Mark 6:3; so Bauckham 1983, 21–27). Parallels between James and the tradition of Jesus' sayings suggest a Palestinian origin (James 2:10–12//Matt. 22:36–40; James 1:22–26; 2:14–16//Matt. 7:21–27; James 1:2//Matt. 5:12; James 1:5//Matt. 7:7; James 1:4//Matt. 5:48; James 3:17–18//Matt. 5:5, 9; James 1:12//Matt. 24:13; James 2:13//Matt. 5:7; 6:14–15; 7:1; James 5:12//Matt. 5:33–37; James 5:2–3//Matt. 6:19; James 1:20//Matt. 5:22; James 2:14–16//Matt. 7:21–23; James 4:4//Matt. 6:24; James 4:11//Matt. 5:22; 7:1–2; James 2:5//Matt. 5:3, Luke 6:20; James 2:6–7//Matt. 19:23–24; so Martin 1988, lxxv; Johnson 1995, 55–57, 119–20). Similar importance is attached to the Old Testament and apocryphal traditions (from 1 Enoch and Test. Moses) in Jude 5–19 (so Bauckham 1983, 4–8), though the use of such apocryphal apocalyptic traditions to announce divine judgment on sinners is quite unlike the combination of apocalyptic and Jewish wisdom traditions found in James. For other scholars, who consider both epistles pseudepigraphical, these considerations do not outweigh the counter-indications of well-crafted Greek sentences and use of rhetorical style in both authors (even Martin sees canonical James as a Hellenistic redaction of the Palestinian James material; Martin 1988, lxxvii; Cargal 1993; on Jude, see Neyrey 1993, 24–31; Joubert 1995; Thurén 1997; Watson 1988).

Whatever decisions are made with regard to authorship and relationships to other canonical writings, scholars agree that the catholic epistles should not be shoehorned into a story of early Christianity that has been established by the Pauline and deutero-Pauline letters and Acts. Instead, the catholic epistles provide valuable evidence for the diversity of Christianity throughout the first century. Since these epistles lack specific references to persons and events, hypotheses about community setting and theological conflict are a consequence of the author's rhetorical skill in establishing an authorial voice and evoking an ethos shared with the implied audience.

Scholars look to all of these letters as evidence for the shared values, symbols, warrants for action, and commitments that bound Christians together in the first century. Each author speaks to strains and crises that threaten the faith. Both 1 Peter and James seek to deepen the audience's faith and practice, as they are faced with conflicting value systems. These Christians have a divided heritage: the ethos of the Greco-Roman world in which they continue to participate and that of their new Christian family.

Jude and 2 Peter present a more somber picture: false teaching and practice that must be challenged within the heart of the community itself. Jude never gives specific details regarding the teaching or moral lapses through which opponents are defiling the communal love feast (vv. 8, 12, 15–16). Nevertheless, the rhetorical task of the letter is to cast these opponents in such a negative light that the letter's recipients will not follow their example (vv. 20–23). Jude's craftsmanship can be judged successful for that purpose (Watson 1988, 78–79). The adaptation of Jude's polemic in the argument of 2 Peter (which apparently drew on the former letter as a source) provides further evidence for its effectiveness.

For 1 Peter, 2 Peter, and James, we will now turn to more detailed analysis. What did it mean to be a Christian at the turn of the century? Though the use of these writings in Christian worship and theology may be slight, they exhibit a strong theological and moral voice at the heart of Christian faith. At the same time, the differences between these letters open up the possibility of divergent forms of Christian life within a single apostolic faith.

1 PETER

1 Peter 1:1–2 includes an expansion in verse 2 that gives theological significance to those addressed. Rhetorically, the depiction of the addressees as chosen and sanctified introduces the thematic focus of the opening benediction (1 Peter 1:3–5). Does the associated geographical notice indicate the churches to which the letter was dispatched? If so, constructing a route of travel between them is problematic (Achtemeier 1996, 83–86). Or has the author chosen the region because it lies outside the Pauline mission as indicated in Acts? In that case, this extension of Peter's apostolic authority does not impinge upon Paul's principle of avoiding the area in which other apostles worked (Rom. 15:17–21; or Gal. 2:7 understood as geographical).

1 Peter's conclusion adds to the Pauline echoes. Though Silvanus and Mark were common names, persons with those names were associated with Paul's mission. Silvanus is mentioned as co-sender (1 Peter 5:12), a function he had in 1 Thessalonians 1:1 and 2 Thessalonians 1:1. The recommendation formula, "faithful brother," can refer to the actual or fictive bearer of a letter (Michaels 1988, 306). Silvanus (= Silas) delivered the letter from the Jerusalem Council in Acts 15:22–23. According to Acts 15:36–41, when Paul and Barnabas separated, John Mark went with the latter and Silvanus took Mark's place. Are these same individuals now close associates of Peter? Or symbolic figures used to provide an authoritative stamp for the pseudonymous letter? Finally, the geographical point of origin, "Babylon" (5:13), probably serves as a symbolic reference to Rome (so Rev. 14:8; 18:2), the city in which both Peter and Paul were martyred. The term "Babylon" forms an inclusio with the opening reference to the churches in the diaspora (1:2; Michaels 1988, 311).

As the place of Jewish exile, "Babylon" also picks up the designation used in the transition from the theological introduction (1 Peter 1:3–2:10) to the communal exhortation (2:11–5:11). The audience is addressed as aliens (*paroikoi*) and exiles (*parepidēmoi*) who must watch how they conduct themselves among the nations (or "Gentiles", *ethnē;* 2:11–12). Some interpreters see these verses as the key to the ethical material that follows (Elliott 1981). They argue that the terms "alien" and "exile" should not be taken merely as symbolic of all Christians living in the world but as indications of the actual social status of 1 Peter's audience. Christians in Asia Minor (as well as those in Rome who sent the letter) are not citizens or native residents in the places where they dwell. Some may be permanent resident aliens, others simply foreigners. In either case, they were particularly vulnerable to persecution if neighbors, business associates, or persons with rights of citizenship decided that Christians were a menace to society. 1 Peter 4:14–16 indicates that the mere name "Christian" could result in abuse or persecution. The persistent references to insults (3:9, 16; 4:14), slander as malefactors (2:12; 3:16–17; 4:15), or hostility (4:4–5) suggest that a Christian never knew when he or she might be challenged to defend the faith (4:13).

Though 1 Peter 4:12 refers to a "fiery testing" that has come on the churches in Asia Minor, nothing else in the letter suggests that the churches were faced with an official edict of persecution. When Bithynia's Roman governor Pliny (around 112–14 C.E.) was confronted with charges against Christians, he had no judicial precedent to follow (Pliny, *Epistles,* 10.96–97; for types of persecution, see Achtemeier 1996, 22–35). Testing of the faithful belongs to standard apocalyptic visions of the end time. Those who endure it are to be delivered by God's coming in judgment (1 Peter 1:4–6; 4:7, 17–19; Perkins 1995, 71–72). 1 Peter insists that suffering patterned on the model of Christ, the suffering servant, will lead to a share in Christ's glory (4:13–14; 5:10).

The suffering Christ provides a model for Christians in every situation of slander and abuse (Achtemeier 1993). 1 Peter reminded Christians of their baptismal call to holiness. Christ's atoning death transformed lives of sin into the stones of God's temple and a holy priesthood (1:13–2:10). Suffering as an innocent person (not through one's own fault, 2:20; 3:17, 21) demonstrates a sinlessness similar to that of Christ. Why? Because to do so, an individual has to be free from passions and be motivated by the desire to do God's will (2:20–24; 4:1–2, taking verse 1b to refer to the Christian; Perkins 1995, 67; Achtemeier 1996, 278–80). Imitation of the suffering Christ has a temporal limit, the revelation of Christ's glory (4:7). After instructing Christian leaders to follow the model of Christ, the shepherd (5:1–6), 1 Peter places the experience of suffering in an apocalyptic perspective. It is a sign of Satan's end-time attack on the righteous (5:8–10; Achtemeier 1996, 302).

The apocalyptic explanation of suffering provides a jarring contrast with the introduction to the hortatory section. There, good conduct holds out the possibility that hostile outsiders will be changed by that example (2:11–12). The first section on relationships to outsiders (2:13–3:12) employs ethical traditions that reinforce social hierarchy and conformity (Balch 1981). Religious warrants and symbolism aside, the mandated behavior represents firmly established values. Governing authorities from the emperor down fulfill God's will by punishing evil and honoring the good (2:13–17). 1 Peter 2:15 even hints that Christian good behavior may enlist the support of Roman officials for their cause (see T. Martin 1992, 196–205). Such authorities will pass a positive verdict on innocent Christians brought before them (Michaels 1988, 126).

The examples of slaves, who remain faithful and obedient to harsh masters (2:18–25), and wives, whose modesty, moderation, obedience and silence aim to win over pagan husbands (3:1–6), ensure that Christians do not exhibit common negative stereotypes of women or slaves. But by so doing, these examples could also legitimate a hierarchy of power that reinforces unmerited suffering. Consequently the critical edge of early Christian egalitarianism appears to be blunted in 1 Peter. For some scholars this development reflects a faith that is adapting itself to the dominant cultural ethos (see Balch 1986). Elliott rejects the negative impression that such a reading suggests. By insisting that "resident alien" and "foreigner" describe the social status of Christians, Elliott concludes that this ethical posture is a necessary strategy for survival. Rejecting the religious traditions of one's local patron, civic authorities, husband, or master was risky enough for persons without rights or status in society. As we have seen, Christians experienced various forms of hostility just for being identified. Consequently the best strategy involved consistent evidence that Christianity fostered high moral standards. Christians may withdraw from former associates, thus indicating that they have not capitulated to social pressures (4:4; see Elliott 1986, 80–83).

This formulation of the alternatives highlights a methodological problem in studying New Testament ethics. It is easy to identify the moral stature of Christianity with teaching that is countercultural, other-regarding, or heroic—as in the reminders that God has chosen those who were once rejected to be a holy people (1 Peter 2:4–10); that Christian leaders should serve with humility (5:2–5), and that Christians should love one another and their persecutors (1:22; 2:17; 3:8–9). But what of the examples in which the New Testament adopts moral standards and arguments that are widely accepted in its cultural milieu? 1 Peter presumes that even the hostile outsider should recognize the innocence and moral integrity of Christians just as one should be able to see that Christ suffered unjustly (3:13–18). Therefore, those who persecute the innocent will fall under God's judgment (3:12; 4:5). For God to condemn the unbeliever, there must be moral insights that Christians share with humanity at large. By invoking the example of Christ, 1 Peter shows that the warrants for Christian adherence to common values have been reshaped by the gospel. Even though good behavior *should* ameliorate hostility, 1 Peter never suggests that it actually does so. Instead, moral integrity places Christians in the Christlike situation of unmerited suffering. This exhortation to accept suffering that results from a firm attachment to the good preserves a critical edge in the ethic of 1 Peter (Achtemeier 1996, 53–55).

Who are these suffering Christians? Elliott's hypothesis finds concrete sociological information in the terms "resident alien" and "exile" and emphasizes the social vulnerability of wives with pagan husbands and of "household slaves" (*oiketai*). This proposal has several weaknesses (see Achtemeier 1996, 56–57, 71–82, 170–82, 212). From the linguistic point of view, the alternative suggestion that "alien" and "exile" are metaphors for Christian life has textual evidence in its favor. The greeting and farewell sections use the terms "diaspora" (1:1, along with "exiles") and "Babylon," which are associated with the Jewish exile. Though 1 Peter consistently depicts its addressees in metaphors used for Israel, they are clearly of Gentile origin and hence not the "exiles of the diaspora" in the literal, Jewish sense. Therefore "alien" and "exile" might also be derived from the Old Testament (Achtemeier 1996, 71). 1 Peter 1:17 clearly uses the phrase "time of exile" metaphorically. The phrase in 1 Peter 2:11 opens with the Greek particle *hōs*, "as," which can introduce a metaphoric comparison. What would be the point of inviting the audience to consider themselves as though they were aliens? Achtemeier suggests that the clue lies in 1 Peter 4:4. Conversion has caused a rift between believers and their former associates and perhaps even a reduction in social prestige (Achtemeier 1996, 56).

Other details also suggest that the Christians addressed could have enjoyed some social prominence. Pliny's report to Trajan suggests that Christians came from a diverse background. Since there was no official policy of seeking out Christians, private individuals who sought to have persons condemned to death by the governor must have some personal reason to gain from such prosecutions. The contentious litigiousness of the upper orders of society even showed up in the Corinthian church (1 Cor. 6:1–8; Clarke 1993). Although the examples are commonplace, exhorting wives to reject the frivolities of wealth makes little sense unless their husbands had the means to provide such (Achtemeier 1996, 212). Similarly the slaves are not addressed with the term "slave," *doulos,* but with the somewhat more specialized "household slave," *oiketēs.* Those with education and training in managing the affairs of a prominent household might move from the margins to the center of society if they were freed. Inscriptions show that slaves often identified with the *familia* to which they belonged (see Bradley 1994, 56–90). Many household slaves enjoyed more material comfort than the poor rural farmer (Bradley 1994, 90–92). 1 Peter indicates that converts chose this vision of holiness and moral renewal in Christ at a price. The epistle presents two possible resolutions to Christian suffering. Either outsiders will be changed by the exemplary conduct of Christians or, as agents of Satan's end-time attack on the righteous, persecutors will fall under divine judgment.

JAMES

The greeting in James 1:1, "to the twelve tribes in the diaspora," suggests that the addressees of this exhortation represent an idealized Israel (compare 1 QS 8:1; Rev. 7:5–8 and the "twelve thrones" of Matt. 19:28//Luke 22:29–30). What follows provides little information that would link the letter to a specific setting. Scholars have often taken James to be a loosely structured compilation of Jewish and Christian ethical teaching (Dibelius 1976, 34–38). Other scholars have argued for a unified literary composition (Cargal 1993; Penner 1996).

Christian faith requires a moral conversion, which James 1:25 refers to as the "perfect law of freedom" (also 2:12). James 2:8 designates the command to love one's neighbor (Lev. 19:18) as the "royal law according to the Scripture." This passage belongs to a section addressed to the problems of partiality toward the rich and neglect of needy members of the community (James 2:1–26; Watson 1993a). Thus, the opening exhortation to a single-minded moral reform that performs pious deeds (1:2–26) is linked to the concrete problems faced by the community (Johnson 1995, 235–36).

A shift in discourse style marks the transition between the opening chapter and James 2. The author adopts a familiar form of Greco-Roman ethical instruction, the diatribe. Hypothetical questions (as in James 2:4, 5, 7, 14, 20) call for negative judgments on particular forms of behavior. James uses this technique to condemn favoring the rich over the poor in the assembly (2:2–3) and failure to obey the law of love (2:15–16). Both can be seen as failures in hospitality. The audience is presented with positive models to emulate in the persons of Abraham and Rahab

(2:21–25; Johnson 1995, 219). Since Abraham exemplified wisdom (Wisd. Sol. 7:27), as well as a tested faith that bears fruit in deeds of mercy, James is not indebted to Paul's use of Abraham to separate faith and works (Martin 1988, 91–95). Rather, the figure of Abraham takes the reader back from the specifics of James 2:1–26 to the general exhortations in chapter 1. Readers are to seek the wisdom that only God can give (James 1:5) in order to have a faith that will endure testing (1:2, 12; Cargal 1993, 134–36). The diatribe style also employs objections from an imaginary interlocutor. Consequently, the allegation that faith or works can suffice for salvation in James 2:17–20 need not represent a challenge to Pauline theology (Gal. 2:16). It has a rhetorical function within the argument made by James. Paul would have agreed with James that Christians must love one another (see Lev. 19:18 in Rom. 13:8) and bear one another's burdens in order to fulfill the "law of Christ" (Gal. 6:2; Johnson 1995, 58–65).

James 3:1–12 takes up another topic from the opening chapter, controlling speech (1:19–20, 26; Johnson 1995, 254). The analogy used to conclude the section picks up another feature of the letter opening, single-minded devotion to God. Moral evils reflect the internal divisions that cause persons to oscillate from one passion to another (1:7–8; Perkins 1995, 98–99). This picture of the wise as above conflicting passions, above angry and rash speech, and able to speak and act with integrity was common in both Jewish and non-Jewish moralists. Once such comparisons have been drawn, Johnson finds two distinctive emphases in James's moral teaching: a more pessimistic view of human behavior and a consistent theological orientation (Johnson 1995, 264–65). Mere human efforts will never rein in so subtle and variable an organ as the tongue (3:8). But James grounds the moral effort in God's word and promise. Consequently, Christians recognize that all they do stands under God's judgment. They know that God gives the wisdom needed to live as commanded, "the implanted word" (1:21). The series of ethical exhortations that follow remind the audience that Christian life requires changing one's allegiance from "the world" to God (3:13–4:10; Johnson 1995, 265).

Since much of the moral advice in James can be paralleled in other ancient sources, turning to God for cleansing (4:8) does not imply a unique vision of what goodness is. Unlike 1 Peter, James never invokes the story of Jesus as an example of Christian morality. God alone is the source of both moral obligation and obedience. But, James does contain some maxims whose closest parallels are found in the tradition of Jesus' sayings (see above). So the audience probably heard Jesus' own voice in those passages. Finally, James follows the epistolary genre in concluding with practical advice (5:13–20). Prayer and anointing will help the sick. James refers to Elijah as evidence for this practice (5:17–18). In the same section, we learn that the quest for moral perfection is not simply an individual matter. Christians will confess their sins to one another (5:16) and will seek to bring others back to God (5:19–20). As in James 2:1–26, this church comprises persons whose lives are intertwined in close face-to-face relationships. The rich and poor, the sick and weak, those making moral progress and those caught in sin all belong to the same church.

2 PETER

2 Peter addresses persons who have a faith "of equal honor to ours" (2 Peter 1:1). This designation reminds readers that their belief is to be measured by the standard of apostolic faith. The letter presents itself as Peter's final testament (1:13–15; see Vögtle 1994, 158–61). Two such testaments are attributed to Paul in the New Testament (Acts 20:17–38; 2 Timothy, Vögtle 1994, 162). 2 Peter 3:14–18 indicates that Paul's letters have been invoked by those who deny the truth of Christian belief in the parousia. Eyewitness testimony to apostolic faith is found in the transfiguration of Jesus (1:16–18). 2 Peter 2:1–3:3 quotes much of Jude 4–18 to describe the arrogance of false teachers and the condemnation that awaits them. Jude used examples from the past to warn against false teachers in the community. 2 Peter shifts the temporal orientation to impending doom. Opponents may scoff at teaching about the day of judgment (2:3, 19; 3:9), but imminent and sudden destruction will prove the truth of this teaching (Neyrey 1993, 188).

2 Peter's arguments are not limited to the authority of scripture and of apostolic tradents. The opposition employed Epicurean polemics against divine theodicy (Neyrey 1993, 122–27). If a rational analysis of the cosmos makes divine ordering impossible, then prophecies and oracles must also be delusions (see Lucretius, *Rer. Nat.* 3.978–1023; Plutarch, *Defectu Or* 420B; Cicero, *Fat.* 9.23). At what points does 2 Peter engage the philosophical assumptions of such critics? 2 Peter 1:3–4 establishes what is at stake from the Christian point of view. God's creative power is the same power by which virtuous human beings come to participate in God's nature (Perkins 1995, 168–69). That salvific power has been exhibited in the knowledge of Jesus Christ. Through it, Christians have become part of an eternal kingdom, not the changing world of Epicurean cosmology (1:5–11). 2 Peter would not deny that people believe many false prophecies and oracles. Consequently, interpretation of the prophetic word of Scripture also requires participation in the Spirit (1:20; Bauckham 1983, 231–32; Fuchs and Reymond 1980, 28–29).

A second engagement with philosophical debate occurs in 2 Peter 3:4. The sameness of the world over time appears as a premise in the Epicurean argument for the eternity of the world against doctrines of cyclic conflagrations (Lucretius, *Rer. Nat.* 1.225–37). 2 Peter 3:8–13 combines the Biblical language of judgment with terminology reminiscent of Stoic cosmology in which the elements are dissolved in fire (3:10–12). For the Stoic, cosmic cycles follow one another as part of the natural process. For the Christian, God will create a new heaven and earth (3:13). Thus the Biblical word of promise provides the overarching framework within which 2 Peter evaluates the cosmological commonplaces of his age.

These cosmological questions pose a major challenge to Christian theology in the twenty-first century (Vögtle 1994, 255–61). Many Christians presume that they hold an apostolic faith equivalent to the New Testament witness when they reduce Biblical eschatology to individual postmortem judgment. 2 Peter would not agree. God's creative power anticipates an eschatological transformation of the cosmos. Christian theologians must bring the conflicting principles of the modern sciences into dialogue with the inspired apostolic testimony of scripture. 2 Peter's opponents have incorporated the antireligious principles of Epicurean science into their challenges to Christian eschatology. 2 Peter marshals counterarguments that combine authoritative traditions with other philosophical and scientific insights. The use of diverse apostles as witness to the tradition (3:1–2) suggests another methodological principle, seeking the common witness of scripture. The author's testamentary format hints at more than the death of a single apostle. The apostolic age itself has come to an end. What remains are the writings by which Peter, the evangelists, Jude, and Paul can remind their descendants to remain firm in the truth they possess (1:12).

Works Cited

Achtemeier, Paul J.
1993 "Suffering Servant and Suffering Christ in 1 Peter," in *The Future of Christology: Essays in Honor of Leander E. Keck,* ed. A. J. Malherbe and W. A. Meeks, 176–88. Minneapolis: Fortress Press.
1996 1 Peter, Hermeneia Commentaries. Minneapolis: Fortress Press.
Attridge, Harold.
1989 *Hebrews,* Minneapolis: Fortress Press, 1989.
Balch, David L.
1981 *Let Wives Be Submissive: The Domestic Code in 1 Peter.* Society of Biblical Literature Monograph Series. Chico, Calif.: Scholars Press.
1986 "Hellenization/Acculturation in 1 Peter," in *Perspectives on First Peter,* ed. C. H. Talbert, 79–101. Macon, Ga.: Mercer University Press.
Bauckham, Richard J.
1983 *Jude, 2 Peter.* Word Biblical Commentary 50. Waco, Tex.: Word, Inc..
Bradley, Keith
1994 *Slavery and Society at Rome.* Cambridge: Cambridge University Press.
Cargal, Timothy
1993 *Restoring the Diaspora: Discourse Structure and Purpose in the Epistle of James.* Society of Biblical Literature Dissertation Series 144. Atlanta: Scholars Press.
Clarke, Andrew D.
1993 *Secular and Christian Leadership in Corinth. A Socio-Historical and Exegetical Study of 1 Corinthians 1–6.* Arbeiten zur Geschichte des antiken Judentums und des Urchristentums XVIII. Leiden: E. J. Brill.
DeSilva, David A.
1996 *Despising Shame: Honor Discourse and Community Maintenance in the Epistle to the Hebrews.* Society of Bliblical Literature Dissertation Series 152; Atlanta: Scholars Press.
Dibelius, Martin and Heinrich Greeven
1976 *James,* trans. M. A. Williams. Philadelphia: Fortress Press.
Elliott, John H.
1981 *Home for the Homeless: A Sociological Exegesis of 1 Peter, Its Structure and Strategy.* Philadelphia: Fortress Press.
1986 "1 Peter, Its Situation and Strategy: A Discussion with David Balch," in *Perspectives on First Peter,* ed. Talbert, 61–78.
Eisenbaum, Pamela M.
1997 *The Jewish Heroes of Christian History. Hebrews 11 in Literary Context.* Society of Biblical Literature Dissertaion Series 156. Atlanta: Scholars Press, 1997.
Fuchs, Eric and Pierre Reymond.
1980 *La deuxième épître de Saint Pierre, L'épître de Saint Jude.* Commentaire du Nouveau Testament, Deuxième série XIIIb. Neuchâtel: Delacheaux & Niestlé.
Johnson, Luke T.
1995 *The Letter of James.* Anchor Bible 37A. New York: Doubleday.
Joubert, Stephan J.
1995 "Persuasion in the Letter of Jude," *Journal for the Study of the New Testament* 58: 75–87.
Lindars, Barnabas.
1991 *The Theology of the Letter to the Hebrews.* Cambridge: Cambridge University Press.
Martin, Ralph P.
1988 *James.* Word Biblical Commentary 48. Waco, Tex.: Word, Inc.

Martin, Troy
1992 *Metaphor and Composition in 1 Peter*. Society of Biblical Literature Dissertation Series 131. Atlanta: Scholars Press.
Michaels, J. Ramsey
1988 *1 Peter*. Word Biblical Commentary 49; Waco, Tex.: Word, Inc.
Murphy-O'Connor, Jerome
1995 *St. Paul the Letter-Writer: His World, His Options, His Skills*. Collegeville, Minn.: Liturgical Press.
Neyrey, Jerome
1993 *2 Peter, Jude*. Anchor Bible 37C. New York: Doubleday.
Paulsen, Henning
1992 *Der Zweite Petrusbrief und der Judasbrief*. Kritisch-exegetischer Kommentar über das Neue Testament XII/2. Göttingen: Vandenhoeck & Ruprecht.
Penner, Todd C.
1996 *The Epistle of James and Eschatology. Re-reading an Ancient Letter*. Journal for the Study of the New Testament Supplement Series 12. Sheffield: Sheffield Academic Press.
Perkins, Pheme
1995 *First and Second Peter, James and Jude*. Louisville, Ky.: Westminster/John Knox Press.
Pfitzner, Victor C.
1997 *Hebrews*. Abingdon New Testament Commentaries. Nashville: Abingdon Press.
Thurén, Lauri
1997 "Hey Jude! Asking for the Original Situation and Message of a Catholic Epistle," *New Testament Studies* 43: 451–65.
Vögtle, Anton
1994 *Der Judasbrief. Der zweite Petrusbrief*. Evangelisch-Katholischer Kommentar zum Neuen Testament XXII. Solothurn: Benziger Verlag and Neukirchen-Vluyn: Neukirchener Verlag.
Watson, Duane F.
1988 *Invention, Argument and Style: Rhetorical Criticism of Jude and 2 Peter*. Society of Biblical Literature Dissertation Series 104. Atlanta: Scholars Press.
1993a "James 2 in Light of Greco-Roman Schemes of Argumentation," *New Testament Studies* 39: 94–121.
1993b "The Rhetoric of James 3.1–12 and a Classical Pattern of Argumentation," *Novum Testamentum* 35: 48–64.

Chapter 11

Revelation

M. Eugene Boring

As I write this, televangelists and fundamentalist sensationalizers are busy making predictions about the end of the world in the year 2000—predictions they claim are interpretations of the "prophecies" of the biblical book of Revelation. If you are reading this in the twenty-first century, their predictions have again been disconfirmed. We should thus be able to study more legitimate approaches to Revelation without having to be bothered, until the next century or millennium, with the sensational claims of "Bible Prophecy" made popular by various fundamentalist and premillennial approaches. If the history of past disconfirmations is any guide, however, this will sadly not be the case.

It is not only fundamentalist premillennialists who have been active in interpreting Revelation in the past twenty-five years. Mainstream international New Testament scholars, especially in North America, have focused their efforts on Revelation. In 1979 an International Colloquium on Apocalypticism was held in Uppsala, Sweden, that both clarified issues and set the agenda for two decades of research.[1] In the same year, the biannual meeting of New Testament scholars in Leuven, Belgium, was devoted entirely to interpreting Revelation and drew contributions from twenty-six prominent scholars in Europe and North America.[2] In 1995 The International Interdisciplinary Symposium on the 1900th Anniversary of the Book of St. John's Revelation was held in Athens and Patmos, Greece. Forty-three scholars from eleven countries made presentations on almost every aspect of contemporary study of Revelation.[3] For several years, annual meetings of the Society of Biblical Literature included seminars on the topics of Early Christian Prophecy, Early Christian Apocalypticism, and Reading the Apocalypse, stimulating research, international exchange of ideas, and publication. Likewise, in the meeting held annually under the auspices of the Studiorum Novi Testamenti Societas, the Seminar on Apocalyptic has attracted scholars of international standing. The presidential address to the Studiorum Novi Testamenti Societas meeting in Göttingen, Germany, in 1987 was entitled "How Christian Is the Book of Revelation?"[4] Scholarly publication on Revelation and apocalypticism during the last quarter-century has included a large number of commentaries and comprehensive treatments of Revelation,[5] dozens of monographs and scholarly books on specialized themes,[6] and hundreds of articles in scholarly journals and reference works.[7]

The status of scholarly research on Revelation that constitutes the continuing agenda for study in the twenty-first century may be summarized in the following seven theses, which will be listed and then briefly elaborated:

1. Most introductory issues have been confirmed and nuanced.
2. History of religion perspectives have been sharpened.
3. Literary approaches have emerged and flourished.
4. The political relevance of Revelation has been rediscovered.
5. The importance of the social location of the reader has been perceived.
6. The hermeneutical role of imagination has been reactivated.
7. Insight into the theology of Revelation has deepened.

MOST INTRODUCTORY ISSUES HAVE BEEN CONFIRMED AND NUANCED

Authorship. Scholarship is now virtually unanimous that Revelation was written by a Christian prophet named John who is otherwise unknown to us. In other words, the author of Revelation is not to be identified either with the son of Zebedee or with the author of the Gospel or Epistles of John. Steven S. Smalley is representative of the tiny minority that still holds to apostolic authorship, while Robert H. Mounce is among the few who leave the door open to the possibility that Revelation was written by John son of Zebedee while acknowledging the stronger case for the other view.[8] J. Massyngbyrde Ford's idiosyncratic view that Revelation is mostly a product of John the Baptist and his disciples has found no response in the scholarly community, and has now been abandoned by its author.[9]

While practically all scholars now consider the Gospel of John and the Apocalypse to have been written by different authors, the relation of Revelation to the "Johannine school" continues to be disputed. The whole business of "school tradition" has become more important in the last twenty years, as scholarship has discovered the role of the Christian community and its tradition in the composition of New Testament documents, with a consequent reduction in emphasis on the role of individual authorship.[10] While some scholars continue to stress the points of contact between Revelation and the "Johannine school" represented by the Gospel and Letters of John,[11] the pendulum seems to have swung in the direction of emphasizing the independence of Revelation from the other Johannine writings. Schüssler Fiorenza's key study not only distinguished Revelation from the Johannine school but properly emphasized its place within developing Pauline tradition.[12]

Date, Unity, and Sources. While an occasional scholar argues for the composition of Revelation as early as the reign of Nero[13] or as late as the time of Trajan,[14] the research of the last twenty-five years has convinced most scholars that the earliest tradition was correct (Irenaeus, *Against Heresies,* 5.30.3, "toward the close of the reign of Domitian," that is, around 95 C.E.).[15]

David Aune presents the most recent and most extensive discussion of Revelation's date, arguing that we should think in terms of a three-stage process rather than a single date: the formation of individual textual units prior to 70 C.E., their combination into a "first edition" about 70 C.E., and a revised and expanded "second edition" in the 90s or just after the turn of the century.[16] Aune claims to be able to identify these pre-redactional units and the history of their redaction. This type of source analysis was popular in the nineteenth and early twentieth centuries, but during the last twenty-five years scholarship has neglected the prehistory of the text and concentrated mostly on its final form, shifting from thinking of the composer as an editor to a creative author. While the majority of scholars would regard as probable the proposal that sources and traditions have been incorporated, they no longer see John as merely an editor who combined these. Aune, who prefers to speak of John as "author-editor," represents a turn away from the current emphasis of regarding Revelation as a unified composition, and something of a return to the nineteenth-century penchant for dividing the book into layers and sources. Aune's theory of dating and sources obviously has far-reaching implications for understanding the book's genre and theology.[17] His commentary is a major work that will be reckoned with for at least the next generation, but it remains to be seen how convincing scholars will find his theories of sources, dating, and redaction.[18]

Language and text. It has always been noticed that the language of Revelation is a peculiar kind of Greek. This has led, in turn, to a peculiar history of the transmission of the text, as scribes were tempted here more than any other place in the New Testament to "correct" the strange language by bringing it into conformity with standard grammar. In the last twenty-five years a strong but not universal consensus has developed that the author was not writing in his native language, but was a Palestinian whose mother tongue was Aramaic or Hebrew, and who migrated to Asia Minor (probably as a result of the population disruptions caused by the war of 66–70). His Greek is thus the language of one who "writes in Greek but thinks in Hebrew."[19] Since there is a fairly consistent system to John's grammatical and syntactical aberrations, his style is not due merely to ignorance of good Greek, but may represent a protest against the higher forms of Hellenistic culture and/or an imitation of the "biblical Greek" of the Septuagint.[20]

Historical context. The increased sophistication in the application of sociological methods to the study of biblical documents during the past quarter century has influenced the study of apocalypticism in general and of Revelation in particular. There is now a debate about whether generalizations can be made about the social world or social context of apocalyptic movements in general, and whether apocalypticism as such can be associated with typical or specific social groups. Paul D. Hanson, for instance, in a number of works, has developed detailed theories that locate apocalyptic documents in specific social situations.[21]

With regard to interpreting Revelation, the issue is whether the document is directed to a particular situation in the reign of Domitian during which Roman officials in Asia Minor persecuted Christians who refused to participate in worship of the emperor. Twenty-five years ago, many scholars would have seen Revelation as an apocalyptic response to precisely this situation, encouraging Christians to hold fast to their faith in the face of government persecution. Perhaps the most dramatic change in understanding Revelation is related precisely to this point. The current state of research indicates no such official persecution ever existed in John's time. The imperial cult and popular pressure to conform to it (especially in Asia Minor) were realities in John's situation, but previous scholarship tended to exaggerate this on the basis of later Christian portrayals of the history of persecution. While John probably thought that the sporadic harassment Christian communities experienced by virtue of being out of step with the dominant culture (including an occasional martyrdom) was the leading edge of a universal and official persecution, the actual threat to the church was more that Christians might drift too much in the direction of assimilation rather than yield under overt persecution. John's role was thus to point out the danger of assimilation by portraying the demonic aspects of Roman culture to a church that was mostly unaware of them, rather than to comfort a church already suffering under Roman cruelty.

The negative picture of Domitian in Roman sources was painted by his contemporary and later political enemies (Pliny the Younger, Tacitus, Seutonius, Philostratus, Dio Cassius). The current view that is becoming dominant is that this picture of Domitian was intentionally distorted and cannot be used as evidence for the background of Revelation.[22] Domitian was not an egomaniac who insisted on being worshiped as a god. That the author of Revelation thought he and his churches lived in the dawn of a terrible persecution is clear; that the recipients of Revelation actually lived in such a situation is no longer clear. Thus, a range of social backgrounds has been projected. Schüssler Fiorenza represents those more oriented to seeing real persecution, with Thompson the polar opposite: John's apocalypse is typical of apocalypses in attempting to awaken the perception of a crisis when none actually existed. Yarbro Collins represents the via media on this issue: there was real social unrest and marginalization of the Christian community, but not active persecution in John's setting. This is probably the most common view now; the uniformity of the Domitian persecution view is no longer presupposed but must be argued for.

Archaeology. An enormous amount of archaeological work has been done in the last twenty-five years to illuminate the text of the Bible, but the value of work done in Asia Minor for the study of Revelation is a disputed issue. Colin Hemer's revised doctoral dissertation published in 1986 was projected as a reassessment of the work of William M. Ramsey's work earlier in this century.[23] Ramsey's books have been celebrated in conservative circles as providing archaeological support for the historical accuracy of the New Testament. Ramsey's study of the seven churches of Revelation 1 — 3 is considered a classic of this genre. Hemer intended to provide a critical and updated version of Ramsey's approach, providing a plethora of geographical and archaeological data presumed to illuminate the message of Revelation to each of the seven churches by showing how well-informed the author was about concrete items of Hellenistic life and culture as they pertained to each particular church. The book also claims that a study of relevant epigraphy, numismatics, and archaeology documents the fact that the crisis faced by John's churches was not merely perceived, but real. The effort has received very mixed reviews,[24] illustrating William Dever's 1985 claim that "New Testament archaeology scarcely exists as a field of inquiry, much less as an academic discipline."[25] While much data exists and more can be uncovered, it is usually dealt with atomistically. Here is a field where academic development in the twenty-first century could prove very helpful in future research on Revelation.

HISTORY OF RELIGION PERSPECTIVES HAVE BEEN SHARPENED

From the point of view of the study of the history of religions (*Religionsgeschichte*), the development of apocalypticism is no longer regarded as merely a matter of adopting Persian dualism or other external traits and materials. While there were "foreign" as well as "Israelite" influences, biblical apocalyptic is now seen as in continuity with Israelite prophecy, not an alternative to it, and "pure Israelite" (for example, H. H. Rowley) vs. "foreign influences" (for example, Wm. Bousset) has been recognized as a false alternative. Gerhard von Rad's derivation of apocalyptic from the wisdom tradition[26] has found only a minimal response and is not the wave of the future.

With regard to Revelation, this means that early Christian prophecy is seen as both in continuity with Israelite prophecy and with prophetic phenomena in the Hellenistic world. Perhaps the single most important new development in the interpretation of Revelation in the last twenty-five years has been the placement of Revelation within the context of early Christian prophecy. This development was long overdue. Old Testament prophetic literature was always interpreted in relation to the phenomena of Israelite prophecy, but our one clear example of New Testament prophecy was, until recently, interpreted as an example of apocalyptic thought without reference to its context in the religious life of early Christianity, that is, as an instance of Christian prophecy. A Seminar on Early Christian Prophecy that continued for several years was formed in 1972 within the framework of the Society of Biblical Literature. Some members of the Seminar published on both Christian prophecy and Revelation, and the work of the Seminar influenced other Revelation scholars, with the result that studies of Revelation and research on Christian prophecy continue to influence each other.[27] There is still no agreement on details, but future studies of Revelation will continue to be influenced by studies of the prophetic phenomenon in early Christianity.

LITERARY APPROACHES HAVE EMERGED AND FLOURISHED

The career of Revelation has paralleled that of other New Testament documents in the last twenty-five years, in that it has been transformed by the impact of literary criticism. While few New Testament scholars have had training in advanced literary criticism, many have nonetheless benefited from the kind of secondary works represented by Norman R. Petersen's 1978 *Literary Criticism for New Testament Critics*.[28] While literary criticism has sometimes been seen as an alternative to and replacement for historical criticism, overreacting to the preoccupation of some historical critics with the prehistory and historical context of the text rather than the text itself, many exegetes have integrated the newer literary approaches with historical criticism.[29] Important recent developments in literary criticism of Revelation deal with genre, text linguistics and the communication situation of the writer, the literary structure of the document, structuralist approaches (which turned out not to be the wave of the future), reader-response criticism, rhetorical criticism, orality, and narratology, only a few samples of which can be discussed here:

Orality. Much study of the difference between oral communication and written communication has been done in the last twenty-five years.[30] Since Revelation is a written document designed for oral presentation in the church (Rev. 1:3), and since the document functions primarily by evoking imaginative pictures in the mind of the hearer, studies of orality are very important for interpreting Revelation. So far, however, no major work on oral communication in the Apocalypse has appeared.[31] This is an important area for future development.

Structure. No consensus has been reached on the literary structure of Revelation, but there has been some convergence toward the view that the series of septets is recapitulation of some kind rather than strictly linear (Collins, Schüssler Fiorenza, Giblin), and that the contents of the two scrolls of chapters 5 (Rev. 6—11) and 10 (Rev. 12—22) are important structural markers. Aune, however, argues that the defenders of "recapitulation" do not mean the same thing by the term, that the evidences of recapitulation fit the traditional units better than the final redaction, and that the final "author-editor's" own intention was to string all the material together into one grand eschatological program. In arguing for a straight linear progression as the structure at the redactional level, Aune is out of step with many other contemporary interpreters, but his work shows that structure, and therefore a main line of interpretation, is not a settled issue among current Revelation scholars.

Genre. Genre is one of the key literary issues on which much progress has been made in the last two decades. The terms "apocalypse" and "apocalyptic" had been used rather loosely and vaguely in previous research. Partly as the result of the specific research conducted in the Apocalypse Group of the Society of Biblical Literature's Genres Project and the 1979 Uppsala conference, communication has been facilitated and there is more cooperative work and less idiosyncratic use of terminology. The thirteen-point "master paradigm" and the definition of the genre "apocalypse" developed by the Group has been very influential as a common reference point for discussion even by those scholars who were not persuaded by the definition itself:

'Apocalypse' is a genre of revelatory literature with a narrative framework, in which a revelation is mediated by an otherworldly being to a human recipient, disclosing a transcendent reality which is both temporal, insofar as it envisages eschatological salvation, and spatial insofar as it involves another, supernatural world.[32]

When Revelation is discussed with regard to this definition, the content seems to fit, but the definition does not do justice to the generic features of a letter. The key study on this topic was done by Martin Karrer, but so far only a minority of scholars have accepted the consequences of this view and interpreted Revelation on the basis that generically it is a real letter (with massive apocalyptic content), that is, that it differs from 1 Corinthians only in degree, not in kind.[33]

The connection between "letter" and "narrative" has also been recently explored from the perspective that real letters represent part of an ongoing narrative and project an implied narrative world.[34] As a letter, Revelation implies and projects a narrative, and belongs to the narrative literature of the Bible. Though the narrative aspect of the genre has been recognized (compare the definition above), this insight has yet to be exploited in the interpretation of Revelation.[35]

THE POLITICAL RELEVANCE OF REVELATION
HAS BEEN REDISCOVERED

Few people realize that the hymn "We Shall Overcome" echoes the song of the oppressed hearer/readers of Revelation ("overcome" was the King James Version's translation of "conquer," a key word in Revelation's theology). Just as Revelation was originally written as a protest against the abuse of power, so it has often been rediscovered by oppressed groups throughout history. The popular caricature of apocalyptic thought as being "other worldly" and providing an "opiate of the people" has been challenged in the work of several influential scholars in the past two decades who have discovered in Revelation a theological affirmation and resource for their own concern for justice.[36] "The main concern of the author is not the interpretation of history but the issue of power. The focal point of the 'already' and 'not yet' of eschatological salvation is not history but the kingdom of God and the rule of Christ." The 1993 Frederick Neumann Symposium on the Theological Interpretation of Scripture at Princeton Theological Seminary was devoted to "Hope for the Kingdom and Responsibility for the World," relating apocalyptic theology to political responsibility.[37]

THE IMPORTANCE OF THE SOCIAL LOCATION
OF THE READER HAS BEEN PERCEIVED

A major development in the last quarter-century of biblical studies has been the increasing awareness that biblical texts are always interpreted by particular readers, and that the social location of readers is important in what they see in the texts.[38] Scholarly study of Revelation has benefited from the awareness that Revelation looks different when read through the eyes of the poor and oppressed peoples of the Third World or eyes sensitized by feminist insights.[39]

THE HERMENEUTICAL ROLE OF IMAGINATION
HAS BEEN REACTIVATED

One of the greatest hermeneutical gains in the last twenty-five years has been the rediscovery of the power and validity of evocative imaginative discourse. It is now seen that Revelation does not offer a steno-symbol code for either past, present, or future historical events. The author did not write code language, but multivalent tensive symbolic language. To be sure, Revelation, like every New Testament document, was directed to a concrete historical situation, but even here, it was not a matter of presenting an encoded message that could have been delivered in more prosaic language. Specifically, the view has been abandoned that apocalypses were written in an encoded cryptic manner so that if discovered, the hostile authorities could not decipher it: Revelation's imagery, like that of Daniel, is transparent, and it would have been a dense Roman indeed who did not perceive the meaning of passages such as 17:9, 18.

INSIGHT INTO THE THEOLOGY
OF REVELATION HAS DEEPENED

At the beginning of the period under consideration, the evaluation of Revelation as a theological document tended to be dominated by the oft-quoted dictum of Rudolf Bultmann that "the Christianity of Revelation has to be termed a weakly Christianized Judaism,"[40] which Bultmann did not intend as a compliment. Books on New Testament theology often minimized or ignored Revelation. The last generation has seen a more positive valuation of John as a theologian, so that, for example, the recent comprehensive *Theologie des Neuen Testaments* by Georg Strecker devotes thirty-five pages to the theology of Revelation, almost as much as to the Fourth Gospel,[41] and Richard Bauckham has even pronounced Revelation to be "one of the great theological achievements of early Christianity."[42] While not all would share this enthusiasm, Revelation is once again seen by many scholars as an important partner for theological dialogue. While studies of Revelation's doctrine of God, christology, the Spirit, soteriology, ecclesiology, philosophy of history, and other theological topics could be listed, space permits only brief discussion of three theological themes:

Eschatology. In 1966 Paul Minear, himself a Revelation exegete of some renown, pronounced G. B. Caird's commentary on Revelation the best book on the subject in English. Many, including myself, agreed. Yet a fundamental linchpin of Caird's interpretation was that the author did not expect the soon coming of the End—the parousia he anticipated in the near future was political, not cosmic. Caird interpreted the bulk of eschatological texts in Revelation in terms of a politically realized eschatology. This interpretation aided many students who had difficulties with futuristic eschatology of any type and were glad to find it interpreted to mean something political to which they could relate. Now, however, the great political crisis seems to have been a projection onto history by Revelation's interpreters (see above) and cannot provide the explanation for the apparent expectation of the ultimate crisis of history in the near future. Thus, with the exception of fundamentalists and others who cannot find any mistaken ideas to have been affirmed by biblical authors, most scholars have accepted the view that John accepted the apocalyptic idea that the end of history was literally coming soon, that he was mistaken in this idea, but that this first-century framework for the way he articulated his faith does not necessarily vitiate his affirmation of the faith itself. Allowing John to be a first-century apocalyptist who has other ideas of cosmology and chronology than we moderns has facilitated a fresh encounter with his message of the book on its own terms.

Universal salvation. The overwhelming impression the book initially makes on the reader is of an ultimate separation in which some human beings (relatively few) are finally saved, while much of humanity is condemned to eternal torment. This initial impression has inhibited many exegetes from even asking whether there is a more inclusive or even ultimately universalistic perspective contained in the book. Yet alongside John's pictures of separation and damnation are pictures in which the persecuting kings of the earth are included in the New Jerusalem, and visions in which everything and everyone finally rejoice together in giving praise to the one Creator and Redeemer of all. Even at the beginning of our period, scholars such as Mattias Rissi contended that John's perspective was ultimately universalistic.[43] This line of interpretation has recently been developed by several scholars,[44] so that John is no longer seen as merely the seer of eschatological gloom and doom, but as a prophet of the final victory of the loving God who wills salvation for all and will not finally be frustrated.

Revelation a Christian book? Not only the awful pictures of divinely perpetrated violence and vengeance, but other aspects of the book such as its anti-Judaism have raised serious questions as to whether the book is actually Christian. Eduard Lohse's 1987 presidential address to Society of New Testament Studies addressed this issue. Many, but not all, scholars and biblical theologians would now accept his verdict that in Revelation we do have a document that poses serious challenges and problems that must be honestly faced, but that nonetheless passes muster as a thoroughly Christian document that will continue to enrich biblical faith.

NOTES

1. The proceedings were published as *Apocalypticism in the Mediterranean World and the Near East,* ed. David Hellholm (Tübingen: Mohr, 1983).
2. Jan Lambrecht, ed. *L' Apocalypse johannique et l' Apocalyptique dans le Nouveau Testament,* Bibliotheca ephemeridum theologicarum lovaniensium 53 (Leuven: University Press, 1980).
3. As of 1997, the essays were still in process of editing and publication.
4. Eduard Lohse, "Wie christlich ist die Offenbarung des Johannes?" in *New Testament Studies* 34 (July 1988): 321–28.
5. David E. Aune's three-volume commentary is the most thorough scholarly treatment of Revelation to appear in any language in the twentieth century, and will be a standard reference work far into the twenty-first century. See Aune, *Revelation,* Word Biblical Commentary (Dallas: Word Books, 1997). Others to be mentioned are G. R. Beasley-Murray, *Revelation* (London: Marshall, Morgan, and Scott, 1974); M. Eugene Boring, *Revelation,* Interpretation Commentaries (Louisville, Ky.: Westminster/John Knox Press, 1989); Ward Ewing, *The Power of the Lamb: Revelation's Theology of Liberation for You* (Cambridge: Cowley Publications, 1990); J. Massyngbyrde Ford, *Revelation,* Anchor Bible 38 (Garden City, N.Y.: Doubleday, 1975); Charles H. Giblin, *The Book of Revelation: The Open Book of Prophecy* (Collegeville, Minn.: Liturgical Press, 1991); Wilfred J. Harrington, *Revelation,* Sacra Pagina (Collegeville, Minn.: Liturgical Press, 1993); S. P. Kealy, *The Apocalypse of John,* Message of Biblical Spirituality 15 (Wilmington Del.: Michael Glazier, 1987); Heinrich Kraft, *Die Offenbarung des Johannes,* Handbuch zum Neuen Testament 16a (Tübingen: Mohr, 1974); G. A. Krodel, *Revelation,* Augsburg Commentary on the New Testament (Minneapolis: Augsburg Publishing House, 1989); Sophie Laws, *In the Light of the Lamb,* Good News Studies 31 (Wilmington, Del.: Michael Glazier, 1988); William Mounce, *The Book of Revelation,* New International Commentary on the New Testament (Grand Rapids: Wm. B. Eerdmans Publishing Co., 1977); Ulrich B. Müller, *Die Offenbarung des Johannes* (Gütersloh: Gütersloher Verlagshaus, 1984); Pheme Perkins, *The Book of Revelation* (Collegeville, Minn.: Liturgical Press, 1983); J. Roloff, *The Revelation of John* (Minneapolis: Fortress Press, 1993); Elizabeth Schüssler Fiorenza, *Invitation to the Book of Revelation* (Garden City, N.Y.: Doubleday, 1981); idem, *The Book of Revelation: Vision of a Just World,* Proclamation Commentaries (Minneapolis: Fortress Press, 1991); J. M. P. Sweet, *Revelation* (Philadelphia: Westminster Press, 1979); Adela Yarbro Collins, *The Apocalypse* (Wilmington, Del.: Michael Glazier, 1979).
6. A small sampling of representative works: David E. Aune, *Prophecy in Early Christianity and the Ancient Mediterranean World* (Grand Rapids: Wm. B. Eerdmans Publishing Co., 1983); Richard Bauckham, *The Climax of Prophecy: Studies in the Book of Revelation* (Edinburgh: T. & T. Clark, 1992); idem, *The Theology of the Book of Revelation* (Cambridge: Cambridge University Press, 1993); Alan Boesak, *Comfort and Protest: Reflections on the Apocalypse of John of Patmos* (Philadelphia: Westminster Press, 1987); John J. Collins, *Apocalypse: The Morphology of a Genre,* Semeia 14 (Missoula, Mont.: Scholars Press, 1979); J. J. Collins and J. H. Charlesworth, eds., *Mysteries and Revelations: Apocalyptic Studies since the Uppsala Colloquium,* Journal for the Study of the Pseudepigrapha Supplement Series 9 (Sheffield: JSOT Press, 1991); J. M. Court, *Myth and History in the Book of Revelation* (London: SPCK, 1979); Paul Hanson, *The Dawn of Apocalyptic* (Philadelphia: Fortress Press, 1979); C. J. Hemer, *The Letters to the Seven Churches of Asia in their Local Setting,* Journal for the Study of the New Testament Supplement Series 11 (Sheffield: JSOT Press, 1986); Martin Karrer, *Die Johannesoffenbarung als Brief: Studien zu ihrem literarischen, historischen und theologischen Ort,* Forschungn zur Religion und Literatur des Alten und Neuen Testaments 140 (Göttingen: Vandenhoeck & Ruprecht, 1986); G. Maier, *Die Johannesoffenbarung und die Kirche,* Wissenschaftliche Untersuchungen zum

Neuen Testament 25 (Tübingen: Mohr, 1981); J. Ramsey Michaels, *Interpreting the Book of Revelation* (Grand Rapids: Baker Book House, 1992); Christopher Rowland, *The Open Heaven: A Study of Apocalyptic in Judaism and Early Christianity* (New York: Crossroad, 1982); Elizabeth Schüssler Fiorenza, *Priester für Gott: Studien zum Herrschafts- und Priester-Motiv in der Apokalypse* (Münster: Aschendorff, 1972); idem, *The Book of Revelation: Justice and Judgment* (Philadelphia: Fortress Press, 1985); Leonard Thompson, *The Book of Revelation: Apocalypse and Empire* (New York: Oxford University Press, 1990); Arthur W. Wainwright, *Mysterious Apocalypse: Interpreting the Book of Revelation* (Nashville: Abingdon Press, 1993); Adela Yarbro Collins, *The Combat Myth in the Book of Revelation* (Missoula, Mont.: Scholars Press, 1976); and *Crisis and Catharsis: The Power of the Apocalypse* (Philadelphia: Westminster Press, 1984).

7. The entire July 1986 issue of *Interpretation* was devoted to Revelation. Space prohibits listing even a fair sampling of other major articles. A good selection may be found in the bibliography of Frederick J. Murphy, "The Book of Revelation," *Currents in Research: Biblical Studies* 2 (1994): 206–25.

8. S. S. Smalley, "John's Revelation and John's Community," *Bulletin of the John Rylands University Library* 69 (1987): 549–71; Mounce, *Revelation,* 25–31.

9. Ford's revised version of the commentary to appear shortly in the *Anchor Bible* series has repudiated the original theory, according to her letter to David E. Aune cited in *Revelation.*

10. See, for example, the discussion by Luke Timothy Johnson, *The Writings of the New Testament* (Philadelphia: Fortress Press, 1986), 250–57.

11. For example, Kraft, *Offenbarung,* and especially J.-W. Taeger, *Johannesapokalypse und johanneischer Kreis: Versuch einer traditionsgeschichtlichen Ortsbestimmung am Paradigma der Lebenswasser-Thematik,* Beihefte zur *Zeitschrift für die neutestamentliche Wissenschaft* 51 (Berlin: de Gruyter, 1989).

12. "The Quest for the Johannine School: The Book of Revelation and the Fourth Gospel," in *Justice and Judgment,* 85–113. Other scholars who emphasize the relative independence of Revelation are Eduard Lohse, Jürgen Roloff, and Ulrich Müller.

13. The problems of the majority opinion are summarized by J. C. Wilson, "The Problem of the Domitianic Date of Revelation," *New Testament Studies* 39 (1993): 587–605, and by J. A. T. Robinson, *Redating the New Testament* (Philadelphia: Westminster Press, 1975), 224–25. Robinson advocates a Neronic date, and Wilson inclines in that direction.

14. Kraft *(Offenbarung)* argues the connections with the letters of Ignatius argue for a date in the period from 110 to 115.

15. Yarbro Collins, *Crisis and Catharsis,* 54–84 summarizes the case for the Domitianic date that is convincing to most scholars.

16. Aune, *Revelation 1–5,* lxxi–lxxxix.

17. Issues of structure, genre, historical setting, and the prophetic experience behind the vision reports are among the items that must be rethought if the book is interpreted in terms of an extensive editorial process rather than the composition of an individual representing a real letter to a concrete situation.

18. Aune's predecessor, R. H. Charles' classic two-volume commentary in the *International Critical Commentary* series (Edinburgh: T. & T. Clark, 1920), has remained indispensable, though Charles's own theories of sources and editing were never accepted by most scholars.

19. Charles, *Revelation,* clii–cliii. Charles's dictum has been often reaffirmed in later generations on the basis of additional study, for example, by Dieter Georgi, "Who is the True Prophet?" *Harvard Theological Review* 79 (1986): 100–26.

20. For the former view, compare Yarbro Collins, *Crisis and Catharsis,* 47; on influence of the Septuagint, compare Daryl D. Schmidt, "Semitisms and Septuagintalisms in the Book of Revelation," *New Testament Studies* 37 (1991): 592–603.

21. Of numerous works, we may list Paul D. Hanson, "Apocalypticism," *Interpreters' Dictionary of the Bible Supplement,* 28–34; *The Dawn of Apocalyptic: The Historical and Sociological Roots of Jewish Apocalyptic Eschatology,* rev. ed. (Philadelphia: Fortress Press, 1979); idem, "Apocalypses and Apocalypticism: The Genre; Introductory Overview," *Anchor Bible Dictionary* 1:279–82.

22. For a representative reevaluation of the sociopolitical context of Revelation in general and the rehabilitation of Domitian in particular, see Thompson, *Apocalypse and Empire.*

23. Colin J. Hemer, *The Letters to the Seven Churches of Asia in their Local Setting,* Journal for the Study of the New Testament Supplement Series 11 (Sheffield: JSOT Press, 1986).

24. The work has generally been celebrated by scholars who had already followed Ramsey's line that such historical and archaeological work is valuable in confirming the historical accuracy of the Bible. For a penetrating negative review, see Steven J. Friesen, "Revelation, Realia, and Religion: Archaeology in the Interpretation of the Apocalypse," *Harvard Theological Review* 88 (1995): 291–314.

25. William Dever, "Syro-Palestinian and Biblical Archaeology," in Douglas A. Knight and Gene Tucker, eds., *The Hebrew Bible and Its Modern Interpreters* (Atlanta: Scholars Press, 1985), 66.

26. Gerhard von Rad, *Old Testament Theology* (New York: Harper & Row, 1965), 2:301–318.

27. Compare, for example, M. Eugene Boring, *The Continuing Voice of Jesus* (Louisville, Ky.: Westminster/John Knox Press, 1991); David Hill, *New Testament Prophecy* (Atlanta: John Knox Press, 1979); Ulrich B. Müller, *Prophetie und Predigt im Neuen Testament* (Gerd Mohn: Gütersloher Verlagshaus, 1975); David E. Aune, *Prophecy in Early Christianity and the Ancient Mediterranean World* (Grand Rapids: Wm. B. Eerdmans Publishing Co., 1983); Elisabeth Schüssler Fiorenza, "Apokalypsis and Propheteia: Revelation in the Context of Early Christian Prophecy," in *Justice and Judgment,* 133–58.

28. Norman R. Petersen, *Literary Criticism for New Testament Critics* (Philadelphia: Fortress Press, 1978).

29. As in Schüssler Fiorenza, "Revelation," in E. J. Epp and G. W. MacRae, *The New Testament and its Modern Interpreters* (Philadelphia: Fortress Press, 1989), 420.

30. Compare the essays in Lou M. Silberman, ed., *Orality, Aurality and Biblical Narrative, Semeia* 39 (Atlanta: Scholars Press, 1987), and the bibliography given there.

31. One of the few exceptions is David L. Barr, "The Apocalypse of John as Oral Enactment," *Interpretation* 40 (1986): 243–56. Compare also M. Eugene Boring. "The Voice of Jesus in the Apocalypse of John," *Novum Testamentum* 34 (1992): 334–59.

32. Discussion of the definition, elaboration of the "master paradigm," and reports of the further work of the Group are found in John J. Collins, ed., *Apocalypse—The Morphology of a Genre Semeia* 14 (Missoula, Mont.: Scholars Press, 1979), with the further work of the group (much of which is specifically devoted to Revelation) reported in Adela Yarbro Collins, ed., *Early Christian Apocalypticism: Genre and Social Setting, Semeia* 36 (Atlanta: Scholars Press, 1986).

33. Martin Karrer, *Die Johannesoffenbarung als Brief: Studien zu ihrem literarischen, historischen und theologischen Ort,* Forschungen zur Religion und Literatur des Alten und Neuen Testaments 140 (Göttingen: Vandenhoeck & Ruprecht, 1986). Karrer was a student of Jürgen Roloff, whose commentary incorporates this view systematically in his exegesis.

34. Compare Norman R. Petersen, *Rediscovering Paul: Philemon and the Sociology of Paul's Narrative World* (Philadelphia: Fortress Press, 1985).

35. A beginning has been attempted in M. Eugene Boring, "Narrative Christology in the Apocalypse," *Catholic Biblical Quarterly* 54 (1992): 702–23.

36. For example, Schüssler Fiorenza, *Justice and Judgment;* Richard Pablo, *Apocalypse: A People's Commentary on the Book of Revelation* (Maryknoll, N.Y.: Orbis Books,

1995); C. Freeman Sleeper, *The Victorious Christ: A Study of the Book of Revelation* (Louisville, Ky.: Westminster/John Knox Press, 1996).

37. The papers are published in *The Princeton Seminary Bulletin, Supplementary Issue No. 3*, 1994.

38. This insight is reflected in James Earl Massey, "Reading the Bible from Particular Social Locations: An Introduction," in *The New Interpreter's Bible* (Nashville: Abingdon Press, 1994) and in the related essays in the same volume.

39. Samples of an enormous and varied literature: Practically all the work of Elizabeth Schüssler Fiorenza; Adela Yarbro Collins, "Feminine Symbolism in the Book of Revelation," *Biblical Interpretation* 1 (1993): 20–33; idem, "Women's History and the Book of Revelation," *Society of Biblical Literature Seminar Papers* 26 (1987); Allan A. Boesak, *Comfort and Protest: Reflections on the Apocalypse of John of Patmos* (Philadelphia: Westminster Press, 1987).

40. Rudolf Bultmann, *Theology of the New Testament,* 2 vols. (New York: Scribners, 1951, 1955), 2:175.

41. Georg Strecker, *Theologie des Neuen Testaments* (Berlin: de Gruyter, 1996), 541–74.

42. Richard Bauckham, *The Theology of the Book of Revelation* (Cambridge: Cambridge University Press, 1993), 22.

43. Matthias Rissi, *Time and History: A Study on the Revelation* (Richmond: John Knox Press, 1966); idem, *The Future of the World. An Exegetical Study of Revelation 19.11–22.15,* Studies in Biblical Theology, Second Series, 23 (London: SCM Press, 1972).

44. For example, Boring, *Revelation,* 226–31, and idem, "Revelation 19—21: End without Closure," in *The Princeton Seminary Bulletin, Supplementary Issue, No. 3* (1994), 57; Bauckham, *Theology* 33–34, 75, 86–87, 101–104, 137–40, 148, 155, 163; Harrington, *Revelation.*

Index of Scripture and Related Writings

Index of Modern Authors